Justice for All

D1557460

JUSTICE FOR ALL

Selected Writings of Lloyd A. Barbee

Edited by

DAPHNE E. BARBEE-WOOTEN

Foreword by

CONGRESSWOMAN GWEN MOORE

WISCONSIN HISTORICAL SOCIETY PRESS

Published by the Wisconsin Historical Society Press
Publishers since 1855

The Wisconsin Historical Society helps people connect to the past by collecting, preserving, and sharing stories. Founded in 1846, the Society is one of the nation's finest historical institutions.
Join the Wisconsin Historical Society: wisconsinhistory.org/membership

Interior images are from the Lloyd A. Barbee family collection.
The silhouette artwork on the cover was produced by Marion Loss for Lloyd Barbee Montessori School in Milwaukee. The frontispiece portrait is by Dennis Morton.

Printed in the United States of America
Cover design by TG Design
Typesetting by Integrated Composition Systems
21 20 19 18 17   1 2 3 4 5

Library of Congress Cataloging-in-Publication Data
Names: Barbee, Lloyd A., 1925–2002, author. | Barbee-Wooten, Daphne, editor.
Title: Justice for all : selected writings of Lloyd A. Barbee / edited by
    Daphne E. Barbee-Wooten ; foreword by Congresswoman Gwen Moore.
Other titles: Selections. | Selected writings of Lloyd A. Barbee
Description: Madison, WI : Wisconsin Historical Society Press, [2017] | Includes index. |
    Identifiers: LCCN 2017009058 (print) | LCCN 2017025039 (e-book) |
    ISBN 9780870208393 (E-book) | ISBN 9780870208386 (pbk. : alk. paper)
Subjects: LCSH: Barbee, Lloyd A., 1925–2002. | African Americans—Wisconsin—
    Biography. | African Americans—Wisconsin—Social conditions—20th century. |
    Legislators—Wisconsin—Biography. | Civil rights movements—United States—
    History—20th century | African American civil rights workers—Biography. |
    Wisconsin—Politics and government—1951– | Reformers—Wisconsin—Biography. |
    Lawyers—Wisconsin—Biography. | African American lawyers—Biography. |
    Wisconsin—Race relations.
Classification: LCC F586.42.K64 (e-book) | LCC F586.42.K64 B37 2017 (print) |
    DDC 328.73/092 [B] —dc23
LC record available at https://lccn.loc.gov/2017009058

Contents

*Publication of this book was made possible
thanks to the generous support
of the Wisconsin Historical Society Press Readers Circle.*

*For more information and to join, visit
support.wisconsinhistory.org/readerscircle*

Foreword

Lloyd Barbee was a state legislator from a district in Milwaukee, Wisconsin, but there was no such thing as a district for Lloyd Barbee. He was statewide. He was nationwide.

I remember him as this extremely brilliant man, hard-working, revered, and respected in the community. He was there. He was not aloof. Even while serving in the legislature in Madison in the 1960s, he was always on the ground in Milwaukee. I saw and experienced it as a girl growing up there, and as one of the young people who was isolated by segregation in the Milwaukee Public Schools. Here was this lawyer, this legislator, this important man who never lost touch with the community he was fighting for.

When I think about my experience in a segregated school, I recognize that I got a good education. Milwaukee really was a leader in education then. But the isolation of segregated schools, and the reality of separate facilities that weren't in fact equal, did have an impact on me and my fellow students at North Division High School. We couldn't do any of the experiments in the chemistry lab because we didn't have the equipment other schools had, for example. I rebelled against that, and we got a new school eventually. But I remember that it was Lloyd Barbee who was fighting, not just for desegregation, but for that fairness, that equal opportunity for all of us.

Lloyd Barbee fought the battle against separate-but-equal schools in Milwaukee with such dignity, such decency, and such respect for his constituents and allies. When I am traveling, I still meet people who worked with Barbee on his lawsuit for desegregation of the schools. He was with us in the neighborhoods, but he reached out nationally on behalf of that struggle. For him this was a national movement, one in which he enlisted the help of lawyers and supporters across the country. That's how important he thought the battle in Milwaukee was.

I was a state legislator before becoming a member of Congress. But I don't think Wisconsin has ever had a legislator as prolific and profound as Lloyd Barbee. He was a pioneering black legislator, a trailblazer, and a true coalition builder. He drew white people, black people, Latinos, men, and women into these coalitions against segregation and injustice. And I think the reason he was so good at building those coalitions was because he really enjoyed listening to people and hearing what they needed. Lloyd Barbee understood that he needed to know what was important to people before he could truly represent them. That's what I mean about how he respected people.

I can't say exactly what Lloyd Barbee would be fighting for if he were alive today. But I think he would still be focused on education, on making sure that Milwaukee Public Schools had the resources to educate its students well. He would be guarding against undermining public education. But he would have so many other struggles. The truth is that we could really use a Lloyd Barbee today. But I like to think we can still learn from him, and can still fight like he did. I know I'm trying.

—Gwen Moore
US House of Representatives
Fourth District
Milwaukee, Wisconsin

Introduction

I am often asked what it was like to be Lloyd A. Barbee's child. My short answer is it was fun and exciting, like riding a wave of history. My brothers, Finn Barbee and Rustam Barbee, and I went on marches for fair housing, participated in protests against segregation in the schools and discrimination at lunch counters, and picketed places that would not admit African Americans, such as the Elks Club. I remember marching for civil rights across the South Street bridge in Milwaukee, with the Milwaukee Commandos protecting the marchers while we were pelted with nails, glass, knives, and other weapons from angry whites who snarled and yelled the "n" word at us on the bridge. Like the marches in Selma, Alabama, marches for civil rights in Milwaukee were met with violent opposition. My father was at the forefront of these protests.

Milwaukee was very racially segregated during the 1960s and continues to be extremely segregated in housing, in public schools, and in workplaces. The city saw riots in 1967 and riots in 2016. My father, who died in 2002, once wrote about the 1967 riots that erupted in Milwaukee in response to police brutality toward nonwhite or lower-income citizens. As excessive use of force by police officers continues to be debated long after my father's death, it is clear that improvement and progress come slowly to places such as Milwaukee. As the children of a local civil rights leader, we learned the power of putting in hard work, taking a stand, and organizing on a grass-roots level. We marched against Bob's Big Boy restaurant when it refused to serve my brother Finn. My father organized the protest, and we marched outside with signs protesting Bob's Big Boy on Van Buren Street. When a friend of mine and I were not served ice cream at an ice cream parlor on the east side, my father drove us both down there and demanded to see the manager. We were able to get ice cream after my father's confrontation with the manager.

We attended our father's speeches on civil rights, often traveling with him around the state to hear him speak. After his speech at Oshkosh, the car he drove got stuck in the snow two miles from home. We had to walk in freezing cold and blizzard conditions to our house. I whined and complained as we walked, but my father told me to keep on moving, and we finally made it home without any frostbite. Walking with him in the snowstorm taught me the lesson to always move forward, even when things are tough.

My brothers and I helped with my father's political campaigns. We knocked on neighborhood house doors for him when he was running for political office. Many of the people invited us into their homes. We passed out political flyers, went to political meetings, attended rallies with him, and were present when he won all of his elections.

He took us to political conventions such as the National Black Political Convention in 1974 at Little Rock, Arkansas, where we met many of the up-and-coming black politicians who had been or became mayors in major cities, such as Carl Stokes (1964, Cleveland, Ohio), George Carroll (1964, Richmond, California), Floyd McCree (1966, Flint, Michigan), Richard Hatcher (1967, Gary, Indiana), and Coleman Young (1974, Detroit, Michigan). It was easier for an African American to be elected mayor of an urban city than to become a state governor, and this continues to be true despite the election of President Barack Obama in 2008. Too few leaders of color are elected to positions of power, such as Congress or governorships. As of 2016 the United States has had only four black governors in its history: P. B. S. Pinchback (1872, Louisiana), Douglas Wilder (1990, Virginia), David Paterson (2008, New York), and Deval Patrick (2010, Massachusetts). This is an especially low total considering that African Americans comprise nearly 13 percent of the US population. Unfortunately, limited electoral success has led many people to believe that America is postracial, in spite of racial discrimination that continues in schools, housing, employment, economic development, and the technology industry.

Over the years, my dad introduced us to important historical figures such as Huey P. Newton and Bobby Seale, founders of the Black Panther Party, Lerone Bennett Jr., Amiri Baraka, Kareem Abdul-Jabbar, and Mohammad Ali. He was friends with Isaac Coggs, the first black representative in Wisconsin. Mr. Coggs and his wife, Marcia Coggs, lived the street over from us on Richards and Meinecke. We lived on Meinecke Street, across from Oliver Wendell Holmes School, where I attended sixth grade. In the early 1960s, my father helped get Isaac Coggs elected as a state representative. In 1964, when Isaac Coggs ran for Senate, leaving his office vacant, my father ran and won, becoming the second African American state representative in Wisconsin. After my father served twelve years in the Wisconsin legislature, he began teaching at the University of Wisconsin–Milwaukee in the Department of Afrocology and continued practicing law. When he left office in 1976, Marcia Coggs ran and won the election, becoming the first female African American Wisconsin state representative. Their daughter Elizabeth Coggs is a family friend and has continued her parents' legacy by being very active in politics and holding several political offices.

My brothers and I worked in my father's law office. We answered the phones, helped him type documents, filed, and did messenger services when he needed it. While he was working with his first partner, attorney Tom Jacobson, I began working in the law office assisting their secretary, Arlene Johnson, who was also a civil rights activist. Her children, Arles, Darryl, Craig, Lisa, and Scotty, became friends of ours. My father later worked as a sole practitioner out of an office located in downtown Milwaukee on Wisconsin Avenue. From there, he represented comedian Dick Gregory when he was arrested while protesting segregated schools and charged with disorderly conduct (see appendix B, page 252). My father had also been arrested for protesting segregated schools. Since he was a legislator at the time, he had immunity and could not be prosecuted.

My dad assisted me in getting a job as a page, or legislative aide, in Madison for state Representative William J. Rogers, a Menominee man from Appleton, Wisconsin. It was an exciting experience working in the Wisconsin Capitol with its marble floors, painted ornate sculptures, and stained-glass windows.

My brothers and I attended dinners with Wisconsin Governor Patrick Lucey and other political dignitaries. We visited the Menominee reservation, the nuclear power plant in Two Rivers, and the Playboy Club near Lake Geneva, as well as Green Bay, the Wisconsin Dells, and museums in Chicago and New York. My father took us to Ireland when his good friend Dr. Sean P. Keane arranged for a speech on civil rights at Trinity College in Dublin. He took us to Oakland, California, to meet Newton and Seale of the Black Panthers. I was too shy to photograph Newton, but I remember him playing chess with my brother Rustam while I stared in awe. Traveling with my dad for these trips was an important part of our education.

In 1968 we attended the Democratic Convention in Chicago, Illinois.

My elder brother Finn joined tens of thousands of Vietnam War protestors while my father, as a democratic delegate, witnessed the intense and at times violent debate over the war inside the convention center. My younger brother Rustam and I watched events unfolding from the hotel and on television. Later, my father talked about being a delegate at that convention and how rude many of the Democrats were toward African Americans and the protestors.

—‖—

My father took us on trips to Mississippi, where his family originated. We have a forty-acre farm in Shannon, Mississippi, which was purchased by my paternal great-grandmother Pauline Barbee after the Civil War. It is located at Barbee Street and Barbee Avenue. My father took us to his birthplace of Memphis and showed us the house where my grandfather, Earnest Barbee, lived on Cannon Street, where my father and his two older brothers, Quentin and Raymond, were raised. He attended LeMoyne College in Memphis, a historically black school, for undergraduate studies. After graduating, he decided to seek better opportunities in the North because of the intense overt racism in the South. He entered the University of Wisconsin Law School in Madison and obtained his juris doctor degree.

While in law school, he became president of the local NAACP branch and began to investigate housing discrimination in Madison. He and filmmaker Stuart Hanisch and photographer George Allez made a film on housing discrimination, for which they sent testers out to try to rent rooms (see appendix A, page 245). African American testers were not offered housing, but Caucasians who applied at the same locations were accepted. When the film was presented at the University of Wisconsin as proof of discrimination, the Board of Regents was highly upset that the film was shown on campus.

During his stay in Madison, my father went with a friend to locate student housing and to serve as a witness to race discrimination. He and a friend knocked on a door owned by my maternal grandmother, Marian Bunting. She had married Basil Bunting, a famous poet in England, and had three children, Bourtai, Roudaba, and Rustam. She left her husband in the Canary Islands and moved to Madison to raise their children. She was a Unitarian and friends with Frank Lloyd Wright. She brought up her children to be liberal. But liberal does not mean free of prejudice. When my father and his friend knocked on the door, my mother, Roudaba, opened the door. They asked her whether the house had a room for rent, and she said yes and agreed to rent it to my father's friend. Soon after, my father and mother began dating, against my grandmother's wishes. My grandmother told my father she had no objections to him except for his race. He replied that since he and my mother were of the human race, there should be no objection. When my mother married him anyway in 1954, her wealthy maternal family disowned her.

Early in their marriage, my father worked as a janitor at the Frank Lloyd Wright Unitarian Church and also worked as a janitor at the Wisconsin State Capitol, a building he would eventually return to as a state representative. After graduating from law school in Madison, my father opened a law practice and successfully sued a trailer park landlord who refused to rent to African Americans. He continued his legal practice while serving in the state assembly, often working fourteen-hour days as he fought civil rights battles on multiple fronts. He brought lawsuits against the University of Oshkosh after it expelled black students who demanded to have black history taught at the university. He filed, litigated, and won the *Amos v. Board of School Directors* desegregation lawsuit in federal court, which desegregated Milwaukee Public Schools. After winning the lawsuit, he was criticized by a federal judge for obtaining attorney's fees for his civil rights work. After finally receiving his fees in 1980, he went to Jamaica, at the urging of Rustam, and purchased a house, Sanspice Villa, near Port Antonio, where my family still vacations. He specifically wanted to spend his fee in a black country.

Because of his civil rights advocacy and legislation, we often received death threats. Our house was broken into several times, and we received hate mail and threatening phone calls. I remember one caller who said he was on his way to kill me, "a little n——." I hid under the bed. When my father came home I told him about the phone call. He told me not to live in fear and that there are hateful people who do not want to see progress in race relations. He also told me to get over it. This advice continues to be useful in my own law practice today.

Late in his life, my father knew much was left to be done and that others would have to take up the ideals he fought so hard to achieve. Years after his death, Milwaukee schools remain racially segregated, offering unequal educational opportunities to those living in primarily black neighborhoods. Issues of race continue to plague the criminal justice system, with allegations of excessive use of force in arrests and the disproportionate incarceration of minorities. In 2013, the Supreme Court struck down a section of the Voting Rights Act that protected the voting rights of minorities in areas with a history of discrimination. Reading my father's writings, one can see not enough progress has been made on many of the issues to which he dedicated himself.

After leaving public life, he began recording his experiences and compiling his many writings for the benefit of those who would follow. In compiling those documents and writings into this book, I have tried to finish this work, both to preserve the record of his perspective on this important time in history and to provide guidance to the activists, legislators, educators, and others who may be able to gain something from his experiences and wisdom.

Lloyd A. Barbee taught me to dream big, follow through, and fight for equality and justice. By introducing and compiling this book, I am proudly fulfilling his goal and dream to share his thoughts and philosophy with all.

—Daphne E. Barbee-Wooten

Publisher's Note

This text includes a selection of documents from Lloyd A. Barbee's political and legal career that have historical importance, continued relevance, or both. Many of the documents, including official statements and press releases, published articles, and speeches, were collected by Barbee himself for the purpose of publishing in book form, with the task being completed by his daughter, Daphne E. Barbee-Wooten, following his death. The documents have been sorted by topic, labelled and dated, and presented in chronological order within those topics.

Many of the documents are labeled as legislative comments, which Barbee wrote and distributed in his official capacity as a state legislator. These often powerfully worded essays covered issues concerning inequality in education, fair housing practices, incidents of violence by and against police officers, prisoner rights, civil rights protests, the equal rights movement, elections and voting, international civil rights issues, and many more issues that were debated during his career. The comments and press releases distributed by his legislative office often were picked up in the media, especially by the black media outlets in Milwaukee, such as the *Milwaukee Star* and the *Milwaukee Courier*.

Also included are pieces of an unpublished manuscript Barbee began writing in 1982 to record his experiences and thoughts on his early life and experiences as an activist, civil rights lawyer, and state legislator. Early sections of this manuscript covering Barbee's pre-political life, from his childhood to his involvement in the Wisconsin NAACP, are included in Chapter 1 of this book. Chapter 2 includes Barbee's more general writings about his experiences as a Wisconsin legislator, from the logistics of working as an African American and member of the minority party at that time to his work on an array of issues. Other pieces of this manuscript pertaining to specific topics are presented in conjunction with the other documents. These are labeled as "Lloyd A. Barbee 1982 manuscript." Some of these provide an overview of a topic, while others comment on a specific incident he wanted to recount in depth.

Barbee's public documents have not been edited except for adding clar-
ifying details in brackets, such as full names or other identifying information that will help today's readers follow the text. His 1982 manuscript has
been lightly edited to fix minor typographical, grammatical, or punctua-
tion errors. A derogatory term used to refer to African Americans in hate
speech, quoted by Barbee in this manuscript, has been indicated by the
first letter of the word and a solid line. Otherwise, Barbee's original phras-
ing and formatting have been maintained as much as possible, both to
present the documents as they exist in the historical record and to preserve
his original intentions and emphasis. Where more clarification is needed,
it has been added as a footnote. Additional historical information regarding events and court cases, compiled by Barbee-Wooten, is presented in
sidebars.

1

EARLY LIFE AND CAREER

INTRODUCTION, LLOYD A. BARBEE 1982 MANUSCRIPT

Since there is a danger in forgetting gains made, I am writing this retrospective. Not remembering often causes us to repeat errors, reinvent wheels, retry things that failed without understanding how or why [they were not] not successful . . . . It is my hope that freedom and justice lovers will build on what is useful and avoid that which is useless. My father often told me to look at his mistakes and avoid them or go around learning.

Hubris has not motivated me sufficiently to write this despite some of my children, relatives, and friends suggesting that I record some of my ideas and tell my story. I started this Project in 1977 but de facto abandoned it. However, my self-image is that of a person with [few] policies but [who is] steadfast without regard to opposition. Often I discipline myself for accomplishing a goal with such tenacity that it is tantamount to stubbornness. This streak in my personality is probably rooted in my upbringing as well as my genes. My father often said to me that everyone is entitled to his opinion but let it be a good one. When I would defend my opinions or notions in an impudent or unconvincing way, he would tell me how my reasoning was defective.

During my obnoxious adolescent days, I almost became extremely dogmatic in arguing about solving racial problems by strikes, creative cooperative protest, direct action, and counter terror attacks. I had answers to all the problems of race, ranging from shaming the Christians and Jews to joining Blacks for reparation coupled with equality,

1

to mass Black copulation and reproduction with two oppressors. Religion and the bedroom would equalize us all. My dad called some of these notions ridiculous. He was more pessimistic about racial equality in the U.S.A. than I. He stressed preparation and education to such an extent that I used to say freedom would be 100 years away and both of us would be dead. A thread which ran through my father's advice was forethought before action. He would say, "Think before you act; look before you leap; consider where you want to go, the way you want to go, the time it should take you, what you need, all before traveling." When I would complain about errors of judgment, back stabber tergiversation, he would say, "Shake hands with that mistake and move on." This writing jars my memory to consider why I succeeded, why I had problems, and why I failed.

Early Beginnings, Lloyd A. Barbee manuscript, June 14, 1985

I was born August 17, 1925, at 5:30 a.m., at 731 Stephens, Memphis, Tennessee, U.S.A. My father, Earnest Aaron Barbee, was born in Shannon, Mississippi. He had four brothers and five sisters. My mother, Adelina "Foxy" Gilliam, was born in Tupelo, Mississippi. She had four brothers and one sister. My father and mother eloped in Tupelo but moved to Shannon and lived with my father's mother, Pauline Althea Johnson Barbee and father Melvin Barbee, for a while.

Dad often told me that he and my mother planted and picked enough cotton to pay off the mortgage for the 40-acre property where the big house was located in Shannon. During the outbreak of World War I, my father, his brothers and some friends built a small house for my mother and himself by the 40 acre tract. The street near our land was named Barbee Avenue. That was where my brothers, Quinten and Raymond, were born October 12, 1919, and August 19, 1921, respectively.

During the fall of 1923, my father, mother, and two brothers moved to Memphis, Tennessee. Carpentry was my father's first trade, and he worked on a crew for my uncle, Pinkney Barbee, who was a general contractor. By the time I was born, my father had become a paperhanger and house painter.

After I was born my father told me that my mother was never well and she prevailed upon him to go back to their little house in Shannon. She died there, March 26, 1926, of "dropsy." Because of her early death, I was often called a motherless child and a half orphan.

My father's sister, Theona, was in an automobile accident in Austin, Texas. He was sent to look after her. My brothers and I stayed with his sister, Gertrude, for two to three months. I recall my father's returning when I was close to two years old, looking into my bedroom at night and saying, "my boy is sleeping." I said, "I'm not your boy, and I'm not sleeping." He laughed and picked me up. When I was 5 years old, my father hired a woman to keep house, cook and look after us three boys while he worked. Her name was Ella Brown. She had been around. Dad married her a year later. She was a bad housekeeper and kept our house in turmoil. Her cooking was insipid and had a taste of straw with salt. She could cook puddings, a sweet batter [that] when baked resembled an uniced cake.

One day, I came home from school and smelled the familiar aroma of what I thought was pudding. After dinner, I asked about the dessert. My stepmother said there wasn't any. Again, I told her my olfactory organs sensed pudding. She said I was wrong and maybe our next door neighbor had baked a cake. I asked the neighbor about a baked cake, she said that she had not cooked one that day.

Later that evening my father and stepmother went out to a party. I told my brother Raymond that the kitchen was full of the odor of pudding when I arrived from school. He was always good at finding things and began looking throughout the house. I was behind him when he found two layers of uniced cake on top of an out room chifferobe. Each of us ate a layer of the cake, washed the plates clean, and replaced them side by side with the cloth napkins over each plate.

The next day after school our stepmother asked me about her cake. I denied knowing the existence of any cake and reminded her that she had told me that there was no pudding, which I interpreted to mean cake as well. When Raymond was asked about cake he claimed not to know what she was talking about. Quinten, the innocent, suspected one or both of us. When he asked us about it, we confessed and had a hysterical laugh for two or three minutes of glee. Our stepmother was too flabbergasted to tell our father. So we got away with our form of justice or payback.

At eight, my first serious attempt at love was with a 91- or 92-year-old, twice widowed next door neighbor. She was an ex-slave [and] told me many things about slavery in the Carolinas. She gained her freedom at age 12. Her trek from South Carolina to Sardis, Mississippi, was detailed by her travels on foot in wagons and buggies. When she settled in Mississippi, she married her first husband when she was 13 years and he was approximately 17 years. She married her next husband after her first one died. When a niece of hers was born, she raised her.

She often spoke of placing this niece in a cracker box for her crib. She brought this niece up as her own. This wonderful woman was known as Auntie. I called her that too. Her niece was called Dump. Dump and my father thought Auntie and I spent too much time together. They tried to separate us but didn't succeed until our family moved to another neighborhood [in] February 1938.

Very shortly after that, Auntie was placed in a nursing home where she died within a month. My early recollection of school is going with my father to enroll in the first grade at LaRose Grammar School and receiving a vaccination. My dad complimented me on not crying when the nurse scratched me with a needle. During the Fall, my father asked what I had learned at school that day. I said "nothing." He asked why I gave that reply. I said they didn't teach anything but ABC's and I knew them before I ever went to school. A friend of my dad's laughed with me at this remark. Fifteen years later this same friend of my dad's reminded me of my quick answer.

School was ordinary and/or generally dull for me until I took my first history course in 4th grade. One day the teacher asked me to recite a section about Roman Civilization. After finishing my recitation, she asked where I got some of my information. I told her the page in the textbook as my source. She opened her book and said the page that I cited had no such information. Therefore I took my book up to her desk [and] showed her the page. She let me read hers. Thereupon I loudly said that her book was old, mine was new, and hers was out of date. She agreed. The class laughed. I became a hero that day, and a good-to-excellent history student through graduation and college.

My father was deeply religious but never fanatical. He said the two best feelings he ever had was love for women and God. At the age of 9, I got that religious feeling, confessed my sin, and was baptized by complete immersion in a basement pool at the First Baptist Church on St. Paul Avenue in Memphis. Dad told me not to tremble and shake as some people did before being dunked. He was pleased that I took the dipping in a dignified manner. At Communion the first Sunday in every month on unleavened bread was broken into small bits and Welch's grape juice was served to represent Christ's broken body and blood. Years later, I considered this a cannibalistic ritual.

One Sunday morning, when I was about 10 years old, my stepmother called her brother to intercede in a protracted loud argument between my father and her. As my father was explaining the origin and reasons for the argument, my stepmother interrupted with her narration. Her brother said, "Sister, I am going to give you justice: Just sit."

Later on, I asked my father what justice meant. He told me it was what a person deserved or what his due was. It might be hard sometimes but also fair. That word and concept stuck with me.

My father, who did not like shopping, delegated that task to me. With some practice [I] became good at it. In 1947, I went to the neighborhood grocery store and bought a can of oysters. The table had a large picture of a Black man about to eat an oyster with a fork. The man's head was black and blue, his lips were red, his teeth were white, his jaw was distended like a door hinge, and the oyster was pearl gray. Written in large red letters was N—— HEAD OYSTERS. In smaller letters were the legend that the oysters were packed in water and salt at Biloxi, Mississippi. I took the label to LeMoyne College, [where I] discussed the racial slur and caricature with the Campus NAACP and the College President Hollis Price. He drafted a short but forceful letter to its Biloxi packer and distributor. No written response ever came.

I left Memphis to attend the University of Wisconsin law school in Madison in September 1949. Sometime between 1950 and 1951 I was visiting my dad and went shopping at another store. On the shelf with fish and seafood were some oysters labeled NEGRO Head Oysters, but the picture was the same.

During the Eisenhower depression, the Wisconsin Interstate Highway Systems was being constructed. Efforts were being made to extend Wisconsin's tourist trade. The Wisconsin Highway Department published an

Official State Map. A Rand McNally map of Wisconsin was used by most petroleum companies. Gousha also published a map of Wisconsin. The Gousha projection of the progressive state of Wisconsin revealed that a lake in Polk County was named "N—— Heel Lake." A quick and simple investigation produced facts that the lake was known by that name since time immemorial and to residents of the area including Southeastern Minnesota thought the lake was shaped like a Black man's heel.

I was president of the Wisconsin State Chapter of NAACP at that time and notified the NAACP's National Headquarters. Most of the NAACP National Office officials were aghast at liberal Wisconsin naming a lake a derogatory name towards Blacks. Simultaneous to notifying the National NAACP, I contacted the Wisconsin Governor's Commission on Human Rights, the new Governor Gaylord Nelson, whose father practiced medicine in Polk County, the Wisconsin Conservation Commission and the U.S. Department of the Interior—U.S. Geological Survey. In keeping my letter to the point with a recommendation, I suggested the lake be renamed Freedom or Opportunity Lake. The issue was resolved in a fashion by the lake's new name, Freedom Lake, which was approved by the U.S. Department of the Interior, and the new name was printed on maps. However, the official state map left the lake unnamed.

I promised to help paint the exterior of my Aunt's house in Beloit, Wisconsin, during the Fall of my first year at Law School. I took a bus to Beloit on a Friday evening in order to get an early Saturday morning start on painting the house.

My cousin Ambrose Gordon, the number two son of my Aunt, secretary to the Beloit NAACP Chapter, had some letters to mail and asked me to ride to the Post Office. I agreed. After dropping off the mail inside the granite eclectic Roman Post Office, which is in the heart of downtown, we decided to have something to eat and went into a small restaurant with a neon sign and "Made Rite Chili." There was a counter with stools and a few tables with chairs. My cousin and I sat down and ordered chili. The woman behind the counter put chili in a paper container. We said we would eat the chili in the restaurant. Thereupon she went through a rear door of the restaurant. A man came out and said we had to leave through the front of his restaurant and go in through the side door, which led to the kitchen, to be served. I said that was discrimination and violated the Wisconsin

Accommodation Law. A uniformed policeman was sitting at the counter. I asked him to enforce the law which contained criminal as well as civil remedies. He said he didn't know about it.

My cousin, Ambrose and I said we were not eating in the kitchen. The man, who turned out to be the owner, said we had ordered chili and had to pay for it. I told him we were not paying for carryouts but entitled to be served inside the regular eating area of the cafe with our chili in the porcelain bowls, like the policeman used.

The owner placed a brown bag on the counter, put the two cartons inside, and told us to take it and leave. The officer did not appear to leave any money on the counter and was about to leave. I asked him to require the man to serve us inside the regular dining area of the cafe. He just looked at me, and I memorized his badge number. Ambrose asked the officer what we should do. He said, "ask him," pointing at me. "He knows all the answers." He left the cafe and rode away on his three-wheeler.

Since we were not going to either eat in the kitchen area of the cafe or take carryouts, we left. Before we had driven two blocks, two squad cars approached us, flashing search lights. One fat policeman in plain clothes said he had a complaint that two colored boys had given Nick the Greek trouble at his chili parlor, and that we should go back and pay our bill. My cousin started explaining the situation. I joined in to fill in some details. The officer wanted to know why I was in town, etc. A black man who knew Ambrose came by to find out what the problem was. The officer also knew this man, [who] said that Ambrose and I should sue the cafe. I said the state should sue him. The officer asked the man if we should go back to pay Nick and he said no. Therefore, the detective said he would let us go.

The next morning we went to see the District Attorney, who after questioning who our witnesses were, said we probably did not have a winnable case. We told him about the police officer and gave the badge number. He said that wasn't enough but called the police officer and was told no report of the incident had been filed. However, he was told that an officer with a badge number did fit our description and was on duty in downtown Beloit using a three-wheeler as transportation. The D.A. asked the Chief of Police [to call back] after talking with that officer. In a few minutes the phone rang and the officer had been at the Made Rite Chili Parlor between Nick the Greek and two coloreds. The D.A. indicated that the officer should write a report of what happened and the time. No prosecution of Nick for violating our civil rights occurred.

After Christmas of 1962, I was told that the Junior Chamber of Commerce, a civic minded group in Whitewater, Wisconsin, was sponsoring a Black-face minstrel show scheduled [for] February 2, 1963. The basic format of the show was to have whites in Black face make up except for the lips and a small area surrounding same and wear white gloves.

I wrote the Chamber of Commerce and Whitewater College, which was permitting the performance on its campus, objecting to the planned performance and requesting cancellation of the show. Some junior chamber officers telephoned me, explained the format, and said they made money from these shows. The College Board of Regents declared that free speech was at issue and [that the] NAACP was asking for censorship, so on went the show.

My approach to Whitewater College and its Regents was to educate or shame them. They confirmed their ignorance, displayed anger, and accused me of trying to embarrass them. The arrogant white snips presumptuously accused us of anti-civil libertarianism.

I led a picket line the night of the Black-face minstrel show for about 4½ hours with people from the Milwaukee and Racine NAACP. It was below zero weather. As the leader and spokesman, I became colder than ever since. My hands, feet, face, and other parts stung and almost became frostbitten. We marched, sang, and passed out leaflets in Whitewater an hour or so before the show began and continued about 45 minutes after it ended.

In addition to dealing with hostile patrons of the minstrel show teachers, students, and ministers, etc., I was confronted by some radio, TV, and newspaper persons who were advocates of Black-face minstrels. Some of the arguments made on that cold February night in 1963 are still strong in my mind.

Factual, unbiased, and wholesome portrayal of the Blacks in American culture is a desirable goal, but one which today remains far from being realized. Instead, public opinion and attitudes are greatly influenced by amateur and theatrical performances that malign Blacks and other racial, religious, or ethnic groups. Such performances depict grossly inaccurate stereotypes which are degrading and encourage prejudice. Not only are such black-face minstrel shows detrimental to group advancement, they are also harmful to the fabric of our democratic society and they have a disastrous effect on our Nation's image abroad, where our adversaries readily seize upon them in their attempts to prove the failure of American ideals. For all these reasons, I deplore the continuance of public performances based on derogatory racial and ethnic attitudes.

The public protest and demonstration was necessary because it is essential that people become aware the performances that mimic and insult ethnic groups are not only reprehensible to the groups so maligned but diminish humanity as a whole.

Our goal was to reduce the audience size for the minstrel [show and to] prevent the sponsors from producing such shows in the future. Some people did not attend for fear of violence. We were dignified and non-bellicose. I remained calm when baited and yelled at. The Black-faced minstrel show was not given any more.

The largest circulated Wisconsin newspaper ran an editorial on February 2, 1963, attacking the protests and instructing us about civil rights issues. Many of the demonstrators were incensed. In response to their pressure, I wrote a letter to the editor and took it to the *Milwaukee Journal*. The newspaper refused to publish it. The editorial was imperious and sarcastic. I was enraged that the *Milwaukee Journal* had the audacity to criticize both the NAACP and the demonstrators, plus lecture us on what to do about civil rights without printing our reaction to their opinion.

I gave a copy of my letter to the *Capital Times*, Madison's liberal newspaper. They published my letter the next day in a boxed column criticizing the *Milwaukee Journal*'s refusal as an example of Milwaukee's monopoly press. The *Journal* and I remained hostile for the rest of my life. Here is my letter:

The Milwaukee Journal Editor
333 West State Street
Milwaukee Wisconsin

February 4, 1963

The Milwaukee Journal is deplorably apathetic in its right cause, and it has no sense of human dignity. This lack makes it sometimes hard to live with.

It was excess of insensitivity, for instance, that led you in your editorial of February 2,1963 to do a major whitewash of the White-water Junior Chamber of Commerce's staging of a blackface Minstrel show, a time-worn but harmless indigenous form of American fun, lynchings on a warm summer night or tarring, feathering and horse-whipping wayward newspaper editors.

There is a difference between rabid racist presentations of white supremacy mythology and the pretense that in Minstrel shows it doesn't exist.

We submit that this parody of your editorial is closer to the truth than is its model. We contend that there is nothing bigger than teach-ing people to be sensitive to human dignity. If this strikes you as humorless, we regret it. We are inclined of late to make up for this lack, however, with droll visions of Milwaukee Journal editors, bellies heaving, tears streaming from their cheeks, as they roar with laughter at the "harmless innocuous" racial stereotypes portrayed in a black-face minstrel show. If this tickles your funny bone, you are welcome to it. So much for your sense of humor.

Gentlemen, either you are lying when you say you have never seen a minstrel show which "ever inflamed prejudice or was cruel or contemptuous or derogatory," or your artistic faculties have been numbed and your critical posture has come to resemble that of an ostrich.

In the meantime, the struggle to improve the shameful civil rights climate in Wisconsin goes on, and our Whitewater protest was only a small part of it. We have attempted to do the State of Wisconsin a service by drafting and having introduced in the State Legislature the only civil rights bill whose substantive and administrative provi-sions are of such scope as to correct problems of discrimination here. We are now trying to get it enacted. The Milwaukee Journal might better spend its time and effort lending a hand. A helping hand or con-structive criticism seems better than your downgrading of serious matters.

You will please reflect seriously for a moment how frustrating and down heartening it is for those of us who are striving to secure a better human rights climate, to discover that those on whom we counted to educate the public are themselves badly in need of education in one of the most prejudice-ridden states outside the south. Yes, we mean Wisconsin. Yes, we do mean you.

Very truly yours,

Lloyd A. Barbee President, NAACP

That was my last letter to an editor. The white owned and oriented media does not serve as a house organ for Blacks and minorities. The pettiness of northern self-styled great "liberal" information was new to me. Once burned, one learns.

One of my most interesting discussions of racism by the greats occurred when R. Voegel of WHA/Wisconsin Radio Education Station, asked me to comment on Mark Twain's treatment of Blacks. I reread *Adventures of Huckleberry Finn* and noted the racial stereotypes in Jim and Huck. The thrust of my five-minute talk was that Twain's depiction of Jim was that of a good darky, dignified and heroic at times, etc., but created with condescension by the author. The word n—— was used so many times that I stopped counting. This benign treatment of a Black character might have been exceptional for 1840. However, in 1958, more was desirable. I did not agree that the book be banned or taken from school libraries as some radical Black groups were demanding then. My supervisor told me the next day that he heard the show and that I hemmed and hawed with dignity.

Wisconsin Conference of NAACP Branches, Lloyd A. Barbee, Wisconsin NAACP President, 1963 Report

Report of year's activities, April 1962 through April 1963

1. The State Conference protested the University of Wisconsin's efforts to suppress a documentary film on discrimination in housing which it had made at the instigation of a citizen's committee which had raised the funds for the film [see appendix A, page 245]. Despite criticism from pseudo-liberal quarters, the protest showed the University's duplicity and hypocrisy in dealing forthrightly with human rights violations. The film contained

thirteen incidents of clear-cut discrimination in housing can-
didly filmed in Madison. In addition, our protest helped focus
the public's attention on housing discrimination and the need
to take corrective measures. Before the film was shot and sup-
pressed, it was the rule, rather than the exception, for public officials, real estate dealers, and the news media to declare that
Wisconsin had no problems whatever with racial discrimination in housing. Such irresponsible statements have virtually
ceased, and have been replaced by widespread recognition of
the existence of the problem. The debate now centers on the
most desirable solution to the "new-found" problem.

2. We succeeded in getting the name "N—— Heel Lakes" changed
   to "Freedom Lakes," pending approval by the U.S. Department
   of the Interior.

3. We succeeded in activating the statutory advisory committee
   of the Fair Employment Practices Division of the Wisconsin
   Industrial Commission, after it had not met for over three
   years.

4. We discovered that a district office of the Wisconsin Employment Service was utilizing an unmarked box on its application
   form as a code to designate the race of applicants and that they
   were accepting job orders from employers who stated racial
   preferences—they even solicited such preferences—all in violation of Wisconsin and federal law. We succeeded in halting
   this practice within a week's time at the local office and witnessed measures to end this practice throughout the state.

5. We protested a black-face minstrel show sponsored by the
   Junior Chamber of Commerce at Whitewater College, Whitewater, Wisconsin, by picketing and distributing leaflets.

6. We introduced comprehensive civil rights legislation, Bill
   49-A, in the Wisconsin Legislature, secured an impressive
   hearing on the bill, and obtained a roll call vote on the measure. Our name appeared on the head of the bill.

7. In September, 1962, a serviceman was the victim of discrimination by Madison trailer parks. As a result, he depleted his savings and suffered other difficulties. Our Legal Redress Committee has begun civil action against several trailer parks.

8. Our Fall and Spring Conferences emphasized equal employment opportunities.

9. We plan a concentrated, comprehensive, and effective voter registration campaign for the next two years.

Why We Protest Black-Face Minstrels

The factual, unbiased, and wholesome portrayal of the Negro in American culture is a desirable goal, but one which today remains far from being realized. Instead, public opinion and attitudes are greatly influenced by theatrical performances which malign the Negro and other racial, religious, or ethnic groups. Such performances depict grossly inaccurate stereotypes which are degrading and encourage prejudice. Not only are such black-face minstrel shows detrimental to group advancement, they are also harmful to the fabric of our democratic society and they have a disastrous effect on our Nation's image abroad, where our adversaries readily seize upon them in their attempts to prove the failure of American ideals. For all these reasons, the National Association for the Advancement of Colored People deplores the continuance of public performances based on derogatory racial attitudes.

The Wisconsin Conference of NAACP Branches lodged appropriate formal protest some time ago with the Whitewater Junior Chamber of Commerce for sponsoring a black-face minstrel show and with Whitewater State College for permitting its facilities to be used in the service of scurrilous racist propaganda designed to perpetuate myths of racial superiority and racial inferiority.

We are now forced to make this public protest and demonstration because we believe it essential that citizens be aware that public performances which mimic and insult ethnic groups are not only reprehensible to the groups so maligned, but further are motivated by un-American attitudes which aid and abet our country's enemies in their struggle to undermine our position. We accuse the sponsors of this performance of being shamefully neglectful of their responsibilities as American citizens.

We urge the decent citizens of Whitewater not to patronize these shows. We urge the sponsors of these shows not to produce them in the future, but rather to seek means of fundraising which are wholesome, positive, and more in keeping with the finest traditions of our American heritage.

We urge the Whitewater State College to cease aiding and abetting affronts to ethnic groups by permitting their tax supported facilities to be used by organizations who sponsor black-face minstrel shows.

In this Centennial year of the Emancipation Proclamation we urge the citizens of Whitewater and, indeed, all citizens of the State of Wisconsin to rededicate themselves to the task of ending second-class citizenship throughout our State and Nation. We ask your help in making tolerance and brotherhood realities, and in eliminating discrimination because of race, creed, or color in housing, employment, and in places of public accommodation.

Finally, we call your attention to the fact that our Wisconsin Legislature is currently considering legislation to achieve these ends through the establishment of a Wisconsin Equal Opportunity Commission. We invite your help and your participation in bringing this attempt to a successful conclusion.

Problems Facing the Wisconsin NAACP

1. HUMAN RELATIONS. Wisconsin's problems are discrimination in employment, housing, and some public accommodations. These problems could be solved by legislation, executive action, and more vigorous private initiative.

2. POLITICAL ACTION. The Negro population of approximately 80,000 is small compared to the total state population. Therefore their problems appear to be undeserving of sufficient attention in the eyes of political leaders for immediate solution. Civil rights is an issue that is inevitably "put off until later" in Wisconsin. The number of qualified Negroes registered and

voting is shamefully small. Negro elected officials are few, and are lacking in patronage. Active Negro participation in both parties at all levels is negligible.

3. WELFARE. There is a swelling wave of opposition to welfare in Wisconsin. It began with a one year residence for relief law passed by the Legislature in 1957. It is presently manifested by a bill before the legislature to jail mothers of illegitimate children.

4. UNEMPLOYMENT. Wisconsin has a high rate of Negro unemployment and a high drop-out school rate.

5. INTERNAL DIFFICULTIES. Although there is general acceptance of human rights, there is not enough active promotion of effective human rights programs in Wisconsin. Young, new leadership is frustrated by old and impotent nominal leaders. Established reputed liberals and currently self-styled liberals dissipate energy by excessive talking, stalling, futile gestures, and even by subverting dynamic persons and programs.

Respectfully submitted,
Lloyd A. Barbee, President
2606 West Fond du Lac Avenue
Milwaukee, Wisconsin

2

MINORITY POLITICS

A MINORITY DOZEN YEARS OF LEGISLATING,
LLOYD A. BARBEE 1982 MANUSCRIPT

Working for change in a state legislature can be like a father-mother team, or a sibling rivalry. Each legislator is a winner in an election but serves as either a father-mother leader or a brother-sister member of the body. Every legislator is a star under the Capitol dome. Many seek to cluster in groups, some wish to shine alone, some are satellites, and others create their own satellite systems. Star battles and star wars occur often enough to polarize participants and observers. Chaos or order reigns depending upon the collective goals, vision leadership, concept of the common good, and the political direction of the moment. The stress of action on behalf of progress or the status quo keeps the stars gleaming or fading.

A few issues and actions from 1965 through 1977, when I was a Wisconsin legislator, are considered with a few conclusions. A complete list of the major legislation offered by me is at the end of this article. While overall progress in civil rights, human services, police-community relations, and state action for justice, equity and peace has not eroded, it must be refueled, readied for blast-off and ignited this decade. As of the date of this article, most black elected officials are in the legislative branches of government. This is good because in a government of laws the writers of legislation are crucial. Since laws have to be made before they are enforced and construed, my thoughts are addressed to those whose concern is political action at the front end of the law making arena. With this in mind, this former solon, who has been a practicing attorney for 27 years, proceeds.

People who know enough about themselves and the world in which they live have a built in advantage over persons who have doubts about their identity and environment. Members of minority groups who recognize majority prejudices and discriminatory behavior possess knowledge of a devil to beat or check. Any deals made should reflect advancement of justice either for all or for some. If it is for all, arguments can be advanced for overall peace and welfare. If it is for some—have-nots—the arguments can be couched in extensions of fairness, justice or mercy toward minorities to secure equal opportunity and buy peace.

Since most legislators are long on rhetoric and short on problem solutions, it takes issue-oriented persons to offer proposals that will resolve problems that are within the province of law-making bodies. There are very few issues that defy the ability of law makers to act. A quick reflection will reveal that law governs pre-birth through post-death of individuals. Laws govern creating, organizing, managing and dissolving all types of businesses from charters, articles of incorporations to stipulations as to what they may and may not do on dissolution. Taxation laws and their enforcement are the life and death of many organizations and even some individuals. All disputes in the United States of America involving individuals, corporations, and government are generally settled in courts. However, legislatures have virtually preempted the common law so that as a result the courts operated under statutory authority, substantively, procedurally and fiscally, from A to Zymurgy. Notwithstanding complaints of judicial encroachment on the legislative branch, the court's role as an interpreter of legislative enactments, or failure to act, gives it the right to rule on issues of constitutionality.

A commitment for positive changes in civil rights protection and expansion of opportunities for people's pursuit of human dignity and self fulfillment requires action. Recognition of persons or groups who are denied justice by the majority is an early step toward choosing a viable solution. Examples of such people are ethnic minorities, the aged, children, women, the poor, the handicapped, the physically and mentally ill, those convicted of crime who have completed their sentences, those with sexual preferences in and out of the mainstream, and creedal minorities.

The incumbent should not wait for persons who suffer or are victims of injustices to initiate changes. Some minorities are so minuscule that their chances of being elected are remote and may continue to suffer for generations. A legislator is in a unique position to make it possible for the have-nots to have what the haves have.

A legislator's effectiveness is often evaluated in terms of results. There are basically two kinds of results that count: the objective and the subjective. The bottom line of objective results is reflected in passage or defeat of legislation. In some sessions, the negative is as important as the positive, because many measures which are detrimental to a legislator's constituency or conscience are offered with a high probability of passage. Killing a proposal can be done by way of procedural and/or substantive amendments. Measures have been referred to committees for burial, or have such a large number of amendments appended or offered that the legislature becomes confused enough to vote for tabling or indefinitely postponing the measure. Filibustering or talking a measure to death are well-known tactics, but there are also tactics of nitpicking, [making] "informational" inquiries, and questioning and cross-questioning a bill's proponent until a sufficient number of inconsistent or ambiguous answers are elicited to cause the measure to be unduly delayed for final consideration. These pitfalls must be guarded against by the proposing legislator or competent colleagues should be relied upon to protect the measure so that it advances through the legislature, which in all but one state is bicameral.

A key to success for any legislator is informed preparation of proposed legislation, knowledge of the issues, pro and con, awareness of the house rules, and anticipation of attacks—obvious and subtle—by opponents. In remedial legislation, the legislator should answer these questions: what is the evil; what is the remedy; what evil, if any, is created by my remedy, and, if so, what is its antidote? If the legislator cannot identify an antidote, then the legislator should weigh the remedy. Evils of depth and scope require drastic remedies either immediately or in stages. Legislators should early identify areas of support from other legislators and thus begin counting votes. This counting should be periodically redone so that the legislator can determine whether or not a coalition of members of the opposing party is needed or whether modifications in the legislative bill might be required for passage. In forming coalitions the quid pro quo should always be mutual interest. This early identification, coupled with periodic re-checks, enhances a legislator's effectiveness in dealing with other legislators during work on the legislative floor where the public is excluded. This access in committees, party caucuses, eating places, etc., permits tradeoffs to occur on an on- and off-duty basis, when and wherever the opportunity arises. Aides and experts are useful in a legislator's preparation, but legislators should internalize such assistance because they alone have entree to sister and brother legislators. During such times they will be expected to know their issues.

A personal example: [my] constituency was always urban [and] low to moderate income, but I maintained a majority rural legislative coalition on civil rights economic and health issues. My farmers' voting record was 100 percent on all issues, except on some farmers' insistence on outlawing yellow-colored oleomargarine. My constituents wanted this inexpensive butter substitute [to be] colored yellow. My rural votes cost my constituents little but benefitted them greatly in the form of a consistent voting bloc in the legislature plus sympathetic lobbyists for a dozen years. In addition, this cooperation and coalition was inherited by my successor and still exists.

The majority wins and the majority rules. Starting with myself, I needed only 49 other votes, or in special circumstances, 67 for a two-thirds majority vote. Only on issues of high principle was it necessary for me to be a lone voter. While objective winning isn't everything, it is equated with power. An evaluation of subjective success does not have to be amorphous. The starting line of subjective success is selecting one's goal and setting a time to a given extant status. In a given session, a legislator may wish to advance appeal of an existing oppressive, unfair law or creating a new liberating, fair law. Abortion on demand is based on the principle that only a pregnant woman should determine whether or not she carries her child to full-term. Any law which violates this right should be repealed. There are legislators who would restrict women's rights to make this decision at various points in time, from pre-conception to delivery. The U.S. Supreme Court has given women protection through the first trimester. The beginning of my legislative career found me the only advocate of repealing Wisconsin's narrow anti-abortion law. This was done without consultation of or cooperation with any other person or group. Within a year, individuals

and groups began to lobby and work for easing abortion restrictions altogether or partially. Their work extended to all branches of government.
Eventually a majority agreed to loosen the restrictive prohibitions against
abortion. Since my voluntary retirement, a majority of the legislature has
joined a regressive movement called pro-life and has passed measures
preventing poor women from utilizing public funds for abortion. The
pro-choice proponents have future recognition of over-population and
over-utilization of the earth's life-support capacity on their side for ultimate victory. Unfortunately, some demagogues continue to advocate
uncontrolled procreation to minorities and third world people because of
the scare word—genocide. People who will not voluntarily control their
population will have it controlled by the government or the dominant
ruling class. This will further erode the chances which some minorities
have for fulfilling their potential.

My subjective success, untold to the public, was, in general, to free
laws from unconstitutional invasions into rights of privacy and from
permitting the denial of economic, educational, health, housing, public
accommodation and due process rights to all. Women are 51 percent of
Wisconsin's population, thus constituting a majority, but are a minority
in legislative halls. The use of one's body is personal and private. In areas
such as sexual intercourse and death, the majority of state legislatures in
the United States of America have been slow to act. However the future
lies with a recognition that consensual body use creates no victim. Thus
lawmaking and/or adjudicating institutions will legally establish a freedom of choice. Bread and butter issues such as income maintenance, reparations for descendants of slaves, constructive enforcement of treaty
violations with Native Americans, desegregating schools, mandating
quality education, equal employment opportunities, adequate transportation system, safe and decent housing, viable and economic energy program, adequate health delivery, prison reform, improved civil and criminal
justice, fair reapportionment, and improved recreational facilities and
opportunities can never be forgotten or ignored by minority legislators.
A perusal of the last section of this article contains a list of this legislator's
proposed solutions.

Progress is the bottom line of subjective success and can be counted
objectively. Has an issue been advanced? Passage, defeat, or amendment

of a bill, introduction of a bill, debating a bill, introduction of a commendatory or condemnatory resolution provides answers to this question. Time, as it passes, ensures the historical fact of your success, subjectively as well as objectively. Since legislation which either passes or fails is a matter of record these days in legislative halls, neither pride nor shame erases a record once made.

Regardless of techniques that a legislator finds effective in accomplishing major priority goals, there are a few rules of dos and don'ts which follow:

- Do identify constituent interests; select issues of conscience, if any; be aware of any conflicts between your conscience and constituent interests; set priorities of those interests; identify other legislators' constituent interests; seek coalitions with those legislators whose constituent interests are similar; seek views of other legislators; work on the basis of principle; seek coalitions with other legislators whose interests may be neutral; work with your leadership when possible; work with the leadership in the other house when possible; keep accurate checklist of past and current commitments; and seek cooperation from the Executive.

- Have a sense of purpose, perseverance, stamina, long memory, goal-setting ability, vision, cooperative spirit, good-working staff, good bladder and bowel control, and good seatmate.

- Don't take constituent interests for granted (you need them to elect and re-elect you); ignore matters of conscience, but rather seek to reconcile them when they exist; let others set your priorities; take any legislator for granted; become complacent; make personal attacks; needlessly bypass leadership; get stopped by vetoes; have poor temper control, poor health without medical supervision, an inability to work with others under pressure, or a lazy or arrogant staff.

Frustrations of legislating are best overcome by remembering why you chose to become a lawmaker. Whether the reasons are lofty or base, a correction course can be put in place soon enough to do what is necessary.

As of today less than one percent of all the elected officials in the United States are black. The 1980 U.S. census shows the black populations percentage to be approximately 14 percent; if one allows for the undercounting, that percentage could be at an 18 percent level. Given the fact that the number of black officials are small, their impact can be great depending on their talent and skill. In my own state, Wisconsin, the number of black legislators is less than one percent. Since the numbers are de minimus, one reviews a legislator's record not merely for effectiveness but for indicating the kinds of behavior important for getting things done.

The first priority in my legislative career was the enactment of a state fair housing law containing a declaration of right to housing, a quick administrative remedy including an investigation and a hearing, injunctive relief, fines against violators, court enforcement, and sufficient budget to adequately implement the law through an independent agency.

My predecessor, Assemblyman Isaac N. Coggs, had pioneered in the legislature with the first fair housing measure in a bill which abolished two civil rights agencies which fought one another with alarming vigor. When Assemblyman Coggs introduced his measure to eliminate the two agencies, one an independent educational agency and the other a fair employment practice division of the Industrial Commission, and to create a strong three-person commission on civil rights, he was opposed vehemently by both agencies. Consequently, his bill was shelved, into the committee which he chaired, and died. He reintroduced his measure the next session as a bill on equal opportunity. The opposite party gained control of the legislature, so Assemblyman Coggs was faced with being a double minority—black and a Democrat. However, he introduced a strong but simple fair housing bill, along with a number of other civil rights measures. Black and liberal white groups joined forces in demonstrating and lobbying for these bills under the banner of human rights. After a favorable series of hearings, rallies, lobby days, and follow-up contacts with legislators in their home districts by some of their constituents (ministers, priests, rabbis, lay leaders, etc.), the issue of need was framed. A legislator, who was chairman of the Judiciary Committee, kept the key measure bottled up in his committee, and announced that it would be buried there until the session was over.

In 1959 I began to work with Assemblyman Coggs, as a voluntary aide, draftsman and factotum and became president of the state National Association for the Advancement of Colored People (NAACP) Conference of Branches in 1961. Wearing these two hats and with a small group of committed people, a drive [began] to save the bill from a sudden white death by conducting a round the clock sit-in in the Rotunda of the State Capitol. The Madison NAACP Board hesitated to sponsor a sit-in. Their reasons ranged from trespass to a bad image. However, there were enough votes to endorse this form of pressure for the enactment of human rights legislation.

In order to counter arguments made by the NAACP Board, the Chairman of Legal Redress was assigned the job of reviewing my research on the issue that state taxpayers were the owners of state buildings and could not be successfully barred as trespassers. In addition, he was assigned the task of finding legal defense for those of us who might be arrested for any reason or non-reason as a result of the sit-in. As a practical preventive measure, a special committee was appointed to call upon the Governor and the State Attorney General, advise them of our plan to exercise our freedom of speech, protest and petition for redress of grievances, and seek their cooperation. Our timing was tight, so that if the Executive Branch would choose to either bar us or have us arrested, our cause would have been advanced. If we were not barred from sitting-in, we would have the opportunity to articulate our position daily to the legislature, users of the Capitol building, and the press. Thus our strategy was a fail-proof one. The Governor, Attorney General, and Secretary of Administration (Housekeeping Officer) were cooperative. So, with some discrete notice to civil rights and political reporters from the media, and a one-page press release, at noon on July 28, 1961, sixteen of us marched into the Capitol with folding chairs and a set of demonstration instructions, wearing 4 x 7 cards bearing the legend: "We are here for human rights." We unfolded our chairs and sat down on the ground floor in front of the sixteen marble columns at the base of the granite Capitol dome, sometimes called the Rotunda. This Wisconsin Capitol dome happens to be the tallest and largest self-supported granite dome in the world.

When relief arrived, I left my seat, spoke to the press, and passed out an information sheet explaining the purpose of the sit-in. Thus the sit-in was generally not interrupted by the television media which tended to be awkward, time-consuming and distracting. Their portable equipment was bulky, their audio level had to be continually adjusted, their film sometimes required changing partway through an interview, and lights had to be adjusted according to hand-held light meters. On at least three occasions, TV film crews returned to reshoot their coverage of the sit-in because of problems in developing their film.

This convinced me that the medium was not the message. The medium was messy, and often it still is. It is important that the messenger handles the media. Accordingly, deliver the message directly, with few modifiers, so that the essence is not encumbered or edited out. Avoid complaining to the media about their oversights and/or misinterpretations; rather inform and educate them about your issues.

The instructions to the demonstrators stressed cleanliness, decorum, non-violence, neatness and dignity. Men were not permitted to have beards and women were not permitted to wear shorts. Known, or seriously suspected, Communists were not allowed to sit-in. While we needed to win more establishment support to get the targeted legislation passed then, I do not favor such a "more royal than the king" strategy now. This position of barring Communists from the sit-in placed me in an incongruous leadership position. Some Russian-type Communists threatened to take over the sit-in one afternoon. When policemen were alerted and brought in to arrest them, the Communists and their cohorts quickly left the Capitol. My position then was, as well as now is, that the people who plan and execute a demonstration must control it by whatever appropriate means. Otherwise chaos or counter production is assured. The demonstrators wore cards so that anyone passing through the Capitol could read the purpose of the demonstration at one glance. A leaflet was passed out at all Rotunda entrances. This information sheet posed the issue—"why we are here"—and went on to solicit support from the reader by requesting that they contact their legislator for our just demands. This sit-in lasted fourteen days, around the clock. The goal of freeing the bill from committee and getting it to the floor succeeded. The measure was debated seriously and voted on the floor for the first time in Wisconsin's legislative history, but did not pass. We remained in the legislature a day after their sine die adjournment in August, 1961, to give the message that we would persevere until a fair housing measure was adopted and improvements were made in the state's fair employment practices and public accommodations laws.

The election of 196[4] resulted in my being the only Black elected to the legislature. My conviction that a fair housing bill could be passed, that the public accommodations law could be strengthened and that fair employment practices could be improved by the legislature was severely tested. With only myself to consult, the Black caucus was never divided in legislative strategy, achievement and evaluation.

A problem developed when one Milwaukee civil rights organization, which was in fact led and financed by whites, chose to discourage co-authors of my strong omnibus civil rights bill by requesting that they support a weak measure, drafted by the Governor's Commission on Human Rights. This group wrote a letter, drafted by a white former law classmate of mine, recommending that I abandon my bill as well. He and other lily-white attorneys, men and women of influence and affluence, told me and others that my name on any civil rights bill was the kiss of death. They did generally praise the strong bill as being well-drafted, and a piece of ideal legislation. These white "friends" of Blacks sought, through sabotage and praise, to maintain leadership by killing or neutralizing black initiative for leadership. Since it was clear to me that these great white fathers and mothers disrespected black initiative, self-reliance, development, etc., I wrote them a letter inviting them to get on the caboose or miss the train. Thereupon, my attention remained with those persons and groups who gave me a chance to consummate the initiative. Eventually this organization joined the freedom train at another junction.

The hearing for this strong bill was so large that the Assembly chambers had to be used. For the first time more people testified for the bill rather than against it. The registrations in favor of the bill were overwhelming. The real estate and some insurance organizations worked against this measure which helps demonstrate the adage that insiders can do more damage than outsiders, particularly when they put their money to use with paid professionals, called lobbyists. Even though this strong ideal bill brought out large numbers of proponents to debate all areas of racial discrimination, there were not enough votes to pass it in the House, which was controlled by the more liberal party. So it served as a lightning rod. The roar of the thunder caught legislators' attention more than the bolts of lightning. This made it possible for me to ask reasonable legislators what they would support. After a visit with the conservative party leadership to get an adequate number of votes to pass a fair housing bill, expand the public accommodations law, and provide more staff to eliminate employment discrimination, [an agreement] was secured in our House. The leadership of that party called in the actual leader of the other House and we struck a deal, which combined my essential ingredients plus a commitment that no referendum would be attached in either House to submit the measure to the public for veto. A referendum would have delayed enforcement at best or ultimately defeated the law at worst. There was also an agreement not to block a new bill procedurally after passage in either House. The Governor, who was not of my party, agreed to sign the bill when it reached his desk. Therefore a bipartisan bill along these lines was introduced. All the agreements were kept, by not too many votes too spare, but by a margin large enough for success. Accordingly, Assembly Bill 852 was passed in the Assembly, September 30, 1965, after 25 amendments, good and bad, were debated. The Senate concurred in passage of this bipartisan measure, October 30, 1965 with 16 amendments debated, more bad than good, and returned it to the Assembly. Since a bill must receive a majority of votes in the same version in both Houses, the Assembly took up the amended measure November 2, 1965, and passed it. I voted against all of the bad amendments, knowing full well that the racists would support unfavorable amendments; my votes against these weakening amendments did not hurt its chances of final passage.

The Governor signed the bill as promised December 10, 1965; it became Chapter 439 of the Wisconsin Statutes. Former Assemblyman Coggs, who was then a Milwaukee County Supervisor, and NAACP representatives were among others, who witnessed this legislative victory.

Thousands of people made it possible to win that legislative battle, but the leadership credit on the state level must go to a few people who banded together and stuck with the job until the statute was passed which eliminated all exemptions from the basic law passed in 1965. This was accomplished in 1972. Credit also belongs to those who are continuing to expand legislative civil rights protection to other minorities such as women, single persons, young and older persons, poor persons, persons whose sexual preferences are in and out of the mainstream, and other handicapped persons.

In subsequent sessions, the civil rights agencies were consolidated into the Department of Industry, Labor and Human Relations. Thus equal

opportunity was expanded to cover fair employment practices, fair housing, public accommodation, and insurance. Timing is important in legislative work. Efforts should be paced so that pressure is applied in the right
places at crucial times for desired results. During the fair housing battle
within the legislature, it was easy to sense honest guilt, concern, and shame
about denial of rights to people based on race. It was obvious that the majority party had no monopoly on virtue. This presented the opportunity
to persuade [members of the majority party]. They seized the opportunity
to participate in a human rights victory by providing the requisite number
of votes. A wider coalition could be built once the black-haters, gradualists,
and the timid had objected to a too-much, too-soon bill. It was logical and
cogent for me to argue for a get-as-much-as-you-can bill for starters. Since
the evil of housing discrimination was pervasive, arguments for a root and
branch remedy were compelling. The fact that Blacks could not rent, lease,
or buy real estate in places of their choosing regardless of economic or
social status was not seriously debated. Rather, a myth was repeated that
Black occupancy resulted in devaluation of real estate and that morality
could not be legislated. The moral right of humans for housing based on
their ability to pay or borrow was thwarted by private individuals. Since
the legislature defines rights and responsibilities of citizens in every session by setting standards in the civil and criminal law, it was easy to insist
that the hour was at hand for action.

   Another aspect of timing impels a legislator to set priority bills early
in each session. This strengthens the legislator's hand in ordering issues
according to importance and ease of passage. With a time advantage, decisions can be made on which issues to advance first, the difficult or the
easy ones. The strategy used in the fair housing issue was to make it my
number one priority, introduce it in its strongest form early, shepherd it,
so that it could be rescued or traded later, but not before the session ended.
Log-rolling [exchanging political favors] is legally forbidden, but effective
legislators trade and make deals all the time. Their style may be beguiling
or galling. But Representative X will not vote for Representative Y's program all the time without reciprocation. The Representatives who promote their programs first have all the advantages that go with initiative,
including keeping a score card on substantive and procedural votes. A
strategy of late timing can be effective particularly when the sessions are

log-jammed. However, this strategy works best when the legislator is working for a single issue and can provide reciprocal assistance on matters which are hotly contested and the votes are close.

Some of my perennial bills concern police reorganization. The final section of this article contains the specific bills on this issue. One of the most interesting perennials relates to repealing an 1885 statute which grants the Milwaukee police chief life time tenure and permitted only freeholders—owners of city property—to complain about police misconduct. The Wisconsin legislature created a 5-member Milwaukee Fire and Police Commission appointed by the mayor and subject to the approval of the Common Council. Commissioners serve renewable five year terms. This commission appoints the police chief by majority vote. The chief was given a statutory term for life and can only be removed for "just cause," e.g., commission of a crime or some other gross misconduct.

The legislative purpose of this Statute was to eliminate political influence and corruption from the police department. In guaranteeing the police chief a term for life, the legislature ensured the potential for accountability. This insurance became reality on several occasions. In 1910, Police Chief John Janssen, who had held office for 22 years, told reform Socialist Mayor Emil Seidel publicly to "go to hell" and continued to serve for 11 more years.

After a couple of sessions, my proposal to permit any aggrieved person to bring a complaint about police misconduct before the Fire and Police Commission was passed and became law. My efforts to repeal the police chief's life-tenure position and create a fixed-term appointment ran into charges of returning politics to the police department and attacking the incumbent tough law and order chief. No police department in this country is realistically devoid of politics. The truth of this statement laid the first criticism to rest early. The personality and popularity of the police chief created an emotional defense which obscured the issue of accountability.

Accomplishment is often a matter of stretching and reaching. In 1965 the major press and media opposed my recommendation for the elimination of life tenure for the police chief. They often cited a 1931 National Commission on Law Observance finding that the Milwaukee police department was a national model for corruption-free police force. The black press and civil rights groups supported me. In 1972 the Wisconsin State Committee of the U.S. Commission on Civil Rights concluded that the Milwaukee Police department's major problems were "attributable to the isolated condition of the department in relation to the citizenry it serves. The responsibility for law enforcement policy making and implementation is concentrated in an office whose incumbent is directly accountable to no one. . . ." Other good government groups and scholars began to look at the issue of accountability rather than the personality of a chief whose popularity had earlier overshadowed it. My strategy was to reintroduce bills to set a fixed term for chiefs, ranging from 4 to 6 years, or permitting the police and fire commission to set a term not to exceed 10 years. During my last two sessions measures were introduced to enable the Common Council to set the term for a period of time less than life. After a prolonged debate during my last session, the bill passed my House and was sent to the Senate. The Chairman of the Senate committee to which the bill was referred had ideological differences, and action was delayed toward the end of the session, despite efforts of friends in the Senate who favored passage and had the votes to do so. The bill was prayed out of committee with a recommendation for passage, but the Senate adjourned before acting.

My successor, Marcia P. Coggs, the first black female elected to the Wisconsin legislature, succeeded in getting the 1885 police chief lifetime tenure law repealed. The bill accomplishing this was identical to the one which died in the Senate in 1976. When the bill was signed into law in 1978 by the governor, comment was made that no one succeeds like a successor.

In discussing the two major bills one can draw some conclusions about effectiveness of minority legislators. Since their number is disproportionately small and the number of issues is vast, accomplishment is possible by: coalitions inside and outside the legislative chambers, speeches, debates, prioritization of legislation, selective use of fiscal power, committee work, and skillful use of the media. The confrontation and controversy strategies are still good but legislators generally can retain their ability to engage in serious dialogue through their office and in the legislative forum. Many issues that were articulated or advanced by me went unmentioned for decades on the legislative floor. My overall policy was to introduce bills which solved problems. Thus the public had access to both the issue and the proposed solution. The education process is a continuous one. Minorities have a responsibility to educate the ignorant majority despite their resistance. Often they know not what they do.

A Black man who wanted to be a Milwaukee County Board supervisor was the runner-up in two successive primary elections. In November 1956, the County Board supervisor, who had won the April general election, died. It was customary for the County Board, which had the authority to name a board member to fill a vacancy created by resignation or death, to appoint the runner-up. [Even though] the County Board was all white, it was expected that they would follow its unbroken precedent and appoint the black runner-up. However the chairman announced before the Board, that "because we haven't had a colored, it doesn't make sense to appoint one." So the appointment went to a white man. In the next election, the Black chose to run again, survived the primary again, but lost in the general election to the white appointee, who was the incumbent.

The next morning, the wife of the Black candidate received a telephone call she relates as follows: "May I speak to Mr. Coggs?"

"He's not in."

"May I speak to Mrs. Coggs?"

"This is she."

"Your husband is a supervisor by over 500 votes."

"We are going to ask for a recount."

"A recount won't do you any good. Investigate the absentee ballots."

Then the call was disconnected.

This black candidate sought a recount and hired an attorney. During the recount, the absentee ballots were sequestered from the regular ballots and it was discovered that a total of 642 absentee ballots were cast, of which fourteen were for the black candidate and 628 were for the white incumbent. Most of the fourteen ballots were from persons who served in the Armed Forces. The majority of the 628 votes were from nursing homes within the district. As a matter of fact, in this district absentee ballots amounted to one third of the entire County's ballots (1,800).

A closer examination of the supplemental poll list showed examples like the following:

Address: 321 East Meinecke Names: John P. Smith, J. P. Smith, J. Payne Smith, Mr. Smith, Alice L. Smith, A. L. Smith, A. Lee Smith, Mrs. Smith, Miss Smith, etc.

Each signed an absentee ballot. These, and similar absentee ballots, cast for the white incumbent, were all notarized by one individual. This situation serves to illustrate how a city and county that prides itself on clean elections is as dirty as anything on earth. The ballots were impounded for court action. The Black candidate, after posting civil bond, paying for another attorney, and other costs for litigating this matter, chose to concentrate on the next election. He did win the next election by 500 votes, the approximate number by which he had lost to the same white incumbent.

Representative [Fred] Kessler and I were successful in prohibiting candidates from witnessing absentee ballots or notarizing them in their own behalf. In addition, notaries were not to notarize absentee ballots, or applications, in absentia. About fourteen years later, a black notary surrendered his seal to the state, in lieu of being prosecuted, for notarizing nominating petitions for a candidate outside the presence of the circulator.

1969 LEGISLATIVE SESSION, LLOYD A. BARBEE 1982 MANUSCRIPT

The 1969 legislative session came to an abrupt end in both houses with the result that many important pieces of legislation died without final legislative action. Most significantly in the closing minutes of the parochial school aid bill to take the bill up and have the legislature stay in session for whatever time was necessary to act on the bill. However, over the objections of the bill's supporters, the majority rammed through an adjournment motion without debate that killed many necessary bills.

The following is a summary of the final disposition of the major legislation considered by the 1969 legislative session:

Human Rights

■ Killed a bill to eliminate the remaining exceptions in the state's open housing law.

Conservation

■ Passed ORAP - 200 which provides for $144 million to help local communities build sewage treatment facilities and $56 million to speed up and expand the land acquisition program for outdoor recreation.

- Passed a bill to ban the sale, distribution, or use of DDT.

- Passed a bill that would reimburse local communities partially for revenue lost as the result of property tax exemption for pollution abatement facilities.

- Passed a bill requiring a jury trial before the State Department of Natural Resources could condemn land for parks, preserves, or other public projects.

- Failed to pass a bill that would appropriate funds to the environmental protection division of the Department of Natural Resources to provide for added staff to fight air pollution.

Crime and Law Enforcement

- Passed a bill to give the Attorney General added powers to identify and fight organized crime.

- Granted law enforcement officers with authority to "stop and frisk" persons they have reason to suspect are involved in a criminal act.

- Passed a bill that would make persons convicted of carrying a concealed weapon subject to imprisonment up to one year.

- Passed a bill authorizing court approved wire tapping for law enforcement purposes in specified cases.

- Revised the state's drug control laws. Reduced the penalty for the use of marijuana, however strengthened the penalties for pushers and repeated users.

- Passed a bill allowing prosecutors to obtain injunctions banning the sale or exhibition of pornographic materials to persons age 17 and younger.

- Established optional minimum standards for law enforcement offices.

Consumer Protection

- Passed a bill to give the Attorney General and district attorney injunctive power to enforce consumer fraud laws.

- Killed a bill to set up a state department of consumer protection to centralize the consumer protection responsibility that presently is divided between the Attorney General and the Department of Agriculture.

Finance

- Enacted a $1.6 billion state budget that included a 4% general sales tax that would cover necessity items such as clothing, household utilities, prescription drugs, and home building materials.

Labor

- Killed a bill to ban the hiring of professional strikebreakers.

- Killed a bill to set up a realistic minimum wage law.

- Killed legislation for improved workmen's compensation.

- Killed a bill that would permit a modified agency shop for public employees.

Agriculture

- Killed a bill to bar the abuses of conglomerate farms.

- Killed a bill to provide for the full state pick up of brucellosis vaccination.

- Enacted legislation to eliminate the state's 5½ cent per pound tax on low butterfat spreads, but not oleo.

- Included the dairy industry in the Unfair Trade Practices Law which made it illegal to sell a dairy product below cost to stifle competition.

- Set up a study group to examine the need for a school of veterinary medicine to report back to the legislature next session.

Veterans

- Passed a bill to assure the direct deposit of 35% of the state liquor tax into the veteran's trust fund for the maintenance of veterans programs. The bill also provides money for the repair of sewer and water systems and construction of buildings at the Grand Army Home at King.

- Passed a bill that would double the payment to the counties for the burial of indigent veterans.

- Passed a bill that would permit veterans to obtain loans from the Department of Veterans Affairs for the purchase of mobile homes.

Other

- Passed a modified Tarr Task Force Bill on county assessors that would make it optional for counties to adopt uniform systems of property assessment.

- Killed the so-called "Dirksen Amendment" that would petition Congress to call a Federal Constitutional Convention for the purpose of amending the U.S. Constitution to allow one house of a two-house legislature to be apportioned on a basis other than population.

- Killed a major revision of the State Civil Service Law.

- Killed a bill for annual sessions of the legislature. It should be noted that the bill could not stand on its own merits because the Senate chose to tie it together with a raise in salary for constitutional offices and a bill for a salary council for legislators that would permit increases in legislative salaries with legislators having to vote on them.

- Passed increased retirement benefits for public employees including teachers, municipal employees, judges and legislators.

- Killed legislation to liberalize the state's birth control laws.

- Killed legislation to authorize 65-foot trucks on the highways.

- Killed a proposal for a boundary review board to decide on municipal annexations.

- Killed a bill that would have removed the tax exempt status of personal property of insurance companies.

- Killed a bill that would have provided tuition grants to the parents of children attending non-public schools.

LEGISLATIVE BACKLOG, LEGISLATIVE COMMENT, JUNE 24, 1971

This week we can see that the Assembly is moving along on its backlog calendar of legislation. However, that legislation designed to help people who need help is being defeated or tabled.

The defeat of the hitchhiking bill was typical of a semi-reactionary state Assembly. It was brought out during debate on the hitchhiking bill that no one appeared against it at the public hearing and only the Milwaukee lobbyist registered against the bill. Typically, there seems to be no desire on the part of the legislature to listen to anybody's argument for the bill.

Obviously, most of the members of the legislature felt that the bill was not important since it affected mainly poor and young people. All this requires is the nerve to solicit a ride and a driver who is willing to give a person a ride either to a short or long destination. I maintain that this is a fundamental right of contract that should not be restricted.

Most of the things that have to do with improving the right of people accused of crimes have not been favorably acted upon, if at all, in this legislature.

The bill to permit discovery procedures for people accused of a crime passed the Assembly and was referred to the Senate Committee on Judiciary where it was recommended for passage. However, the Milwaukee Common Council, the Milwaukee County Board, the Milwaukee City Attorney and its bad police department came to the conclusion that they should oppose the bill. They were successful in having a rehearing. The Police Department, Common Council, County Board and the [district attorney], who were present in full force, succeeded in getting the committee to reconsider its action and delayed the bill.

A fellow legislator commented to me the other day that progress was being made despite the very slow pace of the legislature. I remarked to him that the glacial speed of legislative reform for have-nots is not a credit to lawmaking. The disadvantaged and oppressed will not remain patient to the point of waiting generations for reform of unreasonable impediments on them which reform is prevented by those representatives busy maintaining the status quo.

Black Political Convention, Legislative Comment, March 21, 1972

I shall make a few comments about the National Black Political Convention in Gary, Indiana, last week.

Blacks getting together nationally for political action in this century was a first must. Staying together is a second must. This second must will be harder for some individuals and groups, but successful action requires committed people to work out a plan and implement it.

The quality and quantity of delegates, leaders, and observers in Gary, March 10, 11 and 12 was impressive despite usual convention falderal and confusion. Individualists, collectivists, militants and moderates all had their say and way. Anti-Bussing and anti-school integration resolutions narrowly passed. Thereafter, pro-Bussing and pro-school integration resolutions also passed. A long and controversial platform called a Black Agenda with inconsistent amendments was adopted and referred to an ongoing steering committee to refine, reconcile, and redraft by Malcolm X's birthday, May 19th. A near impossible task and a great challenge.

In summary, Blacks met together, got together, set up a structure to keep together for the benefit of Black political effectiveness. This was an accomplishment worthy of historical note. From the present onwards, it's clear thinking, planning, and working that will result in true political achievement.

Black Agenda, Legislative Comment, April 3, 1972

The U.S. Department of Labor projects that in 1980 there will be more professional and technological workers (15.5 million) with college or post graduate education than factory workers or laborers (15.4 million).

Workers in the professional category are expected to increase 5%; semi-skilled workers will increase 10%. Common labor will decline by 2%; farm labor will drop 33%.

Thus, semi-skilled and unskilled work often used by Blacks to escape from poverty will be more scarce. Poor youth in general, Blacks in particular, will continue to disadvantageously compete for fewer jobs. When one looks at the first year of the Emergency Employee Act, signed by President [Richard] Nixon, July 12, 1971, it becomes clear that the anticipated 150,000 job yield, has not materialized. By Christmas of 1971, 31,000 unemployed were hired. Most of them were in the moderate income bracket of at least $8,500.

The Black Agenda, adopted by the Black Political Convention in Gary, which was referred to a National Steering Committee to clarify and refine, recognizes the economic plight of Blacks in its introduction by saying: "Huge sectors of our youth—and countless others—face permanent unemployment. Those of us who work, find our pay checks able to purchase less and less."

One means of increasing the work force in this country requires a commitment on the part of Congress to make governmental employment more bold and imaginative. For example, the U.S. should either employ the poor directly and pay wages above the poverty level, or permit the private sector to employ blacks in meaningful work, subsidizing any deficits. Non-demeaning or de-humanizing jobs need to be developed in order to make American society human and just. Examples: revitalizing cities, constructing decent and attractive housing; effective ecological programs, para-professional activities, such as ancillary medical, psychological, sociological educational and day-care programs; creative contributions to the arts, architecture and local community development, etc. Drone like jobs such as garbage disposal should be compensated at a level commensurate with their psychological unattractiveness.

A garbage man or street cleaner is more socially necessary than a white collar clerk or an empire building bureaucrat.

REAPPORTIONMENT, LEGISLATIVE COMMENT, MAY 5, 1972

The Wisconsin Legislature managed this year for the first time in 30 years to reapportion itself. I am happy to report that one of my main goals (more Black representatives) was met in the plan.

In 1964 the Wisconsin Supreme Court reapportioned the state according to the 1962 Baker vs. Carr one-man, one-vote decision. This State Court Plan had the effect of reducing the Black delegation in the legislature from 2 to 1. This imbalance has been redressed in the current plan at least.

It will now be possible for the Black community in Milwaukee to send at least two and possibly three representatives to Madison this Fall. It is true that the new plan created some strange-shaped districts. It is [a] question whether or not the new legislative redistricting is a gerrymander. If it gerrymandered the lines to maximize Black electoral power, then I am all in favor of it.

I would add one word of caution: not too many blacks should jump into the race. If a large number of Blacks run against each other, this will simply fragment the Black vote and cede the district to the white community. It is certainly not realistic to expect Milwaukee whites to vote en masse for any Black candidate, except accidentally.

The two easily winnable districts now are districts 17 and 18. District 18 contains the bulk of my present 6th district. This remains predominantly Black, but less than the current 6th district.

District 17 begins at the intersection of North Port Washington Road and West Capitol Drive. It goes south on Port Washington, east on West Vienna Avenue, and along the tracks to East Keefe Avenue. Then it goes west on East Keefe, south on North Richard and west on East Burleigh. From East Burleigh and North Palmer it proceeds south to Hadley Street, west to North 24th Street to Locust, and then west on West Locust.

At the junction of West Locust and North 27th it proceeds north to West Townsend Street, then north again on North 24th Place to West Keefe. The line then runs east on West Keefe, north on North 20th to West Atkinson, then southeast on West Atkinson to North 15th.

From that intersection the line goes north on North 15th to West Capitol and then east to the starting point.

Each of these districts—17 and 18—are clearly within the range of Black candidates. Looking to the future, if a tangible coalition between the black, radical, liberal, progressive, poor communities can be forged, then by the end of this decade we may be able to elect 3 to 5 Black representatives.

I have been aiming at this outcome before the opening day of the '71 legislative session. It is the outcome which favors my constituents and readers. It is the kind of gerrymander, if it is that, which is necessary and desirable.

Racial Discrimination at Private Clubs, Legislative Comment, June 19, 1972

The U.S. Supreme Court dealt a damaging blow to the cause of racial equality through a decision handed down last week. In a 6 to 3 decision, the justices said it was all right for private clubs to exclude Blacks as guests. They refused to prevent states from denying liquor licenses to clubs that openly practice discrimination. A 3-judge Federal court in Pennsylvania said the Moose Lodge in question could not keep its liquor license and at the same time exclude blacks as guests. But the high court said it could.

Ironically, a Black man, although honored by being the majority leader of the state House of Representatives, was judged not good enough to be served at the lily-white Moose Club in Harrisburg. That club and many others in the U.S. make no secret of their hatred of Blacks and specifically exclude them from club membership in their by-laws.

But the court said the membership question was not at issue, only the question of can Blacks be excluded as guests. So, under the court's line of thought, a Black man could theoretically become a member of one of these clubs, but couldn't bring his brother or mother in for a drink.

Fortunately, this step backward in the civil rights movement may not affect actions by the Wisconsin Department of Revenue to revoke the tax exempt status of private clubs in this state which also discriminate against the Black man. Revenue Department officials indicate they will continue the investigation into these clubs, an investigation which has already led to the revocation of tax exemptions for 17 Elks Clubs and one Moose Club.

We cannot continue to function in a society where blacks and whites are divided under the guise of "home rule" or the right of private clubs to serve who they want. Even though Blacks and other minorities are supposed to be equal in education, health, business and government, many of the important decisions governing this country are made by the white bigots in the privacy of their castle-like clubs—fraternal orders, athletic and country clubs, etc.

We must open all institutions, private and public, to all races.

But the facts remain clear. Once again, the high court, packed with the white, upper class reactionary appointees of President Nixon, have scored another victory for those wishing to walk all over the individual rights of Blacks. The justices claim the issuing of a liquor license "does not involve the state sufficiently in the club's practices to bring them under legal state action governed by the constitutional guarantee of equal protection of the laws." Through some cleverly devised rhetoric, the high court, rather than abiding by the constitution, has arrogantly ignored and twisted it and refused to enforce the 14th amendment. The court has thrown its support behind racial discrimination. These clubs and other havens of bigotry are cancers in our society and must be treated by radical surgery, radioactive bombardment or other means.

DISTRICT ELECTIONS, LEGISLATIVE COMMENT, JULY 8, 1971

After an Independence Day weekend the Legislature resumed with a degree of fireworks almost as exciting and polluting as any of the activities on the lake front and the parks of Milwaukee. The proposal to make the Milwaukee School Board more accountable by requiring it to hold district elections ran into great difficulty mainly because one author and one opponent of the bill decided the school board should be partially elected on a district basis and partially on an at-large basis.

I opposed this hodgepodge effort because it has been my firm conviction that Blacks and Spanish speaking people will never be elected to the school board if the elections continue to be decided on an at-large basis.

Further I maintain that the representatives of minorities should be elected by the minorities. The amendment by Kessler and Brown would have reduced the 19 Districts in Milwaukee to 9. Quite obviously, Blacks and the Spanish-speaking candidates would be adulterated by whites and would be completely out of any redistricting plan.

In addition, the redistricting of this new plan will be done by the school board itself. The school board has always been white bigoted and unaccountable to the total community. In good conscience no honest sane critic could permit the board to reapportion itself. I say this not with-standing their election of a man of color as president last week.

On the Muhammad Ali decision by the U.S. Supreme Court last week, I noted that the one race press has praised the judiciary system for being fair.

It is a very callous attitude for Muhammad to have been stripped of his title, harassed because of his religious convictions, and lose more than a small fortune, be told five years later that his religious views should have been honored. This is hardly justice. It proves that justice delayed is not only denied but mocked.

A group which recently organized itself to fight police brutality which is getting worse in Milwaukee is getting off the tract. A number of Milwaukee people have been insulted, had their heads beaten for no valid reason and required to go to court as the defendant for flimsy charges.

We have recently witnessed a youngster being murdered by Milwaukee policemen. Instead of concentrating on that job, the committee has defected and fought for a small amount of money the anti-poverty program has provided Triple O in Milwaukee. I again use my prerogative as an elected official to advise the total Black community that it should not battle over a meatless bone. Blacks must refuse the choice of inadequacy or nothing.

Such a choice is guile and jive.

Committees that want to fight police brutality should keep their real enemy in view and not engage in drawing room fights with brothers and sisters over meager funds this government offers in its attempt to buy the submission of Black people and poor people.

Presidential Nomination, Legislative Comment, July 7, 1972

It is interesting and enlightening to watch this year's presidential aspirants falling all over themselves and each other to get the Democratic presidential nomination. They are like a group of wild college playboys doing their best to impress the pretty, young co-ed that each is more worthy of her affections than the others.

The over-anxious politicians are quick to tell us how they will end the war, poverty, racism, and injustice, in other words, how liberal they are. But I'm sure you've noticed how they all seem to be moving towards the right in an effort to capture the coveted nomination.

Humbert Humphrey, one of the early liberals, has disappointed me by what he calls his "movement to center." This is just a catchphrase for his alliance and catering to the reactionary forces which have put this country where it is now.

The new liberals are not innocent of this maneuvering either. Senator [George] McGovern is as guilty as the rest. Even Sister Shirley Chisholm recently explained on nationwide television before millions of blacks that supporters of George Wallace were not racist.

None of the candidates would go near this southern bigot before he gained such popularity or was shot. But all of them, including Ms. Chisholm have made the journey to his bedside to demonstrate that his preaching of hatred and fear really isn't so terrible. What will these candidates be saying tomorrow? Can we really trust them?

Those who aspire to power possess curious characteristics and contradictions. Out of one side of their mouth, they are decrying the dictatorship of Nixon and how corrupt power has made him. But out of the other side, they are making deals, pressuring delegates, and who knows what else. They call each other names, throw temper tantrums, make threats and empty promises, in order to gain more votes. Then they turn around and tell their supporters in a cool and calm voice, they have the moral leadership and temperance to lead this country. In their quest for power they become corrupt before they attain it—as corrupt as those presently holding it. The amateur politician will prostitute his body and soul to get that power. If virtue is its own reward then the major Democratic presidential contenders will be permanently damned.

Democracy is a difficult principle to implement. Some may lie, say, and think we have a democratic country, but we don't. The bosses and corporate tyrants run this nation. That is why practical politics requires a contrast between the challenger and the incumbent. But the blacks and other have-nots do not have a choice. They just choose between a gnat and a flea.

DEMOCRATIC CONVENTION, LEGISLATIVE COMMENT, JULY 14, 1972

The Democratic National Convention has ended and the more than 3,000 delegates have returned home to either support or oppose the presidential nominee. Which they will do remains to be seen. But it is hoped that the delegates will not forget that the party reforms achieved since 1968 require the continued support of all Democrats. Freedom and democracy is not achieved just once. It must be won time and time again. Those who do not recognize this will soon find they are no longer free.

The 1972 convention was unique in that a greater number of Blacks, women, young people and other powerless minorities were represented. We have finally, but not totally eliminated the old line bosses and party hacks who dictated the choice of the party in years past.

Consider these facts as proof of greater representation: less than six percent of the delegates at the 1968 Democratic National Convention were Black. This year, there were 15 percent. In 1968, only 13 percent of the delegates were women. In 1972, they comprised almost 40 percent of the delegates in Miami Beach. Four years ago, only four percent of the delegate, were under thirty years of age. This year, more than 20 percent were under 30.

But with little doubt, the most significant fact is that 88 percent of the delegates this year were attending their first national convention. This representation is not ideal, but it is a healthy step in the right direction. It is progress towards truly participatory democracy.

But lest we let down our guard, we must fight to maintain and increase the representation of minorities. The large number of young people,

Blacks and women was not won without a bitter struggle against party regulars; and these party regulars are not hesitating in trying to reverse the progress we have made.

Despite the reforms, there were delegations which did not accurately reflect the makeup of the general population. This was accomplished through the bending and subverting of the rules by those machine bosses who bring shame and ridicule to the party. In the name of democracy and under the umbrella of the Democratic Party, they do everything in their power to impede the democratic process. What irony! All the reforms in the world are worthless unless they are enforced through the watchful eyes of the people.

In addition, the reforms won't come about unless those we nominate are held accountable for the promises they make in return for our votes. Blacks should not believe promises until they are fulfilled. But when the leaders are chosen by the people and not just the politicians, there is a greater likelihood that those promises will come true. Backward old type politicians are no longer needed for the new days ahead. I must observe that the new delegates and McGovernites showed a similarity to the old ones from where they came. The poor people's, taxation of the rich, marijuana, sexual freedom between consenting parties and a few other strong planks were not adopted for fear of embarrassing the nominee. If America comes home, principles of freedom, justice and humanity cannot yield to fear or expediency.

Democratic Convention Black Caucus, Legislative Comment, July 19, 1972

The 1972 Democratic National Convention is the second such affair at which the Black Caucus has played a role. Because this year's convention was more open, our influence was greater.

But we did not go to Miami Beach just to choose a presidential nominee. Blacks and other have-nots wanted to press for their needs in a national political arena and to make sure their voices were heard and heeded above all the confusion and debate.

Although two different black caucuses were held at Miami Beach,

Blacks never did develop a workable strategy. One group was the Black Congressional Caucus. Their main accomplishment was hopping onto George McGovern's band wagon once they saw that most everyone else was already aboard. Up to that point, they had fluctuated between different positions and candidates with the end result that they were ineffective in everything they did except talking and partying.

The second caucus consisted of Black delegates and alternates, the group in which I was most interested. Delegates and alternates were the only ones with power and who could deliver their votes. Thus they had the power to have more input in the convention process although the self-proclaimed "Party of the People" successfully rebuffed the genuine needs of the people.

Blacks are participating in the political process in greater numbers and with greater awareness. They are realizing that those persons claiming to be leaders have not been chosen by anyone except themselves. There are those who have been handpicked by whites or small cliques, which is the same as not being chosen at all.

Blacks must begin addressing themselves to the problem of selecting a committee of knowledgeable committed leaders. The short week at Miami Beach was insufficient time for all Black delegates to assess the "would be leaders" without out-shouting, out-accusing, and out-insulting one another. During a short period of competition, frustrated and confused followers do not always choose the most representative or wisest person to lead and speak for them. However the majority of Blacks demonstrated some ability to identify certain national self-appointed messiahs and brokers who claimed to speak for them.

Until a person begins dealing with politicians so enlightened that statesmanship is involved, opportunists, hustlers, con-artists, pimps, prostitutes and jokers will abound.

Now is the time for all of us who want meaningful political solutions to this country's racial and poverty problems to take action. We must work for an open-ended mechanism for Blacks to identify their concerns and apply viable solutions to these problems until the job is done.

At the convention, there were an excessive number of so-called "coming together" meetings contrived only for show. While some may think the invitees let it all hang out, in effect they were used as rope to hang various Black and colored groups for the benefit of so called Black allies and white oppressors.

The goal for Blacks then is leaders who can ably and successfully present their case. But the problem does not entirely stem from the fact that Blacks don't have a voice in this society. It is more appropriate to state that many leaders of this society do not have ears and cannot hear the voice of the oppressed. Thus, we can see that the answer for Blacks and other minorities is to choose their leaders with voices and ears to replace incumbent politicians who have neither.

MINORITIES IN POLITICS, LEGISLATIVE COMMENT, JULY 26, 1972

The political arena is a facet of American life which many persons do not fully understand. This is especially true of many minority groups who often fail to recognize the truth about politics. In reality, politics is an art, a science which has practical applications in the everyday life of all citizens.

There are varied definitions of politics. In a practical sense, it is [a] means of accomplishing one's goals. On the government level, it operates through the elective process. People vote for executives, legislators and often judges on the basis of what these candidates will do for them.

The two major parties are principal characters in politics, except at the local level where contests are often non-partisan. Politics even operates on a less formal, but more personal level in churches, schools and the home.

There are some Blacks who will say that politics is a white man's game played at the expense of Blacks. That is a cop out. Although tremendous pressure has been effectively exerted through sit-ins, boycotts, marches and other forms of protest, Blacks can accomplish more through the direct political process.

It is an accurate evaluation that politics is sometimes, if not often, dirty and devious; but it is entirely possible for a decent and rational person to employ it to obtain reasonable and just ends. The cleanliness or dirtiness of politics depends on the people who participate in it and vote.

Each potential voter has the same power in politics. The machine bosses still have an extraordinary influence in the party structure, but this should be an added reason to work within the party. When more independent active people become party members, the influence of the bosses will be lessened.

However, if a person chooses not to use his vote, he will be treated without a bit of mercy—as powerless. A weak voter is generally influenced by the strong voter. On the other hand, an ignorant voter on emotional issues is not always swayed by the intelligent elector. Hence, we need enlightened and dedicated voters for liberation all the more to end injustice, racism and poverty.

For example, the poor people at the Democratic National Convention prove, that politics can be functional even if they were not successful in their individual struggle. They exerted pressure within the system for platform adoption of a guaranteed minimum income of $6,500. To achieve their end, they presented their proposal through the appropriate channels in the party structure.

They tried to pursue their goals further by seeking delegate seats on the floor. It is important to note that these people cared enough for their goals, themselves and the democratic process to work within the system. Despite the setback, it is clear they will continue to push, in a political sense, for the needs of Blacks and other oppressed groups.

A lesson can be learned from the professional politicians who do not stop until they have succeeded in obtaining their basic goal. Meaningful compromises can only be achieved when the basic issues are laid. Politics is not a static phenomenon, but is dynamic and ever-changing. It changes faster and more fundamentally when the people who want a new order, work and fight hard continuously for it.

The Blacks of this country are demanding action on many fronts in order to improve their standard of living. There are political ramifications in seeking better law enforcement and treatment from public officials and for more progress in economic, housing, educational and health fields. These benefits will only be realized through more, not less, work within the political system. This method can and will work only if Blacks take the initiative to become more involved in each and every step of the political process, including the most important step of voting.

Minority Voting, Legislative Comment, August 2, 1972

Since Blacks and other powerless minorities are demanding a bigger piece of the action, it is imperative that they take advantage of one of the most effective means of achieving that goal. That method is the vote. In order to insure progress, Blacks must cast ballots against those who stand in the way of change and for those persons who will work to eliminate poverty, injustice and other social ills.

Party membership is not a prerequisite for admission to the voting booth. You do not have to align yourself with a political party in order to vote. In fact, it is often desirable not to be affiliated with a party so that you can express your preference independently and be free of possible coercion.

But the exercise of voting rights requires more than making an X in the appropriate box or pulling the right lever. An elector must acquaint himself with the issues and the candidates, especially those who profess to support issues helpful to the people. He or she must be concerned about how the spending of his or her tax dollars actually affects the solution of community problems. It is self-defeating to vote if you do not know who or what you are voting for.

Blacks have an excellent opportunity this fall to increase their representation in the State Legislature. During the primary election in Milwaukee September 12 three Black positions are possible, two State Representative posts and one for a state senate seat. In order for their names to appear on the November ballot, it is necessary for Blacks and whites alike who seek justice to vote for them in September. The likelihood of passing legislation beneficial to Blacks and poor people will be increased when the proportion of these groups in the Legislature approaches their proportion in the general population.

The 1972 elections should be a top priority for Blacks who are dissatisfied with their present situation and are fed up with rich, white politicians running the government without meeting the needs of the people.

Our country is faced this year with a presidential contest that offers a real choice. Since most of us can remember, the Democrats have offered

Tweedledee and the Republicans have offered Tweedledum. This was an exciting choice for politicians and party faithfuls, but it offered nothing for the people.

But this year, there is a difference, because the man that is elected can be held responsible to you if you vote and support him. This is perhaps the most important election point that must be understood by people who want a change. In 1972, society is ripe for a change and it is time the forces against change were thrown out of office and replaced by persons responsive to the needs and will of the people.

PARTY AFFILIATION, LEGISLATIVE COMMENT, AUGUST 28, 1972

For a long time, I have felt that Blacks should be wise, free and flexible enough to support whatever candidate or party best represented their interests. No one party holds a monopoly on pushing for economic and social justice for Blacks; in fact, neither party has done an adequate job in these matters up to now. The interests of Blacks should not recognize party lines.

Therefore, I have no objection to Milwaukee Alderman Orville Pitts switching to the Republican Party, an organization which has by and large ignored Blacks in Wisconsin.

Since Blacks switched to the party of Franklin Roosevelt in the Depression years, Democrats have always considered Blacks their personal property to vote however the party wanted. You might say they were considered slaves of the party. Prior to that time, Blacks had been insanely loyal to the GOP, believing the myth that Abe Lincoln freed the slaves. I am personally concerned that Republicans feel they are getting a bargain in Pitts. They also feel that by buying up and out certain national Black figures, these Black Judases goats will deliver the Black vote to President Nixon, a man who has nixed more programs for Blacks than any president in recent history. The same holds true for the administrations of smiling Dwight Eisenhower and the "above-it-all" Hoover and Coolidge. The latter were sinners of omission. Nixon is a sinner of commission.

My only comment regarding Pitts—who is known to be hard-fighting with strong feelings and opinions—is that he should not be a Democrat for Nixon, as was recently borne out in media ads. He should be a new Republican against Nixon but stay in the Grand Old Party and work hard for meaningful reform. Leave the Democrats and the asses to themselves. It takes more than self-promoters, ego trippers, and entertainers to herd elephants. Go to the GOP for a new SOP or stop.

The case of Alderman Pitts does not stand alone. Black voters should be aware that erstwhile warriors like Floyd McKissick become prematurely weary and seek honor and reward from the very oppressors whom they fought against by accepting money, expertise, and prestige for pet projects and ego.

Thus we see dark-skinned people praising a white President like Nixon who has responded only to White-type Black business and not to the every-day needs of less affluent blacks. All that is being done is subsidizing those Blacks who have opted for the ordinary, crass, white capitalism which exploits most Blacks and the poor all the more.

To switch to the Republican party in order to open it up and work for meaningful reform is an admirable move. But imitating the "King" we hate by self-serving Blacks will only be detrimental to the cause of all oppressed minorities.

Campaign Money, Legislative Comment, September 11, 1972

It is a well-established fact that candidates need a great deal of money to wage a successful campaign for most public offices. Newspaper, radio and T.V. ads, pamphlets, office expenses and other campaign activities are a necessary ingredient in getting a candidate's name and issues before the public, but they cost money. The difficulty is that many suitable individuals do not have the personal assets necessary to finance their campaigns nor the good fortune to have wealthy backers. They must rely on the contributions of their supporters, or go deeply into debt.

Up to 1972, most contributors have been large business firms and other large organizations who have a special interest. But because of a recent change made by Congress, there is a new incentive to contribute to those of modest means.

The change affects your liability for Federal Income tax. For any political contributions you make during 1972, you may claim either a tax credit or deduction.

You may claim credit against your income tax for one-half of the political contributions made during the tax year with a maximum credit of $25 on a joint return. On the return of a single person or a married person: filing separately, the maximum credit is $12.50.

Instead of the credit, you may choose to deduct from your adjusted gross income the amount of political contributions made during the tax year except that the deduction cannot exceed $100 on a joint return. For a single person or married person filing separately, the deduction cannot exceed $50.

Your income and individual situation will determine which is better for you, the credit or the deduction. This is the first year such a tax advantage is available. I urge all voters who are able to contribute to the candidate of their choice to do so. There are two reasons why you should: indirectly, you will be able to receive part of the money back when you claim a deduction or credit on your income tax return.

Secondly, and more importantly, you will be providing needed funds for your candidate, and thus participating in the democratic process.

It would be desirable if an alternative method were available to raise funds for political campaigns so the candidate would not be financially indebted to any special interest.

However, since this is not the case, it is imperative that we provide the means whereby the individual citizen in low and middle income groups can contribute. I think this means is being established through this change. Without the small contributions from citizens, only the rich, the dishonest, and powerful politicians would be able to afford the high cost of campaigning. Faced with the possibility of spending large sums of money and going deeply into debt, what average man or woman can or would take the big step of seeking public office.

Although the new rules of the Internal Revenue Service are not the ultimate or ideal answer to the problem of campaign finances, they are a step in the right direction of taking government from the upper class businessmen/businesswomen and returning it to the people.

VOTER ROADBLOCKS, LEGISLATIVE COMMENT, SEPTEMBER 27, 1972

It is a sad commentary on our democratic society that those wishing to vote must hurdle so many roadblocks just in order to register to vote. The Milwaukee Election Commission has consistently blocked reasonable and sensible proposals to establish door-to-door registration.

It is unconscionable that a commission established to maximize voter participation and promote fair voting procedures would thwart the very purpose for their existence. If this nation is ever to take a giant step into modern civilization during the latter part of the 20th Century, it must make the voter registration process easy and convenient.

The best way to accomplish this is to mobilize registrars to go door to door and take the means of exercising the vote to where the people live. The level of registration for Blacks and other minorities is far below that of other groups. This is no accident. Officials have demonstrated an attitude which effectively prohibits or discourages many Blacks from registering.

In order for a person to register to vote in Milwaukee, he must travel to city hall, a police or fire station or one of the weirdly selected registration centers. What Black would want to go to a fire or police station to register to vote? And how many Blacks can afford the time and cost to travel great distances to register? The answer is very few. Therefore, we must register Blacks at their homes by means of door to door campaign. There would be little or no cost to the city since volunteer groups have offered to do the task—free of charge.

With voter registration so obviously desirable and no logical reason to oppose door-to-door canvassing, why is not such an effort being practiced? Some observers of the Milwaukee political scene feel the GOP dominated commission votes against truly open and convenient accessible registration because Democrats would benefit by greater registration.

One of the more interesting aspects of the voter registration issue is that despite the $28 million fund raising campaign by Republicans, the Grand Old Party is frustrating voter registration. You would think they would permit steps facilitating the registration of the poor, the aged and the weak citizen. Free and open registration should not be a partisan issue; but we have a three man commission with only a lone Democrat supporting the concept of door-to-door registration.

The commission has made some small steps toward voter registration, but only under strong pressure from civic groups. Republican members maintain that if a person wants to vote, he should take whatever steps are necessary to register. That is a formal idealistic but shallow view. Politics has played too large a role for too long in hampering a high level of voter registration. We have opened up the ballot box for minorities in most areas of the country. It is now time to open up and take voter registration lists to the people. To [do] less is plutocracy—rule of the rich and well to do.

1972 ELECTION, LEGISLATIVE COMMENT, NOVEMBER 13, 1972

Much can be and has been said about the national and local elections last week. But two overriding conclusions can be drawn. The majority of voters in this nation are unwilling to support even moderate but necessary change at the presidential level. People are apparently satisfied to accept wholesale corruption, favoritism, racism and oppression by the war mongers and special interest agents in the Nixon gang.

Secondly, the majority of voters do not want to make any great change in the makeup of the U.S. Congress. The status quo is maintained and minorities can expect conservative business as usual. In other words, they can expect not much more, not much less.

However, not all is lost. There are several good signs among all the other dismal omens. Blacks did not support Tricky Dick despite his campaign to buy Black entertainers, hustlers and crass materialistic Black Anglo-Saxons. Happily, most Blacks saw through this political gimmick of Nixon.

Another favorable result is that Nixon's tainted coattails did not extend far enough to produce a shift to the right in other political races. Fortunately, the President did not rise high and wide enough to carry some of his reactionary and conservative cronies into office with him at the local level. So, hope does lie with the people.

Blacks and other have-nots should actively assess the national political mess to determine how their influence can best be used. In the near future, more unresponsive politicians can and should be thrown out of office.

Despite the feeling induced by the Nixon victory, widespread despair [is] not justified. We can go on to victory in the years ahead and build effective political machinery for the interest of Blacks. We do not have to settle on getting out of the hip pockets of the Democrats and into the hip pockets of Republicans as some so-called Blacks are saying. The rumps of both parties will come down hard when they wish to sit on Black rights, needs and aspirations.

Voter Registration, Legislative Comment, March 15, 1973

After eight years of introducing the same measure, I am happy to note that the Committee on Elections last week finally agreed to act favorably on my proposed bill relating to certification of applications for voter registration in cities with a population of over 500,000.

More specifically, the bill would eliminate the requirement that the Milwaukee Police Department verify all statements contained in applications for voter registration and report the voters who have moved or died. Instead, the duties would be assumed by the municipal clerk in verifying voter registration applications.

Although it is impossible to estimate the precise fiscal impact of the bill for Milwaukee, one thing is certain—the measure will have a positive effect on city revenues. The savings would result from the fact that the municipal clerk can perform these functions at a less cost than the police department, because they are more closely related to the routine duties of the clerk.

It's about time that the Milwaukee Police Department be removed from the business of purging bona fide registered voters off the poll lists. For years, Milwaukee policemen have visited the homes of Milwaukee citizens to find whether they've moved.

With the many examples of police brutality in the city districts, many individuals have grown unfriendly toward the city police.

Thus, when policemen inquire whether a registered voter lives in a house, they may not get an accurate answer. The city police have so abused and intimidated Milwaukee citizens that it is no wonder why inner-city residents are overly reluctant to give police any information at all. The Milwaukee Police Department is the worst governmental agency to purge anything other than themselves.

The bill which I authored has only completed the first step toward enactment, but this is farther than the bill has ever gone before in the Wisconsin legislative process.

Campaign Reform, Legislative Comment, October 24, 1973

As we watch Nixon's efforts to again trick the public into believing he can stop his mighty fall in the eyes of white bigots and paranoids, it should take more than surrendering some bugged conversations which were taped to the federal courts to restore confidence in his tainted leadership.

Among the many reasons for King Richard's arrogance and disregard for American minorities and the majority alike is the raw power which he believes is mandated to himself. This false belief is buttressed by the large amount of money put behind his candidacy and which continues to support him for crass materialistic self-interests.

Efforts should be made now to get us out of this mess, and provide assurances that it doesn't happen again. Requests from Blacks and white liberals for Nixon to resign are as futile as making any ego-tripping maniac act sensibly by the mere asking or suggestion. Actions must be concentrated not only to impeach Nixon, but also to change the system which has caused such a one-dimensional person to be elected in a multi-dimensional society.

A good starting place in reforming the system is a drastic revision of our campaign procedures for all public elected officials. This reform, however, must be real and not just labeled so.

Campaign reform needs to encompass many areas. First, it will have to place strict limitations on campaign contributions and spending. The campaign contribution restrictions will have to include donations from private individuals, committees, organizations, special interest groups and the political parties themselves.

A second provision needed for a good campaign reform bill is the full public disclosure of a candidate's contributions and expenditures for the campaign.

Present proposals being discussed in the Wisconsin Legislature have not provided adequate assurances that resorting to illegal campaign acts will be eliminated. The loopholes in the present proposals are big enough to fly jumbo jets through.

3

FAIR HOUSING

THE FIGHT FOR FAIR HOUSING, LLOYD A. BARBEE
1982 MANUSCRIPT

Discrimination against blacks in housing was rampant in rentals, leases, and sales. Arguments against Fair Housing ranged from notions that a man's home was his castle to automatic depreciation of property values if Blacks were permitted to move into white neighborhoods. During Congressional hearings on the Fair Housing Section of civil rights legislation, Attorney General Robert Kennedy argued for little Mrs. Murphy's boarding house exception. The exception would permit an owner-occupied boarding or rooming house to discriminate as long as she or he lived in a unit. This permission to discriminate at a personal level was one of the early disappointments in the Kennedy "New Frontier." Of course the Kennedys got worse during the civil rights marches, freedom rides, school desegregation, murders of many blacks and a few whites who stood up against segregation, and worst, the outward tolerance and inward use of J. Edgar Hoover, whose FBI illicit relations in bed with the Ku Klux Klan, White Citizens Council, and other racist murderers virtually assured no solution to lynchings, bombings, arson, intimidation, harassment, blackmail, and entrapment. State and local law enforcement authorities routinely violated civil rights of blacks and permitted local whites to do the same.

FBI investigation was all too often a cover-up. Some blacks who moved into all-white neighborhoods had not only to deal with threats against their lives but also rocks, bricks, epithets thrown against them, and fires sometimes destroyed their homes. No successful prosecution took place in Milwaukee for these acts.

In large measure this accounts for the fact that most blacks in Milwaukee County live in the near northwest side of the corporate limits of the City of Milwaukee. The 1980 census showed an increase, but while this was dramatic, it was not substantial. For six years, fair housing has been advanced by radicals and liberals as a means to end housing discrimination based on race. I viewed a comprehensive law as a tool to force bigots who were in the business of selling or leasing houses to not discriminate on the grounds of race. Property rights traditionally have yielded to human rights, in this country, as far as our legal system, in theory, is concerned. The post-slavery amendments to the U.S. Constitution, as well as the U.S. Civil Rights Laws, when read along with health, building and zoning codes, attest to this fact.

State Assemblyman Isaac Coggs introduced the first Fair Housing Law in Wisconsin's history in 1957. I committed myself to succeed in getting a Fair Housing Law passed in the 1965 legislative session.

Several lily-white lawyers and leaders were convinced that my name on a civil rights bill would be the kiss of death. To my chagrin, they combined with a few black bourgeoisies on the black Milwaukee Urban League Board, and chose to support a weak Fair Housing Bill, to be administered by an even weaker civil rights agency.

This was tantamount to opposition to the bill authored by me, despite the fact that the League praised my bill as ideal legislation, but, in their view, they supported the weaker measure as a practical matter. When the League sent a letter to me and my co-authors praising us for our efforts but requesting that we withdraw our measure in favor of the weaker one, I became incensed. I wrote expressing my thoughts to the Executive Director, who was a black knowledgeable man, aware of my game plan for passage of the best possible bill. My response was aimed at two sets of people who dominated the Milwaukee Urban League, white liberals who believed they were the surrogates of the blacks, and black bourgeoisie, who emulated missionary-type whites. Both of these groups offered verbose lip service to the plight of urban blacks and parsimonious pittance to alleviate this plight. I told the first group that they offered no leadership to the fair housing legislation movement and their faint praise was not appreciated when it was coupled with the prophecy of failure. I told the second group that the first group not only disrespected black leadership, but would not respect black lackeys who served white masters actively engaged in emasculating black leadership. The Milwaukee Urban League's black Executive Director and the white Board Chairman understood my perturbation over their tergiversation and arrogance.

A middle level management staff person took umbrage and to this day, remains peeved about the letter and its resultant publicity. This staff person was, apparently, not as concerned about sin as the appearance thereof.

The League's letter served as an excuse for some moderate legislators to claim that my ideal bill was too much, too soon, and to scurry for a "too little, too late" bill which I, of course, refused to author, and they refused to co-author. The Democratic party was a fifty majority out of a hundred seat Assembly. It was an eleven minority in the thirty-three seat Senate.

A number of Democrats in both houses were afraid that their constituents endorsed housing biases and would vote them out of office if they passed a Fair Housing Bill. Some of the legislators were themselves real estate brokers and bigots.

Thus a bipartisan coalition was needed to pass the bill. Accordingly I approached the leadership of the Republican Party for agreement on the contents of a bill, which they would support in sufficient numbers to assure passage. After two weeks we had reached an agreement on a measure, weaker than the ideal but stronger than the League supported measure. I received a commitment that no referendum would be attached to the measure by the Republicans and no delayed effective date, upon passage, would become part of the bill. Once the pact was made, the Republicans in both houses adhered to their agreement. Thus, in 1965, the Wisconsin legislature declared that: "everyone is entitled to equal opportunity to find a place to live."

In summarizing this accomplishment, the *Milwaukee Sentinel* wrote:

> Passage of a compromise housing bill after lengthy public hearings
> on the issue, demonstrations, emotion packed debate and dozens of
> votes was perhaps the most far reaching action of the session.

There were amendments offered in the Assembly and some in the Senate. No amendments for referenda were attached. There was an amendment prohibiting testing and there were exceptions for owner-occupied

LEGAL ACTION TO END HOUSING SEGREGATION

In 1964, attorney Lloyd Barbee filed Wisconsin's first housing discrimination case, *Gregory III v. Madison Mobile Homes Park*, 128 N.W.2d (1964),
after an African American plaintiff was denied entry into a camp in Madison, Wisconsin. In this case, the legal issue was whether a trailer park
is a "place of accommodation" such that discrimination was prohibited.
The judge rejected the defendant trailer camp's request for a demurrer,
or a request to dismiss the case because it concerns no valid claim upon
which remedy can be sought. Madison Mobile Homes appealed to the
Wisconsin Supreme Court, which agreed with the lower court that the
case was not demurrer. It found that trailer camps cannot deny a person
admission based upon their race under present federal and state civil
rights laws. This was reinforced by the Fair Housing Act that Mr. Barbee
introduced after his election to the Wisconsin state legislature in 1964.

residences. I introduced bills to remove these exemptions in two successive
sessions of the legislature. The bills passed in the Assembly, but the Senate
failed to act. Consequently the bills died.

In 1971, all the fair housing exemptions were eliminated. This, among
other matters, earned me the reputation as a person who stayed on the job
until it was completed as planned.

SLUM LORDS, LLOYD A. BARBEE 1982 MANUSCRIPT

Slum lords were secure in the habit of violating state and city housing
codes. When citations were issued, many slum lords got numerous ad-
journments in court. After a number of speeches on and off the legislative
floor against slum lords' exploitation of the poor, students and middle
class renters, city planners and civic minded people took an interest. When
the slumlord's property had drastically deteriorated, often no repairs
would be made. The city authorities would have to go through a cumber-
some condemnation procedure to raze the building or board it up. Often

the slum lord would have a property manager who used just enough of their maintenance allowance to keep the decrepit building standing, crowd poor people into the units and charge a rental fee commensurate with, or even exceeding that of adequate housing.

The slum lords had a thriving business in the ghetto. My proposal would enable cities to confiscate blighted property and offer it to poor people for a dollar if they occupied the building and proceeded to systematically repair it and bring it up to code. This homesteading proposal was objected to by a preponderance of the legislature. However, some of the legislators who had concerns about blighted and rotting neighborhoods agreed to sponsor a measure to require a court to appoint a receiver to bring the slum lord's property up to code, lease it, deposit the funds in escrow, and deduct a small fee for services by the receiver. There were many objections on the part of the real estate bar and conventional lawyers in the legislature.

I advanced a rather conventional idea that the city should move against the slum lord's property as a nuisance and have the court award the property to the city. The city could then sell to third parties, rent it, raze it, and/or build green spots, or make it possible for adjoining owners to build garages because the inner-city north and south lots are shallow. The idea of declaring owner's property as a nuisance was viewed as shocking by the same conservative forces who objected to the homestead concept.

The final city fair housing battle started August 28, 1967, and continued for the rest of the year, until a city-wide fair housing ordinance was passed, modeled on the state law. It was to be enforced by the city attorney. The ordinance took effect on December 22, 1968, and provided fines ranging from $10 to $200 for each violation.

The press began to report on some minority housing conditions and blight. The Chairman of the State Industrial Commission made some first-hand investigations of minority housing obstacles. He became an ally in the state fair housing and equal opportunity drive. Since funds were awarded to Milwaukee from federal and state government, I joined the Northtown Planning Association's call for bigger and faster city renewal programs, as a mean to assure that these funds were wisely spent. The mayor accused us of engaging in a plot against him. He had appointed a Director of City Development, who, at a meeting called to study unhealthy conditions such as garbage littered yards and alleys, said:

> Some of Milwaukee's problems might be lessened if unskilled persons not equipped to cope with city life were blocked from, moving here. People who find it difficult to adapt to city life rather than poverty itself were the real reason for crime, violence and unsanitary conditions.

After the meeting this official said he was not only referring to blacks, "I was talking about people who wind up on welfare. This includes people from rural northern areas."

He further indicated that he didn't know people could be controlled, but noted that some European countries required transients to have a job before they moved into new areas. (The US Supreme Court has ruled such requirements are unconstitutional.) Since all of this took place at City Hall, I wrote a letter to the director indicating that he should either apologize or resign. His response was:

> I thought that I had made myself clear, that I was simply raising questions—admittedly provocative—for further intensive study and discussion without taking a position or making unwarranted assertions. For this reason, I do not consider that either retraction or apology is called for; rather I believe that objective dispassionate answers must be given to the questions I have raised.

The final portion of his letter to me indicated that he was willing to discuss the matter further "if you are interested in an intelligent, unemotional exchange of thought."

In my letter to the mayor I asked that he:

> spend more time defending and protecting this city from such ill-advised comments as those made by Mr. Perrin and less time promulgating your poorly disguised, self-satisfying, self-righteous statements. Before this city can hope to launch a war on prejudice

it must rid itself of bigots in government. It is up to you to take the initiative in removing Richard Perrin from his position as Director of City Development. Your failure to do so will be far more damning than any of the misdirection you toss at suburbanites in your game of dodging the snowball of criticism which Mr. Perrin's slum neglect is bringing you.

Since the fact that this man had been the director of city housing, and was now in charge of housing and industrial city development, his record of permitting violations of city housing codes, planning and perpetuating segregated public housing projects, had not insisted on non-discriminatory employment on public housing projects, had permitted daily violations of city housing codes in public housing, and had failed to blast slumlords, the mayor's intent was suspect by such insensitivity.

The mayor had predicted that a Milwaukee "Watts" would march on the suburbs.

I suggested that the "Watts community" should descend on City Hall in view of his refusal to face justified criticism of his development program. The mayor responded by informing me and the media that "the record shows that I was in the field of fighting prejudice long before I heard of Mr. Barbee and long before there was a climate in support of the fight, such as Mr. Barbee has."

A small delegation of civil rights workers and I met with the mayor with a list of remedies which he could implement and recommend. After briefly looking at our list, he told us of his civil rights record and philosophy in a rather lengthy speech. On that note I ruminated that the mayor should declare bankruptcy since his resources were insufficient for the debts or current expenditures needed to operate as chief city executive. A lady in the delegation told the mayor that he was bankrupt in civil rights.

He exploded and attempted to leave the city hall reception room but tripped on television wires and cables. I was able to tell him that the city would remain backwards while he inveighed against the suburban, state, and federal governments, but it was his lack of foresight, courage, and leadership in human rights and government service which was the problem. His slogans, such as war on prejudice, and tantrums did not camouflage the issue. I walked out while he remained ensnarled in the wires and cables.

While the dialogue between the mayor and me was provocative to the audience, it was a communication failure since the interchange of ideas between the two of us was minimal. Members of the group spoke when they could. Later the press told me that the mayor tipped them off that he had a surprise in store for me. The surprise was for him to terminate our conference by walking out on me as I had walked out three years earlier on a school board meeting during a controversy over whether or not the school board administration was biased against blacks. Thanks to the media's paraphernalia, I walked out uttering the last substantive word. I recalled the mayor cursing about "God damn wires," as the civil rights group followed me out shaking their heads in disgust.

OPEN HOUSING, LEGISLATIVE COMMENT, MARCH 4, 1971

The State Assembly has finally given its approval to a bill that would eliminate the remaining exemption in Wisconsin's open housing law. The bill, which passed the Assembly by a vote of 67 to 27, has now been sent to the State Senate.

I am hopeful that the State Senate will give this bill prompt action.

It is essential for those who agree that no person should be permitted to discriminate in selling or renting shelter to contact their State Senators and recommend the prompt passage of this bill without amendments.

We must stop those persons who continue to violate the present housing code. These people continue to make money off of substandard housing.

In line with the Governor's recommendation of $100 million in new property tax relief, I am proposing legislation that would require slum land lords to reinvest their portion of property tax relief in either the up-keep or removal of their substandard properties.

A bill that I have introduced that would provide for election of Milwaukee School Board members by ward is presently in the Assembly Elections Committee, and I am hopeful that this committee will report the bill out soon for floor action.

If the recent Milwaukee elections point toward any order given to the government, it is the need for the black and brown community to maintain real control of its governmental representatives.

I believe that the University of Wisconsin Extension service must now serve the urban community as well as it has served the rural community in the past.

A bill I introduced during the last session of the legislature and that I will introduce during this session would require that a member of the Black community and a woman be appointed to the University of Wisconsin Board of Regents. I am in full support of a bill that has been introduced that would merge the State University Board of Regents and the University of Wisconsin Board of Regents.

It is better to have one good educational system than two mediocre ones.

FAIR HOUSING BILL, LEGISLATIVE COMMENT, MARCH 11, 1971

This week saw an escalation of activity in the state legislature. The fair housing bill which passed the State Assembly two weeks ago was given a public hearing by the Senate Housing and Urban Development Committee with hostile questions coming from only one member of the committee. Pressure for passing this measure must continue.

Again I urge you to contact members of the Senate calling for prompt passage of this bill without amendments.

BUILDING CODES, LEGISLATIVE COMMENT, MAY 17, 1973

One of the actions taken by the Assembly last week was the preliminary approval of a bill that would make it easier for large cities to enforce building codes. The measure would essentially allow tenants or other persons to bring class action suits against a building when building codes are violated.

As a result of the bill, court actions seeking the repair of a building would not cease when the building is in the process of being sold or transferred. This eliminates many of the problems which exist in Milwaukee when trying to deal with slum landlords.

Presently, class action suits can only be brought against the owner. Greedy, crooked landlords, realizing that their necks are in a noose, quickly sell the property back and forth between friends or relatives, thereby making it difficult for the courts to determine ownership. As a result, repairs and prosecution are avoided.

The bill which I co-authored, though, is in limbo because of a motion for reconsideration made and voted for by the fat cat Republicans and a small number of white sheep, rural Democrats. However, I'm still confident that we can get enough votes to send the bill to the Senate when the measure comes up on the calendar again.

It has been far too long that Blacks and other poverty groups have had to live in unfit and unsanitary conditions, caused by avaricious landlords who refuse to spend money for repairs. The courts and laws have been unable to provide a remedy. Passage of the housing code enforcement bill would provide a solution.

Another positive action with a negative twist was the defeat of an emergency powers bill which would give the Governor special emergency powers during riots and insurrections.

Presently, the Governor can only deal with civil disorders by calling out the National Guard or declaring martial law. This bill would give him additional powers, including the right to set curfews.

In the Assembly, I made a motion to kill the measure. The motion did not receive a majority vote. However, when the motion for preliminary approval was made, there were not enough votes to carry it off.

My view is that good governors use imagination, wisdom and intelligence to cope with emergencies. Bad governors use brute power and bully language to control disturbances. Many Southern governors and Rockefeller of New York should serve as good examples of the tyranny which can develop when people in a position of power are given more authority for the sake of "law and order."

Redneck governors, North and South, strive for dictatorial powers to keep the peace by beating citizens in line. This only results in violations of fundamental civil rights.

Governor Lucey is not this type of person. Nor does he need any extra power which could be used as a tool of oppression if put in the hands of a political hack.

Legislative bodies can do their jobs best by passing laws which remove the causes of riots and insurrections, namely racism, prisons, poverty and its attendant inequities in education, health, police abuse as starters.

URBAN HOUSING, LEGISLATIVE COMMENT, NOVEMBER 1, 1973

Urban housing represents a problem, not only for government officials who, many times, only halfheartedly search for solutions, but also for those who must live in poor, run-down houses. There are, however, many ways to overcome the problems of poor housing.

The northern part of Milwaukee's inner city, for example, has a considerable number of houses that are unoccupied and boarded up because the owners are not able or the slumlords are not willing to keep up the property.

At the same time, there are many Black families and poor people living in un-tenantable, substandard housing, who are paying exorbitant rents in proportion to their incomes or are paying off mortgages or land contracts that were higher than the fair market value at the time of the real estate contract closing date.

Many buildings which have been condemned represent an excellent alternative to improving a city's housing situation. Since many of these are structurally sound, the expenses involved in rehabilitating the vacated buildings would be much less than mortgage payment or rental costs or building similar new housing costs. Rather than keeping old, abandoned buildings as an eye sore for the cities and neighborhoods, they could be reclaimed and put back into use for their original purposes.

The most logical method of employing this philosophy is to initiate an urban homesteading program. The Homestead concept is not new. Early American society encouraged the expansion of the country by using the Federal Homestead Act. But an urban homesteading program is considered a new and unique concept. Only one community in this country presently has such a program, and this is in Wilmington, Delaware.

The program works rather simply: A Homestead Board surveys the city real estate and picks the property adequate for homesteading. The properties must be structurally sound and in an environment where rehabilitation is feasible. The public is then encouraged to apply for them.

Since it would take money to rehabilitate the vacated property, it would be necessary for the applicant to have the finances or skills and knowledge for improving it. Once the particular applicant receives the proper qualification and certification, he or she is given a certain time to complete the rehabilitation, and must live in the property for a certain number of years. Then the property deed would be turned over to the applicants and the house is legally theirs.

Depending on how the program is set up, there could be possible pitfalls. Assurances would be necessary for eliminating land speculation. It would also be important to prevent a person from homesteading a number of properties, and after the deed transfer, turning these into multirental homes. If such were to happen, problems with slumlords might substantially increase.

The program in Wilmington has been described as a success for easing the housing shortage and improving the deteriorating housing within the city. Much of the success is due to the financial ability of the people who are given the opportunity to participate in the program. I would rather see such programs directed more toward the poorer families of the city. Nevertheless, the urban homestead program is one of the more imaginative local programs to date.

Because the urban homestead concept is relatively new there hasn't been too much stress for this kind of program. All of us should begin now to bring such possibilities out in the open for discussion and practice. If we can convince enough local officials of the benefits of urban homesteading, perhaps we can get Milwaukee to implement a plan. Since the state should also help in the encouragement of urban homesteading, I am drafting enabling legislation along these lines.

This may just well be a proposal for preserving human and neighborhood resources.

Exclusionary Zoning Subtleties of Racial Prejudice, Speech, State Rep. Lloyd A. Barbee, March 18, 1974

The right to travel and move in this country is a fundamental right protected by the Constitution. Although this right is not explicitly stated, it is entwined with this country's very beginning and has been consistently confirmed in a myriad of court decisions.

For most of our history as a nation, migration has been encouraged and treated almost as a matter of national policy. Now, however, growth restrictions are being considered in many areas and are being implemented in many more.

Limitations on mobility or on developments needed to accommodate a mobile population would strike at one of the principal means which each of us have to control and improve our very lives.

There are many different reasons used to justify restrictions on housing developments and population growth. Some are a response to the dame of urbanization of the environment and the quality of life.

More and more we are becoming an urban people in Wisconsin. From 1950 to 1970, urban population increased by only 60,000. We are now 66 percent urban and 34 percent rural.

Yet, when we take a closer look at these figures we find that less than one-third of Wisconsin residents actually live in cities. Two-thirds of our state population live in suburbs, small cities, villages, and unincorporated areas.

We are urbanizing and suburbanizing land in this state at twice the rate of our population increase. Central cities have grown only 6.6 percent in the last 20 years. And this is mostly from annexation. Suburban areas of cities, however, have grown by 25 percent. The result of this growth is obvious. It is replacing one of the greatest burdens on our environment [that] we've ever had before.

Nevertheless, the great majority of responses to population growth through the restriction of housing developments are leaning over the borderline of racial prejudice. Housing development for well-to-do whites have seldom had a problem for winning municipal approval. But housing developments for the poor and non-whites are consistently voted down. When low-income and minority groups are affected by the response to restrict the development that is needed to contain our population growth, these responses become racist at the heart.

Statistics are showing the effects of these responses. The Bureau of Census reports that in 1968, approximately 95 percent of the inhabitants of the suburbs in this country were white. The statistics are directed at the suburbs of metropolitan areas with populations of at least one million. The movement of whites to suburbia continues to rise. The extent to which cities are becoming more and more predominantly black is also on the rise.

Not only do these population trends exemplify an ever increasing lack of low-income and minority mobility, but they also place a stranglehold on the ability of central city residents to improve their lives while living in the cities which they are forced to reside in.

Along with the white movement to the suburbs also follows the movement of new business and industry away from the city. As a result, the high-paying jobs are being created for those away from the city, while the central city residents become more and more unemployed because jobs become fewer and fewer. The finger-in-the-dike approach that government usually implements to ease the grip of this resulting poverty is to spend more money for poorly administered social programs, which results in higher taxes for those living in suburban rings that surround the central cities.

So it goes, the problems faced by city as well as suburban residents is a result of citizen and governmental short sightedness that has been going on for ages. The future will tell whether we will continue in these haphazard ways, or whether we will repair the resulting ironies and imperfections.

The most often used means for limiting urban and suburban development is through zoning ordinances. Every municipality in our state and country uses zoning laws. To some extent, these ordinances are all exclusionary in the true sense of the word.

The exclusionary zoning laws that we should all be very concerned about, however, are those which prevent the construction and development of housing for low- to moderate-income residents. These are, by far, the worst of our zoning laws because they are preventing the mobility of the disadvantaged and have-nots of our country.

One type of exclusionary zoning ordinance is large-lot zoning. A survey conducted by the national commission on urban problems in 1968 showed that 25 percent of the metropolitan area municipalities of 5,000 or more permit no single family houses on lots of less than one-half acre.

Of course, acreage limitations in large-lot zoning ordinances varies considerably. Sometimes the construction of housing in suburbs is limited to property of four acres or more.

Strangely enough, large-lot zoning has also received favorable rulings by the courts in some cases. There are usually four basic reasons why such zoning laws are accepted. First, there are fiscal considerations that must be made by a municipality, when a community does not wish to pay the costs for an extension of sewer and water lines beyond present development. It may limit development to large lots because the properties can sometimes be served by septic tanks and wells.

Second, there may be certain areas where topographic conditions place limitations on the number of developments that can be constructed under these conditions. Thirdly, specifying minimum lot sizes can give the municipality the ability to time its development of an area until town officials believe it is ready for development. Lastly, minimum lot size requirements fulfill the individual property owners' desire for space and privacy.

I find many of these arguments are rather questionable when applied to large-lot zoning as it is used today. In our present times of skyrocketing land values, the larger the chunk of land, the more it will cost, especially when such properties exist in a rather well-serviced suburb. Furthermore, the greater the cost of the property, the less likely it will be that a low- or moderate-[income] family will settle there.

The costs of development and purchase of property run even higher for a large lot within such an exclusionary zoning ordinance. A builder will simply not develop a small-sized house on a large lot. The opinion expressed frequently is that a large lot requires a large house. Initial purchase of the property for a large lot also falls victim to the general rule of thumb that the price of a lot should be some specified percentage of the total price of house and lot.

From the ecological point of view, large-lot zoning is also a very undesirable method of regulating land development because it disperses housing construction and leads even further to urban sprawl. In fact, large-lot zoning is one of the direct results of what we can call "slurban sprawl," that is, a combination of urban and suburban sprawl. . . .*

However, exclusionary zoning should be considered in a greater sense. It's time that government and people look on this type of zoning for what it really is, a method employed to keep the neighborhood white and well-to-do, a method that clearly demonstrates the subtleties of racial prejudice. The fact that some courts have recognized legality in these ordinances should reflect more on the shortsightedness of the courts rather than on the merits of eliminating exclusionary zoning. Hopefully, as more and more cases of discrimination are documented, the courts in this country will begin to see the light.

One well-documented case that must be decided soon by the courts concerns a rural St. Louis County township in Missouri. In 1970, the township was incorporated as the city of Black Jack. Two weeks after its incorporation, the new city zoning commission recommended a zoning scheme that excluded multi-family residential developments from the city limits of Black Jack. The city council adopted the ordinance.

During the same period, negotiations had been underway with the department of housing and urban development for a 210-unit multi-family housing project in what was before the unincorporated St. Louis County township, but what had become the city of Black Jack.

The Black Jack Improvement Association opposed the development because there was a lack of employment opportunities and transportation, because the project would result in the devaluation of neighboring property, because of projected school deficits and because "crowding low-income families into a closed space would result in disturbances requiring more police support."

We are already witnessing a terrible injustice when municipalities continue to use exclusionary zoning for meeting their own selfish interests. But should these ordinances become clothed in legality because of court decisions, our country will be taking a step towards a constitutional erasure.

---

* A page is missing from the speech transcript here.

In a 1958 court case, *Shapiro vs. Thompson*, the US Supreme Court ruled:

> This court long ago recognized that the nature of our federal union and our constitutional concepts of personal liberty unite to require that all citizens be free to travel throughout the length and breadth of our land, uninhibited by statutes, rules, or regulations, which unreasonably burden or restrict this movement.

In a 1970 Pennsylvania case, entitled The Appeal of Kit-Mar Builders, Inc., the Pennsyvlania Supreme Court became even more direct:

> It is not for any given township to say who may or may not live within its confines, while disregarding the interests of the entire area. If a township is successful in unnaturally limiting its population growth through use of exclusive zoning regulations, the people who would normally live there will inevitably have to live in another community and the requirement that they do so is not a decision that the township should alone be able to make.

The issue that governments and regional planners must take is not whether there will be urban regions, but what form they will take, even though present trends are pointing to a continuation of urban sprawl, the destruction of valuable and critical environmental lands, and racial and economic segregation, the development process for housing can be changed to inhibit the resulting tendencies of uncontrolled, or in some cases, over-controlled growth without denying equal housing opportunities or valid development needs.

Within the framework of urban regions, there is enormous scope for directing the way in which these regions develop, for determining how precious land resources are to be used, and for influencing the quality of life, per se.

There is no need or justification for people or governments to accept a future of blanketing urbanization in which the inhabitants lose their identity or which shrouds the people's pursuit of life, liberty, and happiness. Nor is there a need to limit the mobility of those with modest means, the poor and disenfranchised, the black people, and other minorities. Nor is there a need to accept housing developments that sprawl across what used to be rolling countryside, forests, and farmsteads.

In essence, there is opportunity to have urban regions that contain the natural beauty so necessary for sustaining the aesthetic quality of our lives. The needed quantity of urban development and sufficient space to live can be provided consistently with our environmental, social, and economic values; whether or not it actually will depends on what we demand of the developments that will be built in the next quarter of a century.

URBAN HOMESTEAD, LEGISLATIVE COMMENT, DECEMBER 16, 1974

More than one year has passed since the issue of urban homesteading was discussed as a topic for this column. At that time, much attention was directed toward an urban homestead program that was started in Wilmington, Delaware, and I had introduced enabling legislation in the Assembly.

Since this early publicity of urban homesteading programs, Milwaukee has made some worthwhile efforts to establish its own program to renovate old and abandoned homes in the inner city.

Plans for a homestead program for the City of Milwaukee were initiated last July when Alderman Ben Johnson and Edward Griffin pushed an ordinance through the common Council creating the mechanisms for urban homesteading among city residents.

Last October another step was taken when Mayor [Henry] Maier recommended three of five persons to sit on the Homestead Board created under the ordinance. The five-member board also consists of the city building inspector and the commissioner of city development. The appointments were approved by the Council, giving the program's implementation its first strong push.

Under the urban homesteading ordinance, city residents are given a vacant city-owned house for renovation purposes following payment of a one dollar fee and approval by the Homestead Board.

Within two years, all necessary repairs must be made to bring the home up to city building code requirements, and once the home is lived in by the applicant for a period of five years, the title is turned over to the resident of the home. The ordinance also states that renovation must begin within 90 days of entering agreement with the city for the house and that the occupants must carry fire and liability insurance on the home for the five-year period.

Although the City Development Commission has been accepting applications for the Homestead program and has now received over 1,000, the applications are not being processed until the Board decides the criteria for eligible applicants. Under the ordinance, only a general description of eligible applicants was given.

The Homestead Board must also establish standards on houses for inclusion under the program, as well as continuing work on the general procedures for carrying out urban homesteading in Milwaukee.

Landlord Tenant Act, Legislative Comment, February 26, 1976

One hundred or so people rallied at the State Capitol this past week to demonstrate in support of Senate Bill 392 which would establish a residential landlord-tenant act. More of this active vocal support is needed. The proposed reforms passed the State Senate last June. The bill was referred to my Committee on Judiciary and reported out for debate last September. Now it's being subjected to heavy lobbying pressures from some of the worst slumlords in Milwaukee and south western areas. Landlord-tenant relations have always been contractual, and the duties each owes to the other are usually spelled out in some agreement. These agreements can be oral or written.

Landlord-tenant laws as proposed in Senate Bill 392 serve three basic functions:

1. Establish the prevailing relations between landlords and tenants in those areas which are silent in the contract. Where the rental agreement fails to deal with an issue, the courts should be able to select a solution. A landlord-tenant law can dictate such solutions.

2. Determine the types of agreements which shall not be enforce-
able. Although enforcing agreements should be encouraged,
some private bargains violate good public policy. Landlord-
tenant laws establish this public policy.

3. Specify the remedies which the parties to an agreement may
secure from the legal system.

Under common law, landlords had no responsibility to deliver rent-
able property or maintain it in a fit condition. The tenant took the property as he/she found it and assumed all responsibility for maintenance.
Even if the landlord promised fit conditions, his/her breach of promise
did not relieve the tenant of the duty to pay rent.

Like most states, Wisconsin had modified the common law approach. In 1961, the Wisconsin Supreme Court recognized a limited
warranty of habitability. In 1969, the Legislature also created a limited
duty to repair on the part of landlords. Even so, existing state law is still
solidly in favor of the landlord.

The intent of the proposed residential landlord-tenant act is to put
tenants on a legal par with landlords. Last session, the Legislature debated a much stronger bill, co-authored by me. That proposal failed.
Since then, a compromise measure has been drawn up.

Pauline Althea Barbee was once a slave in Northern Mississippi. After being freed, she and Melvin Barbee purchased 39.5 acres of land in Shannon, Mississippi. They had ten children, including Earnest Barbee, Lloyd's father.

Barbee's mother, Adelina Gilliam Barbee.

Barbee's father,
Earnest A. Barbee.

Earnest A. Barbee is pictured with relatives from Shannon, Mississippi, including Pinkney,
Charlie, Arthur, Theona, Darthula, Gertrude, and one unnamed family member.

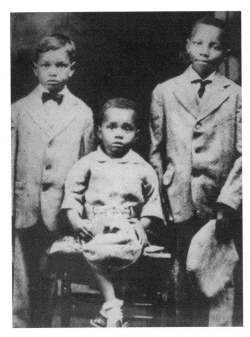

Barbee (middle) with his brothers Raymond and Quinten, in a family photo taken in Memphis.

As a young man in the early 1940s.

Barbee served in the Navy from 1943 to 1946 during World War II.

Lloyd Barbee and Roudaba Bunting Barbee on their wedding day, September 4, 1954.

Lloyd and Roudaba Barbee at their wedding, with Bourtai Bunting Scudder, Earnest Barbee, and Marian Bunting.

(*above*) Barbee with his wife Roudaba and their oldest two children, Finn and Daphne.

(*right*) Playing with his children, Finn, Daphne, and Rustam, on the grass.

(*below*) A family portrait with his children, Daphne, Rustam, and Finn.

As a young lawyer.

Barbee, pictured with his law library, worked as an attorney for the Wisconsin State Department of Labor before entering private practice.

Barbee used this protest sign, now preserved in a frame by his family, at rallies supporting the integration of Milwaukee Public Schools.

Barbee and other protesters are arrested at a protest against segregation of Milwaukee
Public Schools in 1965.

4

School Desegregation

The Fight for School Desegregation, Lloyd A. Barbee 1982 manuscript

The controversy over school segregation in Milwaukee was publicly raised by me in July 1963 at a Milwaukee Junior Bar Association luncheon. Many members of that progressive organization of young lawyers defended the School Board and expressed disbelief that the Board or its Superintendent discriminated against blacks. Some stated that, if there was black bias, it was the result of housing and employment discrimination.

I retorted that, often, the school authorities led the pack of segregationist running dogs, snarling and biting as they fled.

A planned systematic manipulation of the school system, which resulted in both educated whites and undereducated or uneducated blacks, was ignored by the majority of citizens of Milwaukee. To counteract the subliminal repression of this fact, it became necessary to identify blatant as well as subtle acts of intentional discrimination. Since some remedies could be immediately implemented, while others would require a year or two of planning and redirection.

Various proposals were first offered, later demanded, and subsequently litigated. Proposed remedies were: 1) Adoption by the School Board, and implementation within a reasonable time, of an overall plan to eliminate racial imbalance of classes in the public schools, 2) Immediate integration in white receiving schools, classes transported from black schools that were overcrowded, being renovated, and/or having additions constructed thereto. The transported classes were kept separate in the receiving schools, often even separate lunch and recess periods. Generally, the teachers and children were taken back to the sending school for lunch, even when lunch facilities were available at the receiving school, 3) Redrawing of the school attendance and districts to enhance racial balance, 4) Selection of sites so that new schools would not become ghettoized, 5) Use textbooks which reflect black and minority cultural and intellectual contributions to society, 6) Desegregation of faculty and staff, 7) Recruitment of more minority staff and faculty, 8) Upgrading of minority faculty and staff (at that time, only one black was a principal; he was assigned to a school which was reopened to house black students who were in an overcrowded school zone), and 9) Providing a school transfer system which would enhance racial balance. The Board refused all of these proposals.

The Board did agree to mount an annual headcount, which would determine the racial composition of the school system. In 1964, a series of demonstrations including picketing, marches, rallies, sit-ins and boycotts, took place. Petitions, presentations, appearance before committees and the Board as a whole were of little avail.

In 1965, I introduced legislation such as setting standards for racial imbalance; eliminating racial isolation; prohibitions against segregation; mandatory school courses in minority history. I continued to push for education legislation during my tenure as a legislator, culminating in the adoption of Chapter 222.

The issue of intact bussing was brought to the public's attention more clearly when MUSIC (Milwaukee United School Integration Committee) sponsored demonstrations of human chains, sitting down in front of buses which were transporting black children to white, underutilized schools. A total of sixty persons were arrested during the spring of 1960. I was one of the first to be arrested in May 1965. I chose to be arrested, along with eight others, on a Monday when the legislature was not in session and the committee was not meeting. Because legislature was in session at that time, I was immune from arrest. The case against me was dismissed, though I was booked, fingerprinted, searched, and mug shot. While in jail, I observed that the black prisoners' pictures were on a different wall than the whites.

The issue, which needed to be dramatized, was the blatant racial practice of intact Bussing. We succeeded in delaying the buses and getting the Huntley-Brinkley Monday night television news program to explain the issue in two minutes of primetime, which had been obscured up to this time in Milwaukee for eight years. More than a few of my fellow legislators screamed for my impeachment.

In 1971, the School Board voted to integrate the intact bussing classes. The next large demonstration focused on the issue of school site selection. After two weeks of protest at the construction site, twenty-one people were arrested for padlocking themselves to gates at the sites and chaining themselves to forklifts and cement mixers. Three requests were made that the Department of Housing, Education and Welfare (HEW) withhold federal funds until discrimination segregation practices were ended. HEW never responded, though they did eventually get some investigators on a fact-finding mission. They haven't issued a report yet.

The state Department of Public Instruction was requested to order the Milwaukee school system to cease discrimination. The Milwaukee school superintendent promised a reply by Labor Day. He did respond in a timely manner by saying that "segregation is illegal. The Milwaukee school system does not segregate." He said problems were based on housing and disadvantaged children. He didn't say that his department had studied the Milwaukee school system a year earlier and found that several black schools, including a new one, had inadequate facilities and course materials. My role in this measure was essentially that of a lightning rod, to draw the thunder and lightning from entrenched forces and save the moderates to work on passing measures that were palliative and passable.

EDUCATION, LLOYD A. BARBEE 1982 MANUSCRIPT

Issues in the field of education which permeated my work in the Legislature will require some detailed references to a battle for integrated quality education in the Milwaukee Public Schools, which culminated in a lawsuit instituted by me. This battle was won decisively at the desegregation level after the integration of schools issue was won in the field of public opinion but the implementation was snarled by objections to bussings and quotas for racial balance. Because of limitations inherent in a

LEGAL ACTION TO END SCHOOL SEGREGATION IN MILWAUKEE PUBLIC SCHOOLS

Mr. Barbee's most famous case was *Amos v. Board of School Directors*, 408 F.Supp 765 (E.D. WI 1976), also referred to as the Milwaukee School Desegregation Case and by the name of a later plaintiff, Armstrong. For a very long time, Milwaukee Public Schools were segregating students on the basis of race. Black students went to black schools, and white students went to white schools. Busing was allowed to permit white students to avoid attending black schools, or to allow white students to attend private schools. Even in situations where a black school was temporarily closed and students had to attend white schools, the school board would order that the black students have lunch hours separate from white students and sit separately from white students. All of this occurred after *Brown v. Board of Education*. It was de facto segregation.

Mr. Barbee brought suit against the school board in Milwaukee for intentionally creating and maintaining a racially segregated school system. The trial took place from September 1973 to January 31, 1974, before Judge John Reynolds. At the conclusion of the trial, Judge Reynolds ruled in favor of Mr. Barbee's plaintiffs and ordered that the Milwaukee public schools be desegregated. After a long delay and appeals, which were affirmed by the appellate courts, the Milwaukee public schools were able to remain segregated. Even though by law these schools cannot be segregated, education leaders find many ways to get around the law and to perpetuate a racially separate school system under the guise of "school choice," the voucher system, and the lack of specific intent.

In the aftermath of the desegregation case, Mr. Barbee struggled to recoup his legal expenses, which were considerable due to the prolonged legal battles. When a civil rights case has been won, the law allows the attorney bringing the case to obtain attorney's fees and costs from opposing counsel and from the defendants. In this case, attorney's fees and costs were awarded to Mr. Barbee in the amount of $134,103.39. His cocounsel for the appeal, Mr. Irvin B. Charney, who was appointed by

Continued on next page

the court, received $377,918.22. Defendants' attorneys received more than $1 million from the School Board.

Despite the fact that Mr. Barbee received relatively small compensation and had to pay his expert—a statistician who testified that black students were systematically excluded from white schools—from his attorney's fees, the media and judges were in an uproar that Mr. Barbee was to be paid. A Wisconsin federal district judge, Myron Gordon, criticized Mr. Barbee for receiving payment and encouraged an FBI investigation and IRS audit of him. This prompted Barbee to write several letters to Chief Justice Warren Berger concerning the federal judge's comments. Judges are supposed to be fair and impartial, far from disparaging an attorney who fought and won a major civil rights case. However, in the 1960s and 1970s, most judges were white males who felt privileged to attack civil rights protesters, civil rights advocates, and civil rights attorneys by targeting them for disciplinary actions and criticizing them in the media. Judge Gordon's actions are an example of the politically charged acts of the judicial branch of the United States government that affected the civil rights movement. Neither the Bar Association nor the IRS found wrongdoing on the part of Mr. Barbee. Mr. Barbee's complaint about Judge Gordon also resulted in no action.

Mr. Barbee and Mr. Charney endured multiple death threats as a result of the lawsuit to desegregate public schools. The FBI agreed to investigate and prosecute a similar threat against Judge Reynolds, but not against Mr. Barbee or Mr. Charney.

legal forum, desegregation is heavily dependent on remedies which rely on court enforcement of orders to be implemented by local school district politicians and taxpayers who are reluctant to use the most efficient known means of eliminating illegally unequal school systems. This is true whether the remedy must be effectuated by a combination of bussing, redrawing of school attendance areas, magnet schools, creation of expanded regional or metropolitan districts, affirmatively balanced students, faculty and staff at every educational unit, or continual court jurisdiction to ensure effective means to prevent resegregation within each state district or territory within the jurisdiction of the United States.

Since the key reasons for public education rest upon a recognition that schools should not only transmit skills and knowledge for jobs and enlightened citizenship but should also lay the foundation for formulating character of the highest order, our greatest resources should be expended, thought-, technology-, and money-wise. To accomplish this task, better funding of the public school system is necessary. In most of Wisconsin's urban districts, the property tax funds public education.

TIMELINE OF THE MILWAUKEE DESEGREGATION MOVEMENT, ARTICLE BY LLOYD A. BARBEE FOR *INTEGRATED EDUCATION*, APRIL 7, 1977

The wheels of justice in Milwaukee grind slowly and coarsely in both the private and public sectors. This is the author's view of a war against segregated schools which he championed commencing with his conscience raising efforts and ending with a moderate court order. This war covers a 16-year period. After the declaration of war against school segregation, the battleground in board meetings, conferences, negotiations, demonstrations, boycotts, arrests, research and non-legal logistics preceded and then coincided with the 12-year battle in the courts.

January, 1961
The NAACP state president requested that the Milwaukee NAACP Branch study whether or not segregation in the Milwaukee Public Schools was intentional. He suggested that the Milwaukee Public School system was in fact racially segregated and recommended that the branch report back in June. During a spring state meeting the Milwaukee Branch President indicated that no segregation existed and no study was being undertaken. The NAACP at its National Convention in July took a position against de facto segregation.

September, 1961
The State NAACP President spoke at a Milwaukee Branch membership kickoff campaign about symptoms of racial discrimination in the north

generally and Wisconsin particularly, such as bigotry in housing, education, employment, welfare, courts, police and fire protection as well as
public accommodations. The discussion which followed this talk centered
on the wisdom of boycotting Milwaukee 5 and 10 cent stores and chain
merchant stores like Sears which did not discriminate in the services to
blacks. The only educational questions raised concerned employment of
more black teachers at the high school level and possibly hiring black male
teachers at the kindergarten and elementary schools for a masculine positive image to black pupils.

July, 1962

The National NAACP took a stronger position against school segregation
in the north. The Milwaukee Branch President told the State NAACP President that the members of the Milwaukee board were satisfied with school
progress because more blacks were being hired although they were assigned to predominantly black schools. One black male, past president
of the Milwaukee NAACP, had been named principal of an elementary
school. He was the first black principal in the state of Wisconsin and my
cousin, Grant Gordon.

July, 1963

The NAACP State President addressed the Milwaukee Junior Bar Association on the need for lawyers and liberals to work against racial bigotry at
home rather than in Georgia, Mississippi, Alabama and Florida. Since
segregation in the public and parochial K-12 schools was rampant, he said
that clear thinking and hard working persons who knew their local structure, personalities and history were needed to eliminate bigotry in the
governmental as well as private sector.

   The all but one white junior bar association attendees claimed to have
been insulted. The one race Milwaukee press accused the NAACP president
of calumniating the best school system in the nation. Thus the issue of public
school segregation Milwaukee style was joined because the School Board
President created a Special committee to fight integrated, quality education, by evasions, quibbles, lies, specious studies, insults, diversions, token-
ism, etc., with all of the arrogance of entrenched white majority racists.

The State Superintendent of Public Instruction, similar to a state Commission of Education in other states, was asked by the NAACP President to:

- Recognize the existence of segregation in Milwaukee

- Recognize its harmful effects on children

- Issue an order for the elimination of school segregation throughout the state

- Assist local school boards to devise plans for speedily integrating schools

The State Superintendent responded 15 days later in a meeting with the NAACP President and its National Legal Counsel Robert L. Carter, now a U.S. District Judge for Southern New York by stating:

- That compulsory mixing of races in Wisconsin schools would be a complete reversal of present school policy

- That he needed proof of illegal segregation in Milwaukee schools before he could act to eliminate it

- That he would make a detailed reply to the requests after further study by the time school opened in the fall.

August, 1963
The Milwaukee NAACP Branch members supported the State Conference in its drive for true equality in educational opportunity. Since that time and even now, they have remained active in their psychological support.

September, 1963
The State Superintendent wrote to the State NAACP President a letter containing the following points:

- That no evidence was found of any intentional segregation by Milwaukee School officials

- That the Milwaukee situation is the result of a "residential pattern"

- That placement of pupils or altering of boundary lines with a view to changing the racial constitution of the schools "could very well be interpreted as being in violation of Wisconsin Statutes"

- That he reaffirmed his own interest in the problem and called attention to the "free transfer" policy, and the creation of the school board's Special Committee on Equality of Educational Opportunity as signs of the Board's acceptance of its responsibility in the matter.

- That he urged cooperation from the NAACP with the local school board.

The Chairperson of the Special Committee on Equality of Educational Opportunity divided the problem into legal, educational and sociological categories. The State NAACP President asked to appear before the Special Committee on the real problem—racism in the school system.

The Chairperson responded that that committee was then studying education and administration of central city schools but sometime in the future NAACP would be allowed to speak. It was December 10th before the NAACP appeared and submitted a 77 page report.

Milwaukee Teacher's Education Association (MTEA) gave a "special salute to those teachers in the inner core schools whose work and efforts have been under fire by unjust criticism in recent weeks." The MTEA also assured the Milwaukee Superintendent and his staff that they supported him "100 percent" in "maintaining Milwaukee's fine record."

The Special Committee Chairperson wrote the State NAACP President to support the view that the school board's responsibility was educational and not in the area of housing and employment. A Board standing Committee had voting members and staff input from the City Housing planning Commission. The official board hires more people than any other branch of city government. Blacks are still underemployed by the Board. The State NAACP President said that no amount of "compensatory education could eliminate school segregation" in response to the Special Committee Chairperson's ploy.

October, 1963

Ms. June Shagoloff, National Education Director of NAACP visited Milwaukee, studied data gathered, observed some of the schools and encouraged the School Board to abolish its segregated system and become a model for other cities.

December, 1963

The NAACP presented a report, petition, testimony and statements along with Milwaukee Core and Near Northside NonPartisan Conference at a Milwaukee School Board and Special Committee hearing. Deadlines were given by NAACP with the other groups' agreement for an integration policy declaration by January 30, 1964; and for the following by the fall of 1964:

- End to intact Bussing

- A comprehensive integration plan to include district re-zoning,

- Site selection for integration

- Integrating assignments of teachers and recreation staff

Seven plans used in other cities were recommended by NAACP as a guide. It was emphasized that an open enrollment policy placed the burden of integration on parents and was the least effective means of integrating a school system. Representatives of these groups were invited by the Special Committee to return on January 21, 1964, to answer questions by the Special Committee. The school board and the administration said they were color blind, criticized NAACP racial figures and were told to take a head count school by school or accept NAACP's figures. On December 26, the Board announced a census to determine the number of black students enrolled in each school.

January, 1964

The Chairperson of the School Board refused to let representatives of other Civil Rights Groups answer questions on school segregation, claiming the NAACP President was issuing ultimata. The State NAACP President walked out of the meeting and never returned.

No positive action came from the School Board on any NAACP demands by January 30 so the first demonstration against Milwaukee Public
Schools, on a cold day, was a march to a rally at the School board administration building where it was announced that a protest against intact
Bussing would begin, boycotts would be called, other direct and legal
action would commence and continue until segregation was killed, and
integration would be permitted to flourish.

February, 1964

Pickets at three sending and receiving schools began by civil rights groups
protesting intact Bussing.

"Intact Bussing" in Milwaukee was used to relieve overcrowded and
overutilized black schools by transporting mostly black students during
periods of modernization of construction. Using this method, students
were bussed intact as whole classes to overcrowded, underutilized white
schools. The bussed students were kept together and isolated from other
students at the receiving school. In most instances, students who were
bussed intact were bussed back to their home school for lunch even when
lunch facilities were available at the receiving school. It is important to
note that white students bussed to other schools were bussed on a "mixed"
basis and were integrated into the student body of the receiving schools.
The Federal Court found this as a fact January 19, 1976.

March, 1964

Nine hundred citizens at a mass meeting voted unanimously to boycott
Milwaukee's public schools in protest over the failure of the School Board
to act on any of NAACP demands. The Milwaukee United School Integration Committee (MUSIC) was organized to implement all mass action of
the school segregation issue. The State NAACP President [Barbee] was
elected chairman.

A School Board attorney warned the City that if NAACP and CORE
demands were met, it would mean "the beginning of the end" of the neighborhood school system in Milwaukee.

Civil rights leaders toured Roosevelt (100 percent Black) and Wilbur
Wright (99 percent White) junior high schools. They charged inequities
in Roosevelt's textbooks, classroom and shop equipment and library. They
commented on paddles allegedly used to punish Roosevelt students.

April, 1964

The Chairperson of the School Board Special Committee announced that the only demand made of the Milwaukee School Board which could legally be met was an open enrollment policy. In response to the request for a statement of policy favoring integration he stated that such a declaration would only be "a flock of words" and suggested that a policy statement would be "silly." The NAACP President charged the Board with a "lack of insight" and stated that only about 1 percent desegregation would be achieved by open enrollment.

May, 1964

The Mayor of Milwaukee sought to arbitrate the dispute between the Milwaukee United School Integration Committee (MUSIC) and the Milwaukee School Board. The Milwaukee United School Integration Committee agreed to meet with an arbitration committee.

A nine to six vote by the Milwaukee School board rejected the Mayor's proposal.

A mass withdrawal ("boycott") of children from Milwaukee schools conducted by the Milwaukee United School Integration Committee took place on May 18. MUSIC reported 16,000 children attended Freedom Schools staffed by 370 teachers. The Milwaukee School Superintendent reported 13,700 absent from inner core schools compared with 2,562 absences from the same schools on the same day of the previous week.

May 20, the State NAACP President wrote the Milwaukee School Board, asking for dissolution of its Special Committee and asked the board to meet as a committee of the whole with civil rights leaders to resolve the segregation issue. The letter was referred to the Special Committee and placed on file. The oldest Negro attorney in Milwaukee criticized the local NAACP branch and resigned from it as a protest against the boycott.

May 21, Wisconsin Upper Michigan Synod of Lutheran Church in America criticized the boycott, but affirmed the right to demonstrate on racial issues. Its statement also supported open occupancy, unsegregated schools and equal job opportunities for all persons.

May 27, because of the Milwaukee School Board's Special Committee's decision to put aside most NAACP requests, the State President announced that plans for legal action against the board would be pursued.

The State NAACP president retired from that office and became NAACP's State Legal redress chairman but remained chairman of the Milwaukee United School Integration Committee.

June, 1964
Two University of Wisconsin–Milwaukee Professors submitted reports to the Special Committee concerning the consequences of segregated education. Both urged integration and suggested methods of achieving it. They were ridiculed by the Committee.

July, 1964
The school board put aside suggestions made to help integrate schools by the NAACP and by its only Black member Dr. [Cornelius] Golightly. The vote was 9 to 4. On the same day the Governor's Commission on Human Rights appointed a 14 member committee to study school segregation in Milwaukee and make recommendations.

November, 1964
The Milwaukee United School Integration Committee Chairman and former NAACP State President was elected to Wisconsin's Legislature. On November 22, Dr. Golightly warned fellow school board members against complacency regarding the racial situation in the city's inner core schools.

May, 1965
The Milwaukee United School Integration Committee sent notice to the Milwaukee School Board that demonstrations would escalate if intact bussed black students were not integrated by May 15. The School Superintendent claimed that it would be administratively unfeasible to integrate intact bussed students. On May 17, protest of intact Bussing (by persons standing, sitting or chaining themselves in front of busses) began at Brown St. School. Nine people including the MUSIC Chairman, ministers and others were arrested for blocking busses. Between May 17 and June 16 a total of 71 were arrested for this reason. In addition, CORE conducted "sit in" civil disobedience at the Milwaukee School Board administration building, resulting in five more arrests.

June, 1965

A suit was filed in the US District Court by 41 Milwaukee black and white pupils and their parents asking for a decree to end segregation The suit alleged that whites and blacks as a class were irreparably harmed educationally and psychologically as a result of the Board's US constitutional violation.

July, 1965

July 29, the Milwaukee United School Integration Committee sent a nine page letter of complaint to the Department of Health, Education and Welfare (HEW) detailing charges of discrimination and segregation and requested that federal funds be withheld from Milwaukee public schools. No action was ever taken by HEW.

August, 1965

A demonstration march and rally in MacArthur Square took place to commemorate the March on Washington and to protest Milwaukee inequities. The Milwaukee United School Integration Committee chairman announced an extended boycott of schools to take place in the fall.

September, 1965

Congressman [Henry] Reuss urged the Milwaukee School Board to adopt a proposal for a one year pilot project of integrated bussed classes; he also asked the Milwaukee United School Integration Committee to call off the boycott if the project was approved.

The Milwaukee United School Integration Committee refused. This one year test of mixed Bussing resolution was defeated by the board May 20, 1966. On September 5, the Milwaukee Urban League asked discontinuation of intact bussing of classes and urged the assignment of Black teachers to more white classes.

October, 1965

A well listened to white minister called this boycott an "illegal demonstration" but also criticized the school board by saying "Citizens with legitimate concern about the effect of racial imbalance and de facto

segregation upon schools have not been given adequate consideration."
On October 10, a Marquette University Law professor, on TV described the
old Negro Attorney as "not really of this generation." The attorney replied
in a letter to the *Milwaukee Journal* emphasizing an historic role of seeking
legal redress.

On October 11, the Milwaukee United School Integration Committee
Chairman called a meeting of the committee to reconsider its decision for
an extended boycott in light of a proposal to study segregation. The Milwaukee United School Integration Committee voted not to rescind. A three
day prayer vigil was held at the Milwaukee School Board building.

October 18, when parents and students picketed at the home of the Milwaukee School Board President. When they were criticized by the mayor,
his home was picketed the next night for suborning bigotry; the school
superintendent and the Chairperson of the Special Education Committee's homes were picketed the following nights. The Governor was asked
at a press conference about the boycott and indicated that it was a local
problem in which he has "no particular right to intervene." The boycott
of schools begins. School officials estimated that 7,300 more pupils were
absent than usual. MPS claimed over 30,000 students participated. Forty-
nine welfare counselors were used as truant officers. The District Attorney
announced that he planned to prosecute boycott leaders and possibly parents. He never did.

October 22, the boycott ended at noon after three and one-half days.
The Milwaukee United School Integration Committee chairman announced that protests would continue until the school system gave evidence
of implementing a clearly stated policy of desegregation.

December, 1965

A series of demonstrations began at McDowell grade school which was
being constructed. The Milwaukee United School Integration Committee
and others charged that the school would become segregated, have inadequate playground areas and [be] unsafe for elementary children because
it was three stories high.

Demonstrations included numerous cases of civil disobedience (e.g.,
chaining people to forklift trucks, sites gates, etc) which resulted in 21
arrests and the payment of over $2,000 in fines.

February, 1966

The Milwaukee United School Integration Committee secretary and co-ordinator elected to serve 30 days in jail rather than pay $100 fine and $67.50 in costs assessed for assisting a demonstrator to chain himself to a fork-lift truck at the McDowell school site. She chose jail as a protest against the quality of Milwaukee justice.

March, 1966

The Milwaukee United School Integration Committee (MUSIC) called a North Division High School Boycott for March 28. MUSIC announced opposition to a spring referendum which asked voters to approve a bond issue for financing net school construction, remodeling, etc. The referendum passed.

An injunction was sought to prevent the North Division Boycott but was refused by a State Court. The Boycott of North Division High School took place.

MUSIC began exclusive research of school board policies and administration for the lawsuit, parents, students and community groups.

Despite public opposition, defendants leased a school vacated by a Lutheran Church, which they opened as a 99% black school. The school board continued leasing and purchasing schools which extended or maintained segregation throughout the liability phase of a Federal Lawsuit. Defendants formed Jackie Robinson School by reopening 68th Street School and leasing a vacant catholic parochial school adjacent to it. Although Jackie Robinson was located in an all-white neighborhood it opened as a black school because it housed students bussed over 6 miles across town. Defendants purchased a Spencerian College property which was used as an annex for the all black Franklin School and bought a former Seventh Day Adventist school property which was used as an annex for Black Clark School.

1967

The Academy for Educational Development, Inc. studied the public schools. Their study was paid for by the School Board and We-Milwaukeeans men of influence and affluence in Milwaukee. This study found extensive segregation in the schools and recommended that the School Board adopt a policy of reducing racial segregation. The School Board did not act on the study group's recommendations but filed the report. The National NAACP agreed to finance research and offered Legal assistance to the lawsuit. It discontinued both [as] of December 2, 1969.

June, 1967
Depositions became necessary of the outgoing Milwaukee School Superintendent because voluntary production of public school board and administration data and documents were withheld. This Superintendent remained under subpoena until he died of a heart attack while seeking a state legislative office for the [19]69 term.

November, 1967
A recently appointed Milwaukee Federal Judge held a press conference in his chambers praising his friend and candidate for re-election, the Mayor of Milwaukee, for his civil rights record and condemning activists who marched 200 consecutive days for a City Fair Housing ordinance, boycotted schools for integration, etc. The Plaintiff's attorney in the school suit complained and asked the Supreme Court and 7th Circuit court of Appeals to discipline this judge for unethical conduct. The plaintiffs' attorney recommended that this Judge be permanently disqualified from hearing Civil Rights cases involving the city government.

March, 1968
The plaintiffs amended their complaint against the School system adding new and younger plaintiffs and the Secretary Business Manager of the School Board. This amendment coincided with the 100th anniversary of the 14th amendment to the US Constitution.

April, 1968
The School Board hired a private law firm as co-counsel with the city attorney. By the time of trial, September 10, 1973, the senior counsel died but his junior represented all the defendants and continues to do so.

Hence Forward and Backward
The problems of bringing this case to trial from the author's vantage point would fill several volumes of this publication. In summary, one judge was

reluctant to try the matter for 7 years and the judge who tried this case took two years to decide it in 1976.

1979
However, despite all the obstacles, we won and Milwaukee Public Schools were ordered to integrate by Federal Judge [John] Reynolds in *Armstrong v. Board of Directors of the City of Milwaukee* on May 4, 1979.

BUSSING, LEGISLATIVE COMMENT, OCTOBER 6, 1972

Forty percent of all American school children ride busses to school. Fewer than 1% of these are bussed for racial integration—court ordered or other wise.

Nearly 10,000 students are bussed daily by the Milwaukee public school system. At least 10,000 more probably use some other form of transportation, such as Milwaukee Transport. The Milwaukee school board also bussed some 1200 parochial school children to and from school.

- 2465 children are bussed due to hazardous conditions in their districts, while 1300 are bussed due to their distance from school. These children live in predominantly white districts.

- 2808 children from both black and white school districts are bussed to classes for the physically or mentally handicapped.

- 3360 children are bussed out of their districts because of over-crowding. 79% of these children are bussed out of schools which are predominantly Black. Less than half of the children bussed for overcrowding are bussed under the new mixed Bussing pol-icy, and in this category, the majority of the children are mixed between schools which are almost all Black or almost all white.

- 1705 children, out of the 3360 bussed for overcrowding, are bussed into so-called "annexes"—which are vacated buildings no longer used by the districts, and these are some of the oldest school buildings in the city: 68th St. (built in 1928) is used at the Peckham Annex along with what used to be a white, private high school, Francis Jordan; 8th St. (built in 1884) is used as an

annex by the Fulton 7th grade; McKinley school (1885) is used
by 5th, 6th, and now 7th graders from the doubly overcrowded
Auer Av. School.

Although the Milwaukee school board has changed its Bussing of
classes out of schools intact, only one-fifth of the children bussed out of
overcrowded schools are bussed so that some measure of integration
takes place.

As the punsters said of the People's Republic of China: "We don't ask
people if they want to be bussed, we just bus 'em." This is what the school
board has been able to do in the Black community.

The one exception to this seems to be Black parents who wanted Bussing. In Meinecke, parents who secured transfers out of the district when
it opened in 1966 asked that the board fund a bus, and it refused.

The intact Bussing at Auer was reduced for a while four years ago, but
[it] was largely the opposition of the teachers that brought this about—
when they then put up the "temporary" Willis wagons, which are now
being used for the fifth year.

Before 1971, the Milwaukee board bussed thousands of Black children
intact, starting in the late 1950's. It was not until 1964, however, that the
children were permitted to stay at the receiving schools for lunch. Children
were missing hundreds of hours of time because of this every year. At the
same time, somehow it was possible to bus numerous whites by the usual
methods.

Numerous arrests and demonstrations by Blacks yielded nothing. But,
at the behest of new white liberal school board members, the board finally
ended it. The *Journal* applauded it, even though they called our demonstrations in the '60's extremist and reckless. Some of you may remember
my being arrested May 24, 1965, for blocking a school bus at Brown Street
School.

"This practice [intact Bussing] deserves careful reexamination by
school authorities. But let no one delude himself that this is the real issue.
The central problem revolves around the question of how a public school
system can extend a strong helping hand to scores of deprived children,
and, at the same time, encourage racial integration in our society." (*Milw.
Journal* 5-28-65)

In 1963 the Wisconsin State NAACP and C. L. Golightly, a former member of the school board, both suggested methods of integrating districts which did not require any additional Bussing:

- Open enrollment and free transfer policy (such that it would promote integration rather than white flight)

- Redistricting

- Integrated grade centers

- Changing the feeder patterns

- School spotting and judicious site selection

- Teacher and staff integration

- Integration of intact bussed classes

- Comprehensive high schools, or specialty schools which would draw a city-wide enrollment.

In the final statement of the [National Black Political Convention in Gary], the Black delegates rejected getting embroiled in a "politically manufactured issue" of Bussing created by self-serving white politicians.

As for the Nixon Bussing bills, they are blatantly unconstitutional:

- As an interference by Congress with the powers of a separate and coequal branch of the government, namely, the courts.

- As "postponing" enforcement of individual rights under the 14th Amendment, and saying in effect that they can be ignored.

- As clearly against the decision of the U.S. Supreme Court in *North Carolina v. Swann*, declaring North Carolina's anti-Bussing bill unconstitutional.

If North Carolina cannot pass an anti-Bussing bill, it is hard to see how the Congress can. Nixon may already know this, since his own man, Chief Justice Berger, wrote the North Carolina decision.

The bill passed the House on August 17, and managed to unite both CORE and the NAACP in opposition to it, because the funds to be given to inner-city schools were turned down. So after being told by Nixon that the "real solution" was to pump more funds into central city schools, the southern dominated House (with the scared northern liberals either afraid to oppose them or powerless to do anything), rejected the money that was to go into the Nixon bill. In short, the Nixon bill is a fraud!

Needless to say, it is not the education of Black and poor youngsters that concerns any of the anti-Bussing forces. Rep. Ron Dellums (D-Calif.) blasted the liberals who had capitulated, while Parren Mitchell (D-Maryland) stunned supporters of the bill in a late night address in which [he] warned that the Congress was setting the stage for the second reconstruction.

With some more maneuvering by the southern Dixiecrats (primarily Sen. James Allen of Alabama), the bill was set for debate on the Senate calendar, and it will be coming up this month.

Many things other than bussing could be done [in Milwaukee] to begin integrating schools, and they could be done without administrative difficulty.

It is difficult to see how significant integration could be accomplished here without one additional Bussing (although that will be happening anyway). But the need for Bussing is largely of the school board's own making, since it has failed to do anything to integrate for over twenty years.

Since it is not the Black community's fault that Bussing may be necessary, they should not have to bear the whole burden.

There's already been enough one-way Bussing in Milwaukee, and there can be no integration if it is "one-way."

Many whites, and even Black parents to some degree, think integration is essentially designed to give Black children a chance to go to school with whites, but it is the quality of education that is crucial.

Bussing, Legislative Comment, December 19, 1973

The issue of bussing as a means for achieving racial balance and quality education in our schools is involved in a Congressional energy bill. The bussing amendment, however, is a ride backwards. The House bigots who sponsored this rider have lost neither their ingenuity nor energy.

While the fuel shortages have provided an impetus for energy gluttons to review some of their wasteful ways, it has also given additional credence to white bigots and conservatives for halting the Bussing of students to predominantly segregated schools. This is evident in Congressional arguments used for tacking an amendment on the most recent energy bill, an amendment that bans the use of fuel to transport children beyond their neighborhood schools.

During the House debate on this amendment, supporters of the anti-bussing movement stated that 78.3 million gallons of gasoline were used annually to transport children to schools for achieving more adequate school desegregation levels. How many gallons are used for maintaining racial segregation?

When the issue came up for closing some of our schools during the winter months or limiting the number of school days each week, considerable concern was made over the effects of such moves on the child's education.

As a result, these actions as a means for conserving fuel consumption are now regarded as a last alternative.

It appears when the issue is turned around, however, when Black children will be the most affected. Hence concern is not so serious over the possible resulting educational deficiencies.

Bussing is not the only answer to improving Black education. In many ways, bussing is not achieving the objectives of integration and quality education as originally intended. Nevertheless, I would hope that the Senate will act judiciously in dealing with this emergency energy bill before Congress. The anti-Bussing amendment deserves to be stricken.

We may also find a further negative impact with some of the energy legislation being offered within the various levels of government. For example, the same bill discussed above has another amendment that delays the implementation of the 1976 emission control standards called for in the Clean Air Act of 1970. And then there's the increasing support for speeding up the licensing of nuclear power plants and the new shift in authority for setting radiation standards for these plants with the Atomic Energy Commission rather than the Environmental Protection Agency.

Considering that the AEC's past record has shown a definite trend toward promoting nuclear power rather than providing adequate assurances
that public health and safety standards are met, it is obvious that such a
move is undesirable. While Black and poor people live and work disproportionately near expressways and industrial areas, the majority will
choke, get deafer, sicker and crazier too.

While the fuel shortages are heading us in the right direction in some
areas, such as mass transit, they are undoubtedly leading us down the
wrong paths when it comes to environmental considerations. And let us
not forget the issue of racism. Diverting the few social and environmental
gains of the last decade in the name of energy conservation is an example
of serious shortsightedness on the part of private and governmental officials, shortsightedness that may quickly lead us back into the Dark Ages.

DESEGREGATION IN DELAWARE, LEGISLATIVE COMMENT, DECEMBER 6, 1975

The U.S. Supreme Court upheld a Federal District Court's ruling that Delaware schools and housing policies promote school segregation. The state
must submit a school desegregation plan which will include Wilmington
and its neighboring suburbs. Since this decision without comment is taken
as a Thanksgiving present for proponents of metropolitan school desegregation, a few facts of this case should be considered.

In 1968, Delaware's Educational Advancement Act withdrew all school
district lines but majority Black Wilmington school. The legislature subsidized transportation for children attending private and parochial schools
outside as well as inside their own school district boundaries. The trial
judge concluded the effect of this was "a co-operative venture involving
both city and suburbs!" The Federal District Judge found Wilmington's
Housing Authority guilty of fostering racial isolation. In 1972, WHA operated for 2,000 public housing projects within the city limits but fewer
than 40 in the suburbs and no new projects were started in the suburbs
after 1972.

All these activities caused Judge Caleb Wright to say that "governmental authorities are responsible to a significant degree for increasing disparity in residential and school populations between Wilmington and its

suburbs." With the US Supreme Court's decision Judge Wright must decide between a new interdistrict plan or one limited to Wilmington.

Indianapolis and Detroit School Districts are involved in complex law suits over possible city-suburban school desegregation plans. Persons who like to analyze cases should read *Buchanan vs. Evans* along with *Milliken vs. Bradley* because the court said that under certain circumstances an inter-district plan is constitutionally valid.

CHALLENGES IN THE APPROACHING 1980S, REMARKS BY STATE REP. LLOYD A. BARBEE TO SYMPOSIUM ON EDUCATION PROBLEMS CONFRONTING MILWAUKEE, MAY 15, 1974

Twenty years ago, on May 17, 1954, the Supreme Court in *Brown v. Board of Education of Topeka, Kansas*, declared the segregation of school children by race unconstitutional. The decision was unanimous. The legal principle that "separate but equal" was inherently unequal became the law of the land. Today, however, we find a different situation. The pre-occupation with integration efforts is waning. Now, there is more discussion with the desegregation, decentralization of big city school systems, wider citizen participation, and in some cases control of the local community schools. And at the same time, our big city schools, especially here in Milwaukee, are retaining and expanding their segregated characteristics.

The present interest [is] in the decentralization of school with urban education. The rationale behind this desire for more community control in a decentralized school system is because the big systems are failing individuals and that educational progress cannot be made under systems which are too big to identify local needs and serve individuals on an individual basis.

While community control of the schools has never been claimed to be an end in itself for achieving quality education, it has been offered as an alternative to the existing dissatisfaction with the present school system. Is it really a good alternative, though?

In 1967, New York City became the first to experiment with decentralization. They met with disastrous results. Over one million school children were affected by this change, and the resulting pandemonium can easily be attributed to this massive undertaking which was needed to decentralize the New York City school system.

Detroit, however, offers us a different lesson. When the issue of decentralization of Milwaukee schools was presented as a legislative proposal two years ago in the Wisconsin state assembly one of the remarks made was that decentralization should come about only if accompanied by a successful desegregation effort. The experience that the Detroit city school system had, however, was that community control and integration were not compatible.

In order to control a school system, the community must have a tax base great enough to finance delivery of necessary educational goods and services. Decentralization efforts have been underway in other cities, such as Los Angeles, Washington DC, St. Louis, Louisville, and Oakland, California. Yet, neither of these reforms can be considered ideal models to base a possible Milwaukee effort on.

Nevertheless, more community involvement in the Milwaukee school system appears to be the trend today. About three-fourths of the high schools, one-half of the junior high schools, and a smaller number of the elementary schools in Milwaukee have school-community committees or large parent organizations associated with them. About one-fourth of these groups have memberships of one hundred or more, although the number of members in each group can range anywhere from fifteen to four hundred.

In addition, the Milwaukee school board's special committee to study advisory neighborhood school boards has just recently released a report with recommendations on how the school board can provide more community input in the school decision-making process.

The guidelines in the report recommend the creation of advisory neighborhood school boards with complete access to all information and resources, both at the central office and at the local school, consistent with school board policies and state statutes, the advisory boards would also have authority to discuss, advise, and recommend program improvement proposals, student curriculum needs, staffing needs, budget provisions, proposed major construction or school remodeling, and changes in existing school policies. The school board has not as yet agreed to the report's adoption. What's more important is the fact that such boards and committees are advisory only. Thus, they must either rubber stamp or bitch about school administration or policy decisions.

Undoubtedly, this community and parental participation in the educational process can be an important factor in improving the education of Milwaukee school children. Bigness in a school system tends to discourage voter and parental participation in the schools. The advisory neighborhood school boards have little potential of eliminating these discouragements.

Milwaukee's decentralization is a word or phrase only. However, decentralizing the Milwaukee school system and giving parental control over a child's education is a worthy goal for the present time. This type of decentralization has the seeds for becoming excessively provincial and narrow, thus restricting the community's children of broadening interests, experiences, and education in a country and world which is ever expanding. Localized school boards, with fixed attendance areas and no overall relationship with other area boards would perpetuate the racial, social, and economic isolation which exists in the racist Milwaukee school system. To put it simply, community control over unequal and inadequate educational resources is a bad bargain at best and phony at worst.

The educational achievement of children (no matter how generalized this phrase may appear) is the goal for which we should strive. Educational achievement should be based on a series of characteristics which provide a measuring stick for determining how close we are to accomplishing educational progress in our schools.

First of all, educational achievement is determined in large part by the characteristics of a teaching staff, committed to teaching and respecting human beings.

Secondly, educational achievement is determined by the characteristics of the student body, the educational aspirations and backgrounds of students enrolled and attending classes must be a starting point. The underlying assumption must always be that they are educable.

Thirdly, quality education is based on the facilities, curriculum, and other characteristics of the school, itself, committed to the fullest development of students' potentialities and the highest performance of teachers and administrators preparing students to understand and cope with themselves and the world in which they live.

Looking closely at these various determining factors, it's not difficult to realize how far away we are from providing adequate opportunities for educational achievement in Milwaukee inner city schools.

Our schools within the predominantly black areas of this city have the worst facilities, oldest buildings, least experienced teachers, but a student body which is heavily representative of the lower socio-economic groups in our state. These disparities prevent meaningful educational achievement of our children, because of racism, classism, and crass manipulation by the private sector and government. When the worst is given to those in need the most, a bad outcome is surely guaranteed.

Milwaukee's school system was rated one of the five most segregated in the north in a 1971–72 survey conducted by the national opinion research center in Chicago and the center for metropolitan planning and research at Johns Hopkins university in Baltimore. Nothing has been presented yet to show me that conditions have changed for the better. Recent actions by the school board and the MTA reveal that this situation will get worse unless the courts or other arms of government step in hard and fast.

This survey only centered around the extent of racial segregation in the Milwaukee public school system. Poverty goes hand-in-hand with racism and classism.

As we approach the 1980s, I believe there will be a resurrection of the efforts to integrate the public school system in terms of both racial and socio-economic factors not just through the extensive Bussing of school children, through means other than Bussing, such as school redistricting, special schools, etc. This will take work. It will take community participation and input, not community control as a slogan, but community accountability in fact.

Another trend we must work for in the coming years is a reform of our educational financing methods. This would not only make desegregation efforts easier, but would possibly provide the key for making decentralization programs successful by meeting the specific needs of some portions of special community groups. While Wisconsin has already taken steps [in] this regard, we are still a long way off from realizing an equal educational financing scheme.

Hawaii already finances the total costs of secondary education through state-collected taxes. The use of the regressive property tax for funding public schools has been declared unconstitutional by the state supreme courts in California, New Jersey, and Michigan, and by federal courts in Texas and Minnesota.

Just how regressive was the previous way of financing schools? A case in point is Wauwatosa here in Milwaukee County in previous years. It had taxed its residents for schools at less than 75 percent of the tax rate, which was forced on residents of the north side and other parts of Milwaukee. Yet, Wauwatosa was raising enough revenue to spend more than 18 percent above the per pupil cost of education as exists in the poor school districts within the city.

By financing public education in relation to the property wealth of a school district. In other words, through the property tax, the suburban communities and new housing developments were acquiring more and more state aid for bigger and better schools, while the city school districts lacked the property wealth which was the basis for where public educational funding would be funneled.

Today in our state, and in many others, the financing schemes for public education are taking on more equitable characteristics. Rather than financing education relative to the property wealth of a district, there is an attempt at equalizing the public education funds behind each student.

Of course, before additional reforms can occur in Wisconsin for funding public education, there will need to be a change in attitudes among the wealthy outlying suburban school districts. In other words those who claim the educational reforms of this legislative session were "an erosion of local control" must either change their tune or words.

In ruling against the use of property tax for funding public education, the Michigan Supreme Court said:

> This court sees no logical connection between the asserted
> justification of local control and the amount of school funds the state
> distributes or permits to be expended in a school district based solely
> on the fortuitous circumstance that the district has more or less valu-
> able properties per pupil within its boundaries.

Of course, the most effective method for creating a better climate of opinion in regard to educational thinking is for additional judicial declarations of this sort. This, however, will be a long time a-coming, especially in light of the US Supreme Court decision on educational financing.

In March of 1973, the US Supreme Court reversed a decision by a three-judge panel in San Antonio, Texas, that declared as unconstitutional the property tax as a means for funding public education. In an effort to negate the progress made by the previous Warren court in interpreting the constitution, as setting forth a constitutional right to an equal education, yet in the process grant some redeeming grace to innovative methods for financing public education, the Supreme Court said:

> It is not the province of this court to create substantive constitutional rights in the name of guaranteeing equal protection of the laws. Education, of course, is not among the rights afforded explicit protection under our US Constitution. Nor do we find any basis for saying it is explicitly so protected.
>
> Nevertheless, the need is apparent for reform. In tax systems which may well have relied too long and too heavily on the local property tax. And certainly new innovative thinking about public education, its methods, and its funding, is necessary to assure both a higher level of quality and greater uniformity of opportunity. The ultimate decision, however, must come from the law-makers and from the democratic pressures who elect them and not from the Supreme Court.

While not helping our cause, this decision surely didn't put an end to it. Opponents have, at least, identified themselves and the stage is now set for further efforts toward educational financing reform. With a greater infusion of public funds to help buttress the big city educational system, the solutions for providing equal educational opportunities and reaching the goal of greater educational achievement among our children will become much easier to identify.

Blacks must recognize the overall failure of public and private education to serve their interests in every significant respect.

Whites generally do not admit this fact. Blacks can meet the challenge confronting them in education by insisting that political forces work along with parents and students who want a real relevant, human education now.

Integration in Education, Letter from Lloyd Barbee to Milwaukee educator Bill Dahlk, September 4, 1991

Dear Mr. Dahlk:

Below are the answers to the questions you raised August 24, 1991.

1. What are the main reasons why you have been so deeply committed to an integrationist position (in education) as opposed to a "quality-education-in-black-school" position?

The main reasons I am "deeply committed to" integration in education are: Integrated education is learning and interacting with the common goal of eliminating ignorance among persons of differing cultural backgrounds, ethnicity, economic wherewithal, etc., with regular contact of teachers and students. Ideally, this diversity is reflected in both teachers and students in the learning place. At the very minimum the diversity must be present in the student body, faculty and support staff. Segregated, Balkanized, education perpetuates stereotypes and ignorance. The real world is multi-national, cultural and lingual. A school setting must take this into account because some parents are so narrow and ignorant that they will handicap their children. "Quality-education-in-black-schools" is only possible when the municipal government is totally black and will not avail itself of affirmative action. Planned all black male, socalled education, is not only unconstitutional, it isolates students who are already stigmatized.

1b. Was my long NAACP affiliation a major factor? Yes.

1c. My own personal experiences? Yes. My elementary and secondary education was segregated in Memphis, TN. My Navy boot camp and Class A Service School education racially segregated. I have known African American and white American students to undergo culture shock when experienced integration voluntarily or mandatorily.

2. In addition to Ardie Halyard, who were the three or four most influential Milwaukee NAACP leaders in 1963?

Attorneys Clarence Parish, W. Dale Phillips, John Broadnax, Edward Smythe, Mrs. Albertine Warren.

3. In the 1961 State Capitol fair housing sit-in, did the Milwaukee NAACP have any role or just the State NAACP?

The State NAACP conducted the State Capitol sit-in, some Milwaukee branch officers and members joined the protest for fair housing on various days.

4. In the final out-of-court settlement (October, 1978) why were you "willing" to allow twenty-plus schools to remain predominantly black?

The desegregation formula was in terms of percentage of students, not schools, to be integrated. Thus the 83 percent or so student guaranteed enrollment was supplemented by the provision which permitted any minority student to attend a desegregated school. The administration was given the option of submitting to the parties and the court sites where the goal of integration could be realized and those which could not. The Milwaukee minority school population in 1978 was too great to permit 100 percent integration. The only viable desegregation solution was a metropolitan one.

5. In the 1964–66 direct action period, did you/MUSIC ever consider taking the marches or even the civil disobedience downtown, say on Wisconsin Avenue?

Neither MUSIC nor I considered marching or demonstrating downtown on Wisconsin Avenue for school integration purposes only. We joined in the 1965 march for civil rights, police brutality, etc., during that summer. The Police Department refused to issue a marching permit on Wisconsin Avenue. As a result we marched on 3rd to Kilbourne Avenue and ended on the county courthouse steps. MUSIC co-sponsored some welfare rights demonstrations which included West and East Wisconsin Avenue.

5b. If so why was this tactic rejected?

We wished to keep our demonstrations focused on the school board, its members, the superintendent of schools, the mayor, and Judge Seraphim.

6. Was there a preeminent rationale for school desegregation—was it mainly to advance academic achievement by improving resource delivery? Was it mainly to boost self-esteem by eliminating all-black schools? Was it mainly to improve race relations by promoting interracial contact?

The Milwaukee School Board and its administration violated the US and State of Wisconsin constitutions by intentionally creating and maintaining a dual school system: one for whites and one for blacks. They would not voluntarily discontinue [abusing] the rights of residents: students and parents. Aside from the legal argument of racism, I say yes to all the questions in Number 6, plus my answer in Number 1. In addition, the elimination of the false sense of white superiority in all-white schools would facilitate more knowledge about and experience with the excluded minorities and their contributions.

7. Why did the Milwaukee Urban League sponsored Northside Community Inventory Conference not return for the December 10, 1963 Story Committee Hearing? (I sense somewhat of a split regarding remedy: You and perhaps certain Wisconsin NAACP and Milwaukee CORE members being more fervently for a racial balance goal while the NCIC people straddled a desegregation-compensatory education position.)

My memory of the Northside Community Inventory Conference's position is that they were favored by Story's Committee, conservative school board members and administrators. The Conference exhausted their position on compensatory education and an adoption of an integrated education principle. They had nothing more to say. In addition, Harold Story chose to contrast them with the NAACP, CORE, and the Near Northside Nonpartisan Coordinating Community and me as being too extreme and emotional.

8. What do you remember of the Nick Hall Controversy within the Milwaukee NAACP about 1969? Was he too "militant" for Milwaukee NAACP? Was he tending more toward a black power/separatist position than most NAACP people could tolerate?

Some of Nick Hall's positions were antithetical to many Milwaukee NAACP mainliners and could not be accommodated.

9. In one of your letters in your UWM papers you mentioned the Benton Harbor "madness." What was this a reference to? (January, 1975)

I believe the letter is a part of my State of Wisconsin Historical Society's donation, housed at UWM. The reference to Benton Harbor "madness" referred to the fact that a part of MUSIC's research staff sided with an attorney employed by NAACP who wished a higher fee from that organization. When NAACP refused to increase that attorney's fee, that attorney withdrew from the case. The research staff out of loyalty to the attorney who had withdrawn from the case initially refused to turn over their research and documents to the new substitute attorney, hired by NAACP. They persisted, for sometime, in withholding their work product from the lawyer who had to try a school desegregation suit before a Federal judge upon short notice. I thought that such behavior was "madness." This sabotage attempt was short-lived.

10. Two additional attorneys—Theodore Crockett and Holly Cooley—how did they stand regarding support or not for Barbee/MUSIC goals?

Theodore Crockett was generally cooperative, but he was an Assistant City Attorney. Holly Cooley was a senior attorney who died before the Milwaukee case was tried. As an elder Republican black attorney, he was positive.

All the best.

5

RACISM IN EDUCATION

OSHKOSH PROTESTS FOR BLACK HISTORY, LLOYD A. BARBEE 1982 MANUSCRIPT

Ninety-four black students were arrested at Oshkosh State University, Thursday, Nov. 21, 1968, subsequently known as Black Thursday. One hundred or so black students walked into the President's office at approximately 8:30 a.m. and presented him with a typed list of demands which had previously been presented to him in October. The President said that he did not have authority to sign; later he indicated that he needed a progress report from a faculty ad-hoc committee. Since the students saw no reason why the President could not read the report by 1 p.m. that afternoon, they asked him to sign the demands "right now." At about 10 a.m., the president of the faculty senate proposed that the students leave the President's office and go to another meeting room. By 11:45 a.m., all of the students were arrested. Most of the students walked to the city jail. There were at least 120 officers, including a forty-man riot squad, who came to the campus to effectuate the arrest. The students were charged with unlawful assembly and disorderly conduct. I was called to assist the students. Briefly, a number of the blacks attending Oshkosh were from Milwaukee and had been offered scholarships. When they arrived, they were subjected to various acts of bigotry.

Following are some of the comments made at that time:

- A fellow legislator, who represented that district: "It's tragic. They are biting the hand that feeds them."

117

- The common council president: "They have lost the faith, baby."

- Several students and shoppers: "Send them back to Africa."

- An unidentified man: "They should have busted all their clubs on their heads. Why are they (blacks) allowed to do that stuff?"

- A Methodist university minister: "I am deeply disappointed that the feeling of the black students erupted into violence just as meaningful progress was being made concerning their legitimate grievances."

- A local school teacher and John Birch Society member: "If these demands were met, there would be a new set of demands. It's a means of stirring up groups."

- A university professor and former human rights council president: "I hope that the moderates among the blacks will disassociate themselves from the extremists. There are some white militants on campus and in the city who are in favor of kicking all the black students out of town, and there are some blacks who will say 'Oshkosh is a racist town,' and just leave."

- A junior: "All I can say about this is, if they want to be equal, they should act like the whites do on campus."

- An unidentified student: "I am for the civil rights movement all the way, but when harm is done to my well-being, that's when it's got to stop."

The only students who were harmed were some black protesters who were roughed up on the way to the jail.

Some tables were overturned and windows were broken; an initial estimate of the damage was placed at over $25,000. The judge who was to try the misdemeanors as he had jurisdiction over these students initially, was asked by me to disqualify himself, because, on August 6, 1968, he referred to some burglary suspects appearing before him: "They talk like n——, they swallow half their syllables." The judge refused to disqualify himself, and indicated that a number of blacks used that word when referring to themselves. He set appearance bond at $250 cash or property bond. The university peremptorily suspended 94 of the students without notice or hearing. We went to the Federal District Court and got an order that the university either reinstate the students or grant the students a hearing. There were four white students arrested; they were not suspended because no one said that they had taken part in the demonstration inside the President's office. When the judge would neither disqualify himself nor dismiss the case on motions, the case was transferred to the Circuit Court, based on ninety-two affidavits of prejudice.

One of the Oshkosh newspapers suggested that I might use my legislative position to delay the transferred case indefinitely. In the end it was learned that the amount of damage allegedly done was minimal and placed at $710. The juvenile students were placed on probation; the adult student's case was handled in an amicable manner.

The State Assembly's education committee was little interested in two bills, which I introduced, aimed at attacking racism in the public schools, as opponents argued at some length that the matters should be taken up by the Department of Public Instruction rather than by the legislature.

One bill would require that a teacher pass a course in the history of minority groups in America before being licensed to teach in this state. The other would require that elementary and night schools in the state require courses in Afro-American, Indian, and Spanish-American history. Public education in Wisconsin is only perpetuating the racism that children are learning from their parents, movies, television, radio, recordings and newspapers. They learn about Columbus and the white men who supposedly discovered America, while blacks, Indians and Spanish-speaking Americans are maligned. The picture of blacks from television is nothing more than lies and half-truths; what most can expect from school is nothing better.

The State of Wisconsin is racist. If it desires to do anything about it, it cannot continue to teach children that all things good in America and the world are white. A child, particularily coming from a bigoted home, needs something to take back home indicating that the true history of America is not the one seen on television. As school systems are run now, children do not get this.

The Democratic controlled and supposedly progressive education committee favored leaving the matter to the Department of Public Instruction.

STUDENT PROTESTS AND DUE PROCESS

In 1968, during the student protests at University of Wisconsin–Oshkosh, where African American students were requesting black studies and a black studies union, the Board of Regents summarily dismissed and suspended all of the students involved in the protests without any hearing. Mr. Barbee stepped in as the attorney. He sued the university for violation of due process. In *Marzette v. McPhee*, 294 Fed. Supp. 562 (W.D. 1968), the federal district court decided that the students' due process rights had been violated. The court required the University Regents to provide "a due process hearing" before taking any discipline actions against the students. This case was hailed as one of the paramount cases in the state and the country for students protest rights. The court ordered that the university must reinstate the students or conduct a hearing. The Regents, all of whom were white, opted to conduct hearings, after which they expelled all students, who were black. After the students were expelled, the University of Wisconsin–Oshkosh was once again all white. Mr. Barbee commented, "It's like the original sin . . . they had made WSU-O lily white again . . . we have always had to deal with white bigots whenever we find them . . . they have to be challenged and eliminated."

Although the students were expelled, history shows that the protests were effective, and now the University of Wisconsin–Oshkosh provides black studies and black history, has black faculty members, and promotes diversity. Students have the right to have a hearing before they are summarily dismissed from school.

In a similar case involving a high school in Benton Harbor, Michigan, Mr. Barbee assisted in protecting the civil rights of black high school students who were suspended from school for demanding black history courses. As in the *Marzette v. McPhee* case, the school conducted no due process hearings before the suspensions. As in Marzette, Mr. Barbee forged the path for due process hearings in public schools before students can be expelled.

The legislature would set a "dangerous precedent" if it set standards for teachers, argued one member. The committee undoubtedly felt that teaching that everything good in America or the world is not white would indeed be a "dangerous precedent." They tabled the bill, in an attempt to bury the measures before they got to the floor of the legislature.

In discussion of the matter, the state's Assistant Superintendent of Public Instruction said that the number of districts offering teachers seminars and special programs to prepare them to teach black and Indian history had increased in the past three years from five to 40 percent of the state's school districts. He promised to furnish more extensive and detailed information on the subject. I argued, on the other hand, that it was the legislature which would have to tell the department that it was not setting standards for teachers high enough. The real issue was whether or not the state was going to do anything substantial to combat racism. If the state legislature wished to do something it would have to see that school teachers were given the tools they needed to do the kind of teaching that would tell children of the real and actual contributions that blacks, Chicanos and Indians made to America. The role of the Department of Public Instruction had to play was one of tying together various curricular materials and bringing resources together to develop programs for teaching black and minority history.

Minority History, Legislative Comment, February 9, 1971

The first weeks of the legislature were active but not in all instances constructive. Two bills that I authored were tabled by the Assembly Education Committee.

The first bill would have required all state certified teachers to take a course in minority history. The other bill would have a course taught in all public elementary and high schools that would accurately reflect the contribution of blacks, Indians and Spanish-speaking people to American history. I introduced these bills because I felt that action was in order to stem the white racist strains pervading our school curriculum.

The regrettable fact is that history courses taught in many schools either ignore or depreciate the contribution of minority groups to the development of our history.

It was argued in the hearing, that the bills were not necessary because the Department of Public Instruction, by administrative rule, could set these requirements. What those advancing that argument failed to recognize was that "what D.P.I. giveth, D.P.I. can taketh away."

In short, the Department could well modify or rescind such rules without the consent of the legislature. Further the D.P.I. has not promulgated any rule on its own initiative. I feel that the matter was of sufficient urgency to require the force of legislative action to assure these corrective steps would be taken.

UNEDUCABLE LEGISLATORS, PRESS RELEASE, WISCONSIN ASSEMBLY, SEPTEMBER 30, 1971

Two items concerned with educational needs have come out of Madison last week. One had to do with uneducable legislators, the other with two education bills.

Before we take a look at the state legislators' reactionary reactions I would like to report on two education bills which I have authored that had a hearing before the Assembly Education Committee two weeks ago.

One of the bills before that committee would require that Afro-American history and history of the American Indian be taught in our elementary and high schools. There is a need to see that public schools reflect the fact that African achievement predates that of Europe. Presently only the most enlightened schools treat this subject truthfully and they tend to be schools of higher educational levels.

The other bill before that committee would allow any person 15 years or older to cease attending school if that person could pass a high school equivalency test.

It seems to me that those legislators who have been berating the welfare mothers and Father [James] Groppi prove to be in contempt of justice by using Father Groppi as a scapegoat.*

---

* Father James Groppi led the Welfare Mothers' March on Madison in September 1969 in response to proposed cuts to the state welfare budget. The week-long, ninety-mile march

As if that wasn't bad enough, these same legislators refuse to recognize that they precipitated Monday's march and "takeover" by making totally unconscionable cuts in the budget and by passing tax increases which adversely affect the poor.

I welcome the welfare demonstrators to the Assembly Chamber and it is my belief that if the reactionary and cowardly leaders of the Assembly had welcomed the demonstrators and requested representatives of the welfare mothers to address a Joint Session of the Legislature, perhaps some of the less informed and more callous members of the legislature might have had their eyes opened.

This would have displayed not only hospitality, good manners and a decent approach to justice, but would have averted the escalation of tempers which caused the temporary delay in commencing the special session called to permit the legislature to drop a pebble on the beach of humanity, while dropping boulders on themselves.

This legislature may have restored $16 million dollars in welfare cuts. I cannot understand why we invite astronauts, go-go girls, and amateur singers to perform before the legislature, but we won't listen to the cries of the people.

I attempted to persuade the Speaker, the Republican leadership in the Assembly, and Governor [Warren] Knowles to proceed with the special session once the demonstrators cleared the chamber so that all the legislator's seats were available and the podium was clear. Although I was not surprised, I was extremely disgusted when all the aisles were clear, session was called to order, and by a pre-arranged signal immediately adjourned.

Father Groppi rightly told Speaker Froehlich not to push the welfare mothers and himself too far against the wall. Speaker Froehlich and this establishment pushed the panic button and brought out their bag of tricks to make their problems disappear.

Father Groppi has been scapegoated by mad, justice hating legislators, who prefer to beat him and the poor rather than face up to their prejudices and commence making meaningful changes in this system themselves. And because they choose this alternative, the changes will be forced from without.

---

to the Capitol culminated in demonstrators taking over the Assembly chamber for eleven hours. See Stuart Stotts, *Father Groppi* (Madison: Wisconsin Historical Society Press, 2013).

Far too many legislators forgot about law and order and voted against every principle of decency in voting to jail Father Groppi without a trial or the opportunity to defend himself before an impartial tribunal.

In my welcome address to the welfare protestors, I indicated that the legislature had no intention of working because the legislature has not worked this entire session except to keep from working. This reactionary legislature has stalled and copped out on every opportunity to pass meaningful legislation by giving long emotional speeches against the university, the poor, the students, welfare, and the courts. The only other time the legislature seems to get interested is when there is a motion to adjourn on the floor.

REPEAL COMPULSORY EDUCATION, LEGISLATIVE COMMENT, SEPTEMBER 30, 1971

This week I have introduced into the Legislature a bill that repeals the compulsory school attendance laws. This bill would apply to elementary schools as well as high schools. Its effect would be that no parent would have to send his child to school at all if he did not wish to.

On the surface many people will scoff at this because they have been brainwashed in to believing there is great value to the schools that their children are subjected to today. They have been badly misled. The premise behind my proposal is that schools are so irrelevant to the "education" of children as to be totally useless and a waste of time for any child.

What are our schools? What are they doing to our children? As I see it the schools of today are the nursery of society's racism. Schools do nothing more than desensitize children's minds to drain them of any belief in human decency and bathe them in the hate mentality that their parents live day in and day out. With racist administrators and teachers who either share this racism or who are too feeble to counter it, our schools have become death houses, assembly lines crippling what few positive impulse in the nature of children and turning out distorted replicas of the collective biases that make up the current social mentality.

Until this perverted system is changed, until some semblance of decency the current hate and ignorance that passes for a curriculum, it is pointless for parents with a mature sense of decency to send their children

to such schools. If people want schools that do nothing more than repli-
cate and perpetuate racist middle-class values then they should by all
means send their children off to school. But if parents are more concerned
with the development of human values in their children more than the
befuddling of their minds with a disjointed collection of out-dated notions
called an educational program, then they will spare their children the
agony and keep them home. At the side of such parents children would
have far more chance to develop a sense of decency than in the school
system. Children with such a value system will be the educated men of
tomorrow.

POLICE IN SCHOOLS, LEGISLATIVE COMMENT, FEBRUARY 24, 1972

The proposal to hire 130 more people to patrol the halls in Milwaukee
schools has the support of the School Board, its President, the Mayor and
the *Milwaukee Sentinel*.

I hope all Blacks will refuse to take these uniformed gestapo goon squad
jobs. My often repeated characterization of the Milwaukee Public Schools
as death houses, prisons and anti-education institutions will be proven if
more and more "aides for oppression" are hired. Some school authorities
and teachers want to hire Vietnam Veterans to help teachers curb disrup-
tions and preserve the physical integrity of Washington High.

Alderman Pitts referred to the hiring of aides as turning schools into
an armed camp. While the guards won't initially be armed they will clearly
have citizens arrest powers.

It is only a matter of time before detention by physical force and weapons will be used. Recently, an off duty guard killed a Black Vietnam Veteran
in a Chicago school.

Education has fallen on the spikes of ignorance and para-militarism in
Milwaukee. City white fathers and their colored step-children are seeking
federal funds to finance the employment of these aides. It is one thing for
Judas to take 30 pieces of silver to betray God, but quite another to seek
crime in the street money to police students in school buildings. I trust
our communality will insist that our schools function to educate students,
not intimidate, repress, terrorize, imprison or even tranquillize them.

STUDENT DEMONSTRATIONS, LEGISLATIVE COMMENT, DECEMBER 5, 1972

Prior to celebrating Thanksgiving of '72, the University of Wisconsin system again witnessed demonstrations by Black students who are demanding to be treated as human beings in an educational environment. They are justifiably insisting on an atmosphere which is conducive to study.

Most observers, regardless of their bias, are aware the University of Wisconsin–Superior campus is essentially a white, Northeastern school, accustomed neither to seeing nor dealing with Blacks except through the mass media. This ignorance is always a perfect background for racial oppression and harassment.

The uncontroverted facts in recent occurrences at Superior are as follows:

Some university officials saw fit to recruit Blacks to attend the institution this fall. Out of 2,836 students, sixty are Black, with 2,590 being white. Most of the Blacks are from large cities (Chicago, Newark) as well as the Milwaukee ghetto.

The minority position in which Black students found themselves led to the recent happenings. Blacks at Superior had been taunted and called names typically associated with white bigotry. A teacher in an English composition course even went so far as to complain about the Black race, Malcolm X, and other facets of Black culture.

Tensions broke wide open when a white counselor shoved a Black student, forcing him through a window, suffering numerous cuts. When the student questioned the white counselor on duty, he received no explanation for the attack—a frequent result when Blacks attempt to get answers regarding the conduct of whites. The student chose a natural alternative and struck the counselor, whereupon the lat[t]er sought and obtained a criminal complaint against the student.

The following day, a second, similar incident occurred. A female Black student was shoved by a white girl, precipitating a fight between the two. The white student signed a criminal complaint which was issued by the D.A. against the Black, accusing her of an act categorized as a felony with a maximum penalty of 5 years.

After these two unprovoked attacks by whites on Blacks, the chancellor of the university herded all the Blacks out the back door of a building at night, into a bus and transported them across the river to Duluth, Minnesota, for their own safety. The local DA has not prosecuted any white person. No white person has been suspended by the University.

Something can be learned from this series of events. White institutions which want Black students minds and bodies from Soulville will have to pay a higher price. They will have to display extra sensitivity to create a continuing educational atmosphere, including a greater awareness of the real educational needs of Blacks. Special counseling and remedial tutoring must be offered as well as other dues to pay for the sins of white racist elementary and secondary miseducation.

Blacks too must pay a price. The first requirement is a realization that higher education is a racist vehicle for maintaining the status quo, a fact with which Blacks are all too familiar.

Attending such colleges and universities will never alter this fact in the short run. However, Blacks can and must learn how the screwers screw as well as who, what, and when.

With this lesson in mind, Blacks can bring about systemic and procedural changes based on knowledge and experience.

African American Center in Madison, Legislative Comment, May 25, 1973

Too many dark-complected people are fighting over meatless bones and scraps thrown out by white, affluent "dogcatchers." Two recent examples exemplify this.

After a protracted Black-led student Madison strike in 1969, an Afro-American Center was set up. The center has always been underfunded and several threats have been made to its existence, ranging from cutting its budget and phasing it down to outright abolishment.

This year the squabblings have increased. Once again, the central issue is money and charges of racism. The new biennial budget for the Afro-American Center, listed under the heading of "multi-cultural programming," amounts to $90,000. This programming is responsible to the UW Dean of Students.

Native American students, who also have been given a center of their own, are asking for $67,000. Latino students want $100,000 to operate a cultural program. With these requests, the University is facing the problem of where to delegate funds which are earmarked for the education of minority and disadvantaged students.

The only Black on the University of Wisconsin Board of Regents has taken the position that the university's programs for minorities and disadvantaged students should be only educational in nature. He is also saying that Black students are being prevented from learning to live in an integrated society because of the basic policies and programs coming out of the Afro-American center.

Some of these old-time Madison Blacks are complaining that Kwame Salter, head of the Afro Center who earns about $19,000 annually, is using the center as his personal power base. This near tragic drama has been played before.

Amongst all the scraping over funds from a predominately white, reluctant, tax-paying public, and an increasingly conservative Board of Regents, it is a political question of who axes all of the multi-ethnic centers. Will it be the University Chancellor, the UW President, or the Board of Regents?

Since the Chancellor's power is closest, he may do it on his own or as a result of orders from the President or the Regents. If the centers are closed because of stingy bureaucrats in the University system, the future of minority students will be in question. In an alien and competitive environment such as what exists on the Madison campus, there is a need for minority centers that consist of people with common problems and goals. This is not separatism such as charged by white bureaucrats in the University administration. Rather, the centers represent self-determination on the part of its members.

On another note, Milwaukee Blacks are reacting to a racist school board and its crafty administration by squabbling over where a new North Division High School should be built. Meanwhile, these anti-Black educational planners are having a ball watching the name calling and the fights between Blacks. Black students enrolled at Old North Division are faced with a serious educational problem daily. Either they boycott classes or attend the death house on Center Street where the doors are deadlocked in violation of city and state fire safety codes.

REFLECTION ON EDUCATION, LEGISLATIVE COMMENT, MAY 31, 1973

The time of year for commencement oratory has finally approached us. It would, therefore, seem appropriate that we develop a different understanding of the importance of education in our present day society.

No longer is education the principal means for attaining economic stability and material success. Job opportunities in many areas of higher education are diminishing rapidly. Because of sagging economy and limited resources, the competitive nature of society is working against man's social and economic environment. There's not enough to go around anymore. It would seem better in the long run if we throw away some of our materialistic values and replace them with values of a higher reality.

Education can best serve as a key to human liberation and comfort, not only for groups, but for individuals as well.

Truth, justice, fairness and equality can best be implemented by a free search and pursuit of knowledge. This is the heart of any educated human being.

The Watergate revelations at least point out the fact that espionage, harassment, and cover-ups come to light when people persevere for personal gain. Here is an example of various individuals supposedly high on the technically skilled ladder, who fanatically worked for a goal detrimental to most other human beings and good government. Perhaps they need to be really educated.

Members of minorities can be somewhat assured that it is possible not only to expose these misdoings, but also to correct corrupt government. This, however, can only come about when learning is applied for something better than the current, mediocre and de-humanizing state of things.

Education should be a tool for "enlightenment," for improving character and better living. It should give us the knowledge for understanding and helping our fellow human beings, not just for competing against them.

Let's leave material success as an ultimate goal for shallow thinkers and social climbers, because, sooner or later, the rungs of their ladder will break.

Victimless Crimes, Speech to UW–Oshkosh Students by State Rep. Lloyd A. Barbee, December 3, 1973

I appreciate the opportunity to speak and answer whatever questions you may have following this presentation on nonracist civil rights matters.

From the invitation which I received to speak tonight, one of the issues of interest here in Oshkosh is the student user fee study provided for in the 1973 State Budget.

The new state budget directed the UW Board of Regents to study ways to utilize user fees to defray the GPR [general program revenue] costs on non-instructional activities. The provision, as it left the budget conference committee, specifically stated that the user fees were not to apply to students. The Governor, however, struck out the language excluding the student.

It's not necessary to speak long on this issue. However, I voted to uphold the Governor's veto. My reasons are based on the premise that non-instructional activities like sports, etc., have become business and should not be supported by students and taxpayers who do not participate, thus the users or participants should defray the costs. Little of this matters, however, because the Assembly on October 26 acquired the majority necessary in overriding the Governor's veto. If the Senate does likewise, then the issue of student user fees will be eliminated at least temporarily as a possible threat to the existence of extracurricular collegiate activities.

The issue that I find to be much more interesting and one that many of you probably have come in contact with in some way or another is the concept of victimless crimes. The question is: Should they be eliminated from our statute books? The Declaration of Independence states that we are "endowed by our Creator with certain unalienable rights, that among these are Life, Liberty, and the Pursuit of Happiness." While I'm not sure that I have been endowed by my creator (I always thought my parents carried out this function), I do recognize my unalterable rights to life, liberty, and the pursuit of happiness.

Although these "rights" are rather broadly defined, who has the authority and proper judgment to say how these rights are to be interpreted so long as our actions do not deprive another of practicing the same rights?

The right to live, the right to liberty, the right to pursue happiness—these concepts must be open to some individual interpretation.

In our own double-standard society, it doesn't appear to work this way, however. If we look into the Wisconsin Statutes or in the federal law books, we find a conglomeration of rules that prevent us or penalize us for doing actions that are harmless to those around us, actions which in the eyes of religious and governmental leaders go against the moral fiber of the social majority. They are often inhibited. Perhaps "anti-social" majority is a better term, ignorant, and hypocritical. It seems strange in a country originally founded on rather broad, democratic principles that our government can punish people for committing actions which harm nobody, crimes that are without victims, crimes that take nothing away from other people. True, most other countries have similar laws, especially in the area of drug use. Nevertheless, the institution of victimless crimes is one of the many functions committed by governments to undermine the basic rights of life, liberty, and the pursuit of happiness. In most places of the world, we can expect as much especially when the culture has been developed over periods of hundreds of years and the values have been rather traditionally defined. Our own country, however, was originally designed to be different, designed to allow for a diversity of values, opinions, and lifestyles. Yet we, too, observe a flurry of victimless "crimes" that have been written into law. And as ironical as it seems, instituting such actions as crimes actually creates victims. This is obvious in two ways. First, the person becomes a victim of the victimless crime by being unable to practice that individual choice. Second, the person can become a victim by attempting to circumvent the law. The individual can be arrested and pay a penalty for a harmless deed. Or the individual, able to avoid law enforcement, becomes a victim as an indirect result of the action or the purchase of services that is termed illegal under the law, such as seeking an abortion from a horse doctor, consuming an impure street drug extorted for homosexuality or using the services of a prostitute. For the remainder of this presentation, I would like to speak of more specific victimless crimes.

Let's take the issue of drugs. I whole heartedly support the legalization of the sale and possession of marijuana. The evidence, first of all, in support of its safety is overwhelming. It creates no victims, except perhaps through its illegal sale when the consumer gets poor merchandise. Make marijuana legal and you eliminate the victims. To go further on this issue, my belief is that drugs, not just marijuana, should be legalized. The only desirable goal of the state in this field is to set standards and regulate the purity of drugs, in other words, to protect the consumer not from himself, because this is none of the state's business, but from unscrupulous racketeers and drug peddlers. Beyond seeing that the consumer has quality drugs, unadulterated and uncut with either harmless or harmful substances, the state has no business in prohibiting what a person can partake in. If one believes that drug use (excuse the pun) is a way to pursue happiness, then that person should be allowed to pursue that choice. As far as limiting what a person can do under the influence of drugs, then the state, once again, should retain their lawmaking powers. Anytime a certain act has the effect or potential for taking away another's right, then the state has the authority to prohibit such acts. Until that point, an individual should be left alone to do as he pleases.

Throughout the history of this country and this state, there have been numerous attempts to regulate and legislate personal morality of the individual. "Prohibition" is merely the most notable example of the complete failure of these policies. I do not mean to suggest that because these efforts have failed they therefore are wrong. But there is an old saying that "one man's meat is another man's poison."

Take the gambling issue as another victimless crime. It seems ludicrous, in my opinion, to prohibit gambling because too many people would waste their money through card games, slot machines, or, what have you. That's their choice to make. Gambling, to many people, is merely a form of entertainment, no different from television, the theatre, or a good book. Is it the responsibility of the State government to determine what form of entertainment they must enjoy? Do we have the right to channel anyone's paycheck in any direction we so choose?

On the other hand, some people regard gambling as a disease. But, I ask you, can we stop these unfortunates from gambling simply by making it illegal? Facts seem to suggest otherwise. Moreover, by making their weaknesses into vices we merely brand them as criminals rather than trying to help them in their efforts to kick the gambling habit. We can apply this to any habit a person might have. These individuals need our help and sympathy, not our sermon. There is also another issue involved with gambling, and for that matter, with drugs, too. Whether legal or illegal, drug use and gambling will continue. And as long as it is illegal, the profits are drained off into the hands of the more criminal figures.

Legalize the activities mentioned, and the people of this state could at least be assured that these profits through taxation were used for schools, health care, and benefits for the poor. All could benefit from the use of this money which now only serves to line the pockets of a few corrupt individuals.

Other areas of criminal law that need reforming are the "sex statutes." It's time the government is taken out of the bedroom. We should remove all state curbs on sexual activities between consenting parties, married or otherwise. This would keep sexual matters where they should be, in the private realm of personal choice between individuals.

Specifically, we should remove the criminal penalties for homosexuals, adultery, fornication, cohabitation, and possession of "indecent materials" when such actions do not involve minors, under 14.

It makes little sense for governments to condone and support the necessity of war while at the same time, make illegal various acts of love. With the sex statutes as they are written today in this state, we've probably got a populace of criminals. And this is absurd.

Do you realize that sexual perversion is defined as "the committing of an abnormal act of sexual gratification involving the sex organ of one person and the mouth or anus of another"? Evidently, whoever had written this law was thinking in terms of sex solely as a function to have children. Such a narrow view has no place in our present-day society. Each and every one of us needs sexual gratification in some form or another. In fact, the lack of it can often lead to more serious psychological problems. The fines and imprisonments delegated to these various sexual acts among consenting adults are also beyond my comprehension.

Fornication, defined as sexual intercourse with a person not a spouse, can result in fines of $200 or prison terms of six months. Adultery can result in fines not more than $1,000 or imprisonment for not more than 3 years. And sexual perversion, as described above in vivid detail, can lead to fines not more than $500, or imprisonment not more than five years or both.

We should also permit the legalization of prostitution. This would at least allow the individual prostitute to operate under the free enterprise system and on the basis that they and their clients are consenting parties. Making prostitution legal, and eliminating the so called houses of ill-repute would also be the end of a very lucrative business for organized crime. We could also go one step further in legalizing prostitution by requiring that each member of the trade be licensed with the state. In this way, we could also insure that periodic check-ups are taken for preventing and detecting venereal disease.

So also should a man or woman be allowed to have more than one spouse if he or she chooses. Of course, it would be necessary to provide that in such a group relationship the husband or wife is able to support the spouses and children. But definitely, state law makes no sense or provides no justifiable social purpose for forcing people to live monogamously. Although the monogamist relationship can be a useful and happy one for many people, so can a variety of other forms. To require that all people adhere to a one spouse, opposite sex ideology is as absurd and repressive as to require everyone to go to the same church. Allowing a polygamist relationship would finally bring our state's marriage laws under the rational principle that marriage is a contractual relationship between parties for their mutual benefit and happiness, a principle that can only be defined according to the individuals by their own terms. I've never quite understood the reasons, at least in rational terms, for limiting sexual relations between consenting adults. An individual's sexual drive is not diminished by marriage, nor is a person's natural desire for sexual relations affected by criminal laws.

Laws which require policemen to stick their noses into bedrooms, parks, cars, and restrooms make degenerates out of policemen. In many cases, some of the policemen in this state, especially in Milwaukee, are already on their way to becoming this. Why should we help to develop these characteristics by allowing a public corps of professional voyeurs or "peeping toms" to help enforce these ridiculous state laws.

What we have learned from such ill-fated attempts to legislate the prohibition of alcohol, certain sexual relations, marijuana, birth control, and equal rights, is that we cannot legislate morality. It is our changing society and our changing values and environment which are responsible for our morality. Changes in our legal code are merely responses to these changes. And these responses must continue if our legal system is to re-main credible to the people it is supposed to serve. Repeal hypocrisy & double standard.

Democracy does indeed imply morality. However, the type of morality required in a democracy is implied in the golden rule. This is a morality which is responsive to the rights and needs of one's fellow human beings. Looking at our present situation, it seems to me that we in this country have a great deal to learn about the world which is said to be representative of our government structure.

As a final note, we should also eliminate victimless crimes because of its time-consuming effects on our court system. The courts in Wisconsin currently occupy so much of their time deciding victimless crime cases that efforts toward dealing with more serious crimes involving unwilling victims have been seriously negated. Which is more important?

Thank you.

EDUCATION FOR A CHANGING SOCIETY,
LEGISLATIVE COMMENT, NOVEMBER 13, 1973

A deteriorating environment, crime, poverty, racism, ignorance, nation-alism. . . . these are only a few of the problems that governments and cit-izens who make up the governments have attempted to solve.

For over a hundred years, this country has come upon dead end after dead ends in search of some way to solve our daily problems. We are no nearer today than we were back then. Why? Because to know the answers, we must first understand the questions.

Our society is undoubtedly changing. The things around us are con-stantly being altered. Yet if we are to survive as a human race in such a fast-evolving world, we must begin now to prepare ourselves for what may exist in the future. We have to begin a change in attitudes in preparing for the 21st Century. We should begin with our educational system.

In a new book, "Toward the 21st Century: Education for a Changing World," Edwin O. Reischauer, author and Harvard professor, raises the question of what we are to do with our lives. Are we to begin educating for the future, or are we to continue educating for the past?

As Reischauer states, the cushioning space that once absorbed the potential human conflict between nations and individuals is gradually disappearing. As technology and population growth continues, there is a greater concentration of people who come in contact with one another. With this greater concentration is a greater potential for conflict . . . the possibility of which must be eradicated if we are to survive.

We are living too close together and in contact with too many people, attitudes, and events to continue in the retaining of old American attitudes of individualism, self-reliance, and nationalism. We are all dependent on other governments and other people for the things we need in our daily lives. This dependency of which things revolve around should be resulting in a feeling of cooperation between people and nations. Yet we retain the "attitudes and habits more appropriate to a different technological age" as Reischauer describes. He makes a very valid point.

Beginning with a new educational approach in our schools, we can, in time, relate knowledge about the outside world and of other people that would provide the essentials necessary for understanding the future . . . the essentials necessary for human survival. A new realization has not been ingrained within the people of this country. In our nation, when we look at the amount of money allocated to defense as opposed to that appropriated for social services, we can readily see the gap that must be bridged. The role that government plays in helping people to cope with their day-to-day problems must be expanded. The amount of money allocated to education must be increased. Allocations today are meager, indeed. And on the local level, the means to finance education and various social services is becoming less and less.

If we educate ourselves for the future rather than the past, we can more successfully deal with the many problems which we will have to face in the years to come. The intellectual lag between generations is a result of fixing our eyes to the ground while walking . . . an analogy of knowing how we progress rather than where we are progressing to. Education must do more than that.

The Milwaukee educational system, for example, employs the Band-Aid approach to education . . . an approach relying heavily on competitive attitudes and an individualistic nature . . . both of which are losing their place in a world where competition and individualism are becoming more and more of an impossibility.

It is time we begin to learn how to cooperate with one another, not how to compete with one another. These are the philosophies that can and must be incorporated in our education system.

STANDARDIZED TESTING, LEGISLATIVE COMMENT, NOVEMBER 30, 1973

Standardized achievement and IQ tests have often been used in the past to rank students within our elementary and secondary schools into various learning levels. Of course, school districts in Wisconsin now have been slowly backing off from this rigid procedure. In fact, we have become so advanced that we've changed the name of IQ tests to "scholastic aptitude" exams. It sounds better.

Sarcasm aside, these tests which claim to measure intelligence, achievement, or mental ability are not too valid or fair to testees. And when used as a determinant for class ranking, they become a chief factor of a segregated and racist educational system.

Ranking students under certain achievement levels using results of achievement tests and applying a curriculum to their "abilities" actually perpetuates low-level achievement by segregating the "slow learners" from the higher achiever. When we analyze just who these "slow learners" are, we become capable of understanding how racist and materialistic our educational system can become.

Because IQ and achievement tests are of standardized form, they are unable to provide accurate results of the achievement and intelligence capabilities of children from different cultural and socio-economic backgrounds. For the most part, these kinds of examinations are orientated toward a white, middle-class background. Black children, Spanish-speaking children, and others from lower socio-economic classes have different cultural, social, psychological attitudes and experiences from those of the majority and establishment class. Because of this, the children of poverty and non-establishment class families appear to perform generally poorly on these examinations. And as a result, they are placed in a lower achievement level within the school system.

The standardized tests used in our classrooms to examine intelligence, personality, and achievement levels actually foster conditions that do irreparable damage to the self-esteem, self-confidence, and the capacity for academic achievement among our poverty children.

Critical Blacks say "it is not our capability to learn that prevents us from achieving. It is the way in which education is directed toward our socially and culturally determined attitudes, which is against us." As mentioned earlier, school districts in Wisconsin have been backing off from the use of IQ tests and rigid procedures for ranking students. Nevertheless, their use still continues. Worse yet, there are no state agency rules setting standards for what these tests can be used for. Federal law, in fact, requires that the Department of Public Instruction offer one standardized test to each school district below the 12th grade. And in each case, the local school district retains the prerogative over how these achievement and intelligence tests will be used.

Rather than limiting the use of the IQ and achievement tests, it seems more sensible to eliminate their use altogether. Of all the educational tools which children are subjected to within our school system, the aptitude and achievement examinations have become one of most repressive.

There is no actual fool-proof method for testing intelligence capability. Present testing methods only breed more prejudice and racism. Eliminating such testing procedures and adopting an open curriculum schedule may be the most efficient and appropriate way for providing fairness and equality in our educational system. The majority can learn from the minority in a true learning situation.

The culturally deprived, disadvantaged, or different child has been oppressed long enough.

Higher Education, Speech to the Fourth Annual Conference of the National Council for Black Studies, March 1980

Good morning. I am extremely pleased to be here at the fourth annual Conference of the National Council for Black Studies, participating in this exciting, learning opportunity. My goal of this particular panel discussion is to address, in particular, the issues and problems affecting the national efforts to desegregate traditional black colleges and universities, and its general effects on the black community at large.

Executive, legislative, and judicial actions to eliminate racism and discrimination in state systems of higher education in the south are beginning to have detrimental effects on all black colleges and universities which at one time were the only sources of higher education for almost all blacks. And at this time in our history, desegregation efforts appear to be putting black institutions completely out of existence.

This should be of immediate concern to all of us who value the quality of black higher education across this country. Beginning with the *Brown v. Board of Education* decision in 1954 and the Civil Rights Act of 1964, it has been portrayed by many that black Americans have made tremendous advances in their educational, social, and economic conditions. Yet in reality, this has not always been the case. The improvement in college attendance rates has been quite outstanding in recent years yet this so-called progress is deceptive. We cannot believe those who tell us that equity in education has been achieved when more black youth of college age are not enrolled in any school than the number enrolled in post-secondary education. Beyond this issue of access, there remains an even more fundamental concern

Regarding choice, the completion of undergraduate education, and the opportunity to continue on for graduate and professional training, thus, special attention must be paid to federal desegregation efforts which will not really constitute equity in education.

Today, serving all students of all races, the nation's thirty-four traditionally black public colleges and universities enroll more than 126,000 students; and their student bodies are comprised of more than seventy percent of all students enrolled in the 107 black institutions of higher education in the United States. All of these institutions have multi-racial student populations, faculties, and administrations. The Office for Advancement of Public Negro Colleges of the National Association of State Universities and Land Grant Colleges has reported that "approximately fifteen percent of the total number of students graduating from historically black public colleges are classified as non-black," few predominantly white colleges have desegregated to that extent. Black colleges also accept a greater portion of the burden of educating the economically and educationally disadvantaged than white colleges do nationally. The average parental income of students in these institutions is little more than $5,000 annually yet federal agencies only awarded 4.9 percent (or 240 million dollars) to black colleges. In the fiscal year of 1975, although they awarded close to 5 billion dollars to all educational institutions, figures reveal that the total number of students earning degrees in 1977–78 at the traditionally public black colleges and universities totaled over 17,400. And public black colleges continue to be the major producers of black professionals, for example, a recent study conducted by the institute for services to education—a Washington-based educational research firm—indicates that black colleges are leading most four-year institutions in preparing students for entry into careers in the health sciences. Throughout their existence, black colleges have increased the quality of black higher education as well as influencing the number of blacks able to participate successfully in institutions of higher learning and in the broader American society. Thus, the federal government must take a leading role in preserving and strengthening the historically black colleges and universities which continue to carry a disproportionate load in helping blacks enhance their educational and economic condition.

Now, national decision-makers—in an attempt to apply their version of justice—have identified the traditionally black colleges as the ones that are preventing the desegregation of public higher education systems, and many people are claiming that the continued existence of black colleges is inconsistent with the goal of a racially integrated society. Yet this well-sounding resolution for a racially integrated society is intended only to satisfy the concerns of whites rather than fulfill the needs of blacks.

States are continuously pressured to create racially balanced systems and through this our black colleges face extinction through abandonment or merger. The best-known case attacking the dual state systems of higher education is the 1970 suit now referred to as *Adams v. Califano*. In this particular case, civil rights lawyers charged HEW [Department of Health, Education and Welfare] with failing to enforce Title VI of the 1964 Civil Rights Act, which says that federal funds may not be given to institutions that discriminate on the basis of race.

The courts agreed and then ordered ten states to file plans for the desegregation of their colleges and universities. The court's guidelines required states to create a unified system out of the present racially unbalanced dual system—desegregating student enrollment, academic, and non-academic personnel, and the administrative and governing board in each institution.

The National Association for Equal Opportunity in Higher Education (NAFCO) filed an amicus brief disagreeing with the need to establish a unitary system as the remedy for the state's past discriminatory policy. The brief also denied that black colleges were segregated and discriminating against whites.

The issue as NAFCO saw it was not equal educational opportunity but equal educational attainment. And this requires the continued existence and enhancement of traditionally black public colleges.

When the Adams litigation was heard in 1973, the appellate district court issued a supplemental warning that the desegregation process should not place an even greater burden on black colleges—yet HEW still requires that the states "increase the total proportion of white students attending traditionally black institutions"; evidence supporting NAFCO's claim is already available in some states where desegregation efforts have been introduced. For example, Florida A&M University (FAMU) opened in 1887 to produce black teachers for segregated schools. In 1953, the student body was well over 5,000, and now, HEW has forced the university to end programs and transfer them to the predominantly white Florida State and the University of Florida. In return, FAMU received new programs in business, health, journalism, and graphic arts—and, critics believe that this was an attempt to attract more white students.

The plan worked. FAMU's faculty went from no whites to 30 percent in thirteen years; the student body went from 1 to 16 percent in only four years—mainly because of a program that subsidized the tuition of "non-minority students." FAMU President Walter Smith, who originally opposed the subsidies, has said that there has been a recent drop in white enrollment and this evidence supports his belief that paying whites to attend FAMU is the wrong way to desegregate. The program was not funded for the 1977–78 school year—yet program merger rather than student preference remains to be the main strategy in Florida.

In the merger of FAMU and Florida State programs, more than half of FAMU's agricultural programs were dropped or merged into Florida State departments; Florida State lost only its industrial arts and vocational education programs to FAMU. According to press reports, programs were added "to upgrade the school and to attract a racially mixed student body to the predominantly black campus."

Thus, for black colleges operating under state control, desegregation has become a very clear and immediate danger.

Let me remind you—I am not opposed to integration—I just believe that genuine integration calls for strong black institutions alongside the white, where black students as well as whites can get a first-rate education in the institution of their free choice.

Desegregation should not be defined as requiring racial balance per se in white or black institutions nor as the only satisfactory result in the desegregation process. The focus should be on the increased delivery of better-quality education of blacks. Attention should be given to the number of educated blacks with baccalaureate degrees as opposed to just focusing on the number and percentages of white students on black campuses and the numbers and percentages of black students on white campuses.

Benefits from higher education flow to all, or nearly all, persons in the United States directly or indirectly. Yet there is no precise or imprecise method that exists to even begin to assess the individual and societal benefits against public costs. The general national acceptance of equality in education must be the balance in the distribution of overall costs between traditionally black and white schools as compared with the distribution of benefits, and the basic responsibility for equalizing educational opportunity must be carried as a public cost and not as a cost assessed against individual institutions of higher education or against students. We must continue to provide a substantial proportion of diversity that has always marked American education.

We must broaden the range of institutional choices for all students and create a better climate for the co-existence of predominantly black and white schools. And as a community, we need to develop new concepts of desegregation that emphasize such ideals as diversity and pluralism to prevent the potential dangers already arising as a result of the *Adams v. Califano* case.

Charles V. Willie, in his article entitled "Black Colleges Redefined," has stated that one possible further function for black colleges is that of serving as settings where whites may enroll as the minority, in a pluralistic society everyone may be part of a minority at sometime. In schools, whites should learn not to fear the consequences of minority status—and blacks and browns should learn to be comfortable with the responsibilities of majority status. Willie continues by asserting that student bodies should be diversified rather than strictly balanced—some schools would have a majority of whites in the student body with a sufficient number of blacks that have educational impact on the total system. Other schools should have a majority of blacks with sufficient whites to have a meaningful influence. Whites can only experience minority status if there are predominantly black institutions in which to enroll. Thus, the retention of predominantly black colleges and universities is for the benefit of all. Desegregation must be beneficial to all. Higher education is an investment in the future and such opportunities must be available for those who would benefit from it. We must not attempt to save black institutions for blacks nor should we have to cooperate in our own oppression by remaking our schools in the image of whites. Our best insurance is to support all higher education, and every amount of support generated from the traditionally black colleges means improved programs, facilities, and opportunities.

Thus, black colleges must be preserved for their value to our black community and to society as a whole. Thank you.

6

CRIMINAL JUSTICE

RIOT OF 1967, LLOYD A. BARBEE 1982 MANUSCRIPT

On July 30, 1967, Sunday night, a group of young blacks threw rocks and bottles at whites, or persons who looked white, on Third Street, between Brown and Center, broke windows, looted some stores, burned some cars which appeared to be owned by whites, and started a few fires in vacant and occupied business establishments. The mayor and the white press characterized this event as a summer riot, which spilled out of the ghetto and virtually shut down the city.

Actually the mayor shut down the city by imposing a curfew and stopping traffic and people coming into the city, ordering grocery stores and retail establishments closed in the inner city.

The police moved their headquarters to an abandoned department store in the black community. The governor called out the National Guard; residents breathed a sigh of relief, because members of the Milwaukee city police are notorious bullies, night stick and trigger happy storm troopers. A gun battle developed when police and firefighters converged on a burning house. When the fire and bullets subsided, a policeman and a 77-year-old widow were dead, another policeman was blinded. A 55-year-old black man was charged with the murder of one policeman, eight counts of attempted murder, and the wounding of several other policemen. No one was charged with the murder of the elderly black widow. The black man was subsequently convicted of the first-degree murder of the policeman and sentenced to life imprisonment. The police were so busy shooting into the burning house, it is hard to believe they did not kill their fellow officer.

I, for one, suspect that the black man was railroaded as a coverup for the police's reckless use of weapons. A policeman shot and killed an 18-year-old student who, the police claimed, threw a fire bomb at a paint store. It was later learned that the student was never involved in fire bombing or any other illegal activity but was, in fact, in his backyard when he was killed.

The mayor received criticism from merchants, so he lifted his ban on beer and liquor as well as grocery store sales, toward the end of the first week. He appeared on television and presented a 39-point plan for socio-economic reforms, which would eliminate the cause of the disorders.

After the police set up their command post, the National Guard established their temporary headquarters in the same abandoned department store building. When two or more snipers opened fire, the occupation forces cringed. They sent out their shooters but they never apprehended the snipers.

Some self-appointed "Martin Luther King, turn the other cheek" types took to the streets urging blacks to pray, behave, love, and forgive whites and not engage in physical confrontation, looting and damaging of property. I stayed home with my children, worked on legislative drafts, legal briefs, read, listened to music, and reflected. When the metropolitan state of emergency was lifted nine days later, three persons had died of gunshot wounds, all three by the police. Approximately 100 people were injured and property losses were estimated at $570,000. One thousand seven hundred forty (1,740) individuals were arrested during the emergency, mostly for curfew violations.

The legislature met to adopt measures designed to assist Milwaukee in solving the cause of the racial disturbances. One measure was to provide money for "cool it" programs. The city fathers and mothers, white and black, pimps and hustlers, united to beg for "give me" proposals. I had to almost single-handedly oppose funds going to the police for armored vehicles, dogs, etc.

Some money was appropriated for black business development, educational remediation, job development, and financial counseling. The Chamber of Commerce and other groups met to provide jobs from the

CIVIL RIGHTS PROTESTERS

Mr. Barbee participated in protest marches for fair housing, against school segregation, against restaurants who refused to serve customers of color, and against clubs that did not allow African American members, amongst other civil rights violations. Although his own status as a legislator protected him from legal repercussions, police, prosecutors, and judges often targeted civil rights protesters for exercising their First Amendment rights of free speech and assembly. On several occasions Barbee represented protesters who were arrested for picketing in Wisconsin. In one case, a protester was arrested for carrying a sign in a crosswalk on a green light. Judge Christ Seraphim found the protester, Ms. Dorothy Huley, guilty of obstruction of justice. This guilty verdict was thrown out on appeal. Other protestors who staged a sit-in in the Milwaukee County Board of Supervisors office were similarly arrested for disorderly conduct. Mr. Barbee represented Clara Weaver, Arlene Johnson, and Jerry Berndt in these cases. The judge found them all guilty of trespassing.

Mr. Barbee represented Dick Gregory, the famous comedian and civil

private sector. A survey sponsored by the Milwaukee Voluntary Equal Opportunity Council revealed that 148 companies had a total of 12,499 non-white employees, out of a total of 151,956, or 8.2 percent of that total. In 1965 the survey revealed that 106 companies employed 8,572 non-whites, out of a total of 125,808, or 6.8 percent of the total. Both surveys were conducted by certified public accountants.

LAWS THAT TARGET THE POOR, LEGISLATIVE COMMENT, FEBRUARY 9, 1971

The Assembly also defeated a bill which I authored that would repeal the State's ban on fortune-telling. It was not my purpose to make any judgments as to the relative merits of fortune-tellers, mystics, or astrologers rights activist who joined civil rights protests for fair housing, to eliminate discrimination in public accommodations, and to end school desegregation (see appendix B, page 252). Despite his celebrity status, Mr. Gregory was arrested for disorderly conduct and prosecuted. The case went to trial on November 22, 1967. The judge found Mr. Gregory guilty of obstructing traffic by engaging in a protest, despite Mr. Gregory's testimony that he was leaving the protest line to go home. Judge Seraphim fined Mr. Gregory one hundred dollars, the maximum monetary fine. According to the trial transcript, Mr. Barbee questioned whether the maximum fine was appropriate for a first-time offense. The judge responded: "I am fining him a hundred dollars, and that is what it is going to be in this case, which have been the fines, white and colored, in this . . . " Mr. Barbee interjected, "You haven't always on the first offense done that, though." The Court: "No—for Mr. Gregory, he can afford more than the average poor defendant."

Judge Seraphim, who always found civil rights protestors guilty, was the subject of a bill Mr. Barbee sponsored requesting that judges must recuse themselves when they have demonstrated bias.

but merely to see the law repealed because it has been used too often as an indirect weapon to unfairly cite people as imposters or crooks.

Present Law 947.02 (4) defines fortune tellers as vagrants and imposes a maximum 6 months jail sentence upon them.

I do hope that the legislature gives swift approval to my bill to remove all the exemptions that presently exist in the State's open housing law. This bill has passed the Assembly in the last two sessions but has been killed in the Senate.

It is my belief that taking the bill up early in the session adds pressure upon the Senate to approve it so we can successfully get the measure enacted into law.

Certainly Governor [Patrick] Lucey, who has been an outspoken advocate of total open housing legislation, will sign the bill into law.

The time is long overdue for a firm commitment of the State's resources to eliminating all vestiges of housing discrimination everywhere in Wisconsin.

Prisoner Rights, Legislative Comment, March 4, 1971

This week I introduced a bill which would recognize prison inmates' personal, private visitation rights.

I view depriving prisoners of an outlet for their sex drives to be cruel and unnatural punishment. We must stop this unjust practice. Prisons should furnish facilities that will provide adequate privacy for sexual intercourse. An alternative in my proposal would be to provide inmates with furloughs from prison to relieve this forced chastity.

As things now stand, prisoners have only masturbation or homosexual activities as an outlet for their lack of female companionship.

I will address myself more to the concept, which I explained earlier, of removing the state from intruding into our private lives through criminal laws.

Attica Prison Riot,* Comment, September 16, 1971

[New York] Governor [Nelson] Rockefeller has proved to be more ruthless and wasteful of human resources than his grandfather. At least his grandfather did it for money and apologized later by giving some of his blood money back to society and seeing that his children were trained, to save his conscience.

Everybody knows that the United States locks up more offenders, for more different types of offenses, for longer periods of time, than any other country in the world.

For Governor Rockefeller to secretly permit slaughters, with "White House" approval via telephone to move in on the signal of [Corrections

---

* The September 13, 1971, Attica prison riot was fueled by overcrowding, deteriorating and inhumane living conditions, and allegations of racism by white guards toward black and Puerto Rican inmates. After setting fire to several buildings and taking hostages, the prisoners demanded better conditions and federal control of the prison. Twenty-nine inmates were killed when state troopers retook the prison. ("The Rockefellers: Attica Prison Riot," PBS.org, http://www.pbs.org/wgbh/americanexperience/features/general-article /rockefellers-attica/)

Commissioner Russell] Oswald, Wisconsin's contribution to inhumanity is a wanton and disgusting act of courage.

It's interesting to note that the white press so far has been more sympathetic with the actual slaughterers than with the convicts and hostages. The prisoners had grievances that were conceded by Oswald to be just, but he indicated they were to be convicted at some future time. United States' prison reform is long overdue. New York and California are employing genocidal prison guards against the rebel reformers and calling them "militaristic and hard-core radicals."

From the [Charles] Lindbergh kidnap case on up to the most recent case of which I am aware, no one has considered killing the hostage in order to kill the kidnappers.

One reason that I think those blood thirsty, vengeful murderers chose to use tear gas and bullets on convicts and hostages alike was based on the Black and Puerto Rican make-up of the prison inmates. Another reason for this overkill was based on a psychopathic love for the establishment's law and order. Actually, law was sacrificed for order. This type of order requires increased repressive ruthlessness from the state and police. Thus, judicial justice (law) is lost.

Government must always apply the rules of due process and fairness before it punishes anyone. If it does not the oppressed must use the necessary means for redress to survive, let alone thrive.

We expect mobs and vigilantes to execute first, lie, scare, investigate later, and apologize next if necessary. The slaughterers killed first and lied to the public. The white press published a lie that nine hostages had their throats cut by the prisoners. The truth was told later that all nine hostages were not killed by the prisoners, but by the police, sheriff and prison sharp shooters. The inmates had no loaded guns.

I submit that what has happened in New York will be repeated across the nation unless the real freedom lovers rise up and take action for criminal law reform and prison reform. Those civil reforms and elimination of racism are part of the same war for justice.

Some of the early commentators on the horror at Attica indicated that the racial tensions and rebellion common to American society have just seeped into prison and that a hard core of black militants have become politicized and defiantly claim racist prosecution at every turn. Any fair critic of the US prison system will know that Blacks have been punished more often, for a longer period of time than any race and this has been true since the time of slavery. So it's not at all a new thing. What is somewhat surprising to me is that it has taken so long for prisoners to demand decency and be willing to take a real revolutionary stand. I applaud them and wish there were more like them. If perdition exists, I hope the slaughterers are condemned to see, inhale and live in the festering gore created by their misdeeds.

Shut Down State Prisons, Press Release, Wisconsin Assembly, October 14, 1971

All Wisconsin prisons should be shut down.

They would be sold at minimum prices to minority groups. All inmates should be released.

And those persons considered dangerous would be sent to special rehabilitative institutions to receive psychological treatment or job training at prevailing wage scales. Their confinement could extend only for the balance of their original sentence.

These are the main points of a bill introduced by State Representative Lloyd A. Barbee.

"This is the first shot in what will be a long war to make people understand that prisons are neither necessary nor helpful," Barbee said. "What we must do first is understand that we haven't always had prisons in this country. People were punished, often quite brutally, since there was no theory of rehabilitation, but there were no prisons. Prisons, as we know them, did not develop in this country until the nineteenth century.

"Now that we have prisons, we must take a hard look at what they're supposed to do and what they are actually doing. They are supposed to rehabilitate wrongdoers. In fact, they are brutalizing them—as well as the guards—and making convicts that [are] much more dangerous to themselves and society when they are freed. A few statistics suggest the gap between intention and fact. Five cents of every dollar spent in penology is for rehabilitation and crime reduction. Ninety-five cents is spent on custody. So not only are the prisons not doing their job but they are stupidly eating up our tax money.

"But prisons are not only not helpful; they are unnecessary. Most of the people in prison do not belong there. What they need is psychological treatment and educational and vocational training.

"Finally, prisons are wrong in principle. They are pens and cages for members of oppressed minority groups, who are the victims of social wrongs and who cannot afford good attorneys.

"What we must understand is that convicts have as much right to be treated humanely and decently as anyone else. To throw them behind high walls, mistreat and forget them is just plain barbaric.

"It is for these reasons, that I have introduced this bill."

The Barbee bill prohibits the state or any of its political subdivisions from imprisoning anyone for the violation of a statute unless his record, as viewed by the sentencing judge, indicates that the individual would be dangerous to himself or to society if released on probation. Individuals sentenced to confinement may be sent only to institutions providing psychiatric treatment and educational and occupational therapy and must receive fair wages for whatever work they do during confinement.

Any person imprisoned after the bill takes effect would have to be released either unconditionally or serve the remainder of his term on probation unless the Health and Social Services department decides the individual's conditional release would pose an immediate physical danger to himself, or others. He would then be sent to the special rehabilitative institutions.

Further, the department would be required to dispose of its prison property. After a minimum fair market price is established, a prison property would be offered for sale to minority groups. "They could use the former prisons as schools, recreational centers, or minority enterprises," Barbee said. If there were no sale within 90 days, the property would be put up for public auction, with the proceeds going to the general fund.

Contempt of the Legislature, Lloyd A. Barbee 1982 manuscript

The bill, sponsored by myself and Rep. Manny Brown (D-Racine) was prompted by the contempt citation and jailing of Rev. James Groppi of Milwaukee. Reverend Groppi was cited for contempt of the legislature after he participated in a takeover of the Assembly chambers during a welfare protest. The legislature debated the contempt citation, but the accused was not given the chance to defend himself. Under the existing contempt statutes, a person can be jailed for up to six months or the duration of the legislative session.

The bill drastically changed the procedure used by the legislative houses to cite persons for contempt. Under the proposed law, the legislature would have to allow a person cited for contempt to have an attorney and that attorney, or the cited person himself, would have the right to cross-examine the accusers. A special committee would be empowered to recommend a penalty for the contempt citation that would have to be acted upon individually. The original decision to issue the contempt citation would be a separate process.

CONTEMPT OF THE LEGISLATURE, LEGISLATIVE COMMENT, APRIL 26, 1971

The proposition that I introduced for the second time since Father [James] Groppi was convicted of contempt of the legislature would require that before any person could be jailed for contempt of the legislature he would have to be given a fair hearing.

This hearing would be an opportunity to give his point of view to the legislature and show that his conduct may not in fact have been contemptuous, but may have been a dramatic means of communicating a given point of view to the legislature. I think that inherent in due process is the concept of fairness.

It is never fair for a body to decide someone is contemptuous of it and put him in jail without a chance to make some kind of defense. Legislators like judges are public officials and should not be too thin skinned or hypersensitive.

I must report with great disappointment that the State Assembly has refused to give its approval to this measure, thus the Legislature will continue to serve as a witness, prosecutor, judge, jury, and jailor. Speedy action against disruptors was a main argument against my bill.

Haste makes waste of justice when 100 angry men punish one man immediately. Such behavior is most contemptuous of the rights of a defendant to have a fair hearing before being jailed.

The body voted against the very principle of justice on which it claims this country is founded.

PAROLE, PRESS RELEASE, WISCONSIN ASSEMBLY, JANUARY 25, 1972

Convicts who have been sent back to prison for parole violations would be given new encouragement to work for a second chance to go straight under a bill introduced by State Representative Lloyd A. Barbee (D-Milwaukee-6).

The Milwaukee lawmaker, author of many prison reform bills, explained the details of his latest measure.

"The bill provides that when a parolee is returned to prison for a parole violation, his remaining sentence would consist of the original sentence less the good time spent in prison and time spent on parole.

"At present, a returning parolee gets no credit for the time spent on parole. This, of course, is heartless and overly primitive. Whatever the infraction that causes him to be sent back to prison—and many times, it is a minor one—it is stupid not to count the time when he was behaving himself on parole.

"The main point is, the man's hope and society's safety. If a parolee is sent back to prison, he's liable to be a bitter man, for many reasons. The bitterness increases if he feels he is no further down the road towards prison release than he was before he was paroled.

"But if the parole time is included in that time knocked off his original sentence, he is not likely to be as bitter. He can look at himself and society more rationally. He can begin preparing himself again for his eventual release. When he is paroled again or released, he may be a more balanced person if he feels society gave him an extra opportunity to reduce his sentence and become a free man again."

EXCESSIVE BAIL, LEGISLATIVE COMMENT, JANUARY 25, 1972

The Black man is faced with many kinds of discrimination from the state and one variety is the kind of bail that is offered to Black people who are arrested.

In setting bail, a judge offers three options. He can ask the suspect to put up all the cash money set as bail. He can ask that 10 percent of the cash bail be put up. Or, he can request a so-called surety bond which usually represents 10 percent of the total bail figure.

Now, in theory, the judge determines bail according to the seriousness of the case and the likelihood that the defendant will make all his court appearances, not the color of the suspect's skin or the size of his wallet. So for a serious crime, he would ask the suspect to deposit in cash the total amount of the bail figure. For less serious cases, he asks for 10 percent of the cash amount of a surety bond.

In practice, however, the Black or poor man gets the worst of the deal. It's not likely that the average Black suspect can put up the total cash figure of bail. So a judge can offer him the choice of either paying 10–12 percent in cash or buying a surety bond.

Nine times out of ten, the judge will offer the Black only one option, the surety bond. This is unfair.

It is unfair because the wealthy people who can afford to put up all of the cash or 10 percent of the cash of the bail figure get their money back when the case is over. But not so with the surety bond. A Black man who has to buy a surety bond won't ever get his money back.

Now, that is a very good deal for bondsmen who thus get a captive clientele. But it is a raw deal for the Blacks and students who are thus given further cause to believe that justice is for the rich; prisons and penalties for the poor.

We must put a stop to this vicious discrimination. And so I have introduced a bill which would no longer permit judges to offer surety bonds as one kind of bail procedure.

Under my bill, the judge would have to treat Black men the same way he treats white men. He could offer total cash bail or—the more realistic alternatives for Black men—10 percent in cash of the bail figure or release on a man's own signature.

The courts are the first place where we must stop the privileged well-healed few from trampling the poor and disadvantaged. My bill would help root out some of Wisconsin's discrimination against the poor in courts.

Jobs for Persons with Records, Press Release, Wisconsin Assembly, January 27, 1972

A bill that would make it easier for people to get jobs who have been arrested but who have been acquitted or released without being convicted has been introduced by State Representative Lloyd A. Barbee (D-Milwaukee-6).

"This is one more of the reform bills I have introduced during this session that seeks to help people who have been stigmatized by old-fashioned prejudices," Barbee said.

"This latest bill would make it an unfair labor-practice to ask a job applicant if he has an arrest record," the Milwaukee lawmaker continued.

"While the aim of the bill is to help all persons who have been arrested but not convicted, it is directed principally towards ghetto people who are most often the victims of unnecessary arrests. With those arrests on their records, they have a more difficult time of getting jobs, even though they have not been convicted of any crime.

"The bill requires all arresting authorities to give all arrest records to persons who have been acquitted or released without being convicted. And it requires those authorities to expunge those arrest records from their own books.

"Under the bill, the arrest information could not be given or made available to any person or federal, state or local governmental agency except the arresting authority and the court hearing the arrested person's case.

"The measure would also prohibit the state and other public bodies from entering into a contract with any employer who has denied employment to a person because of that person's arrest record. Anyone violating this statute would be subject to a fine and loss of the contract.

"Clearly, this bill is intended to reduce the obstacles to ghetto residents already beset with the consequences of society's neglect and discrimination. To make a man suffer because of an arrest for which he was not convicted is to invite more bitterness and more contempt for the law from society's have-nots," Barbee said.

PRISON REFORM, LEGISLATIVE COMMENT, FEBRUARY 1, 1972

All the current hue and cry about prison reform, with a dozen legislative bills and a Governor's task force all aiming at the same goal, are simply missing the point: The perpetuation of a bad system, however it is "reformed," is counterproductive and futile.

And there is no doubt about it—it is a bad system and should not be perpetuated.

The extremely high number of recidivists—persons released from prison who shortly return for repeating their criminal behavior—is proof enough of that.

If, as we claim, the goal of our prisons is rehabilitation, then we must begin to rehabilitate. Educational, psychological, and occupational therapy facilities must be provided for those who are restrained for their own safety or the safety of others. But most convicts now in jails in this country do not fit that definition. They pose no threat to anyone except a vengeful racist and sadistic society.

It is the institution that threatens society, by creating misfits, neurotics and repeaters. Until the institution of involuntary imprisonment is eliminated altogether, it will continue to perpetuate the very things it is supposed to eliminate.

The ultimate goal of prison reform must be the elimination of the institutions themselves. As they exist now, in the most enlightened state and with the most progressive administration, they are schools for crime, breeding grounds for drug addiction, dependency, and forced homosexuality. The human frustrations and anxieties created within prison walls are so great that the frequent venting of those frustrations as riots within the walls and as recidivism outside the walls—must be viewed as virtually inevitable.

In modern zoos, we have eliminated the bars while still keeping the animals caged behind invisible barriers. This assuages the guilt of the captor more than it eases the frustrations of the captive.

Similarly, halfway attempts at prison reform, removing the cage but not the separation from society, eases the guilt of society without appreciably increasing the effectiveness of the penal system.

There is a movement stirring to attempt to move prisons from suburban and rural areas to core city areas. Some Black leaders can be heard favoring these moves. Whether this acquiescence is witting or unwitting, it demonstrates complicity in a bad system. In opting for these so-called "reforms," they ignore and obscure the real problem.

Prominent Black leaders can be heard calling for replacement of white wardens and guards with Black wardens and guards. They hope that this will make the present institutions more livable for Blacks. Again, this shows a willingness to submit to a permanently bad system of injustice imposed from outside the community. Reform means a change for the better.

A few Blacks keeping their brothers in prisons is worse. Any modern civilization which tolerates prisons is the worst.

Prison Reform, Press Release, Wisconsin Assembly, February 3, 1972

State Representative Lloyd A. Barbee (D-Milwaukee-6) and other Black legislators across the country will meet in New Orleans shortly to consider prison reform.

"I am a member of a Prison Reform Sub-Committee of the Black Legislators Association," Barbee explained. "The sub-committee will hold hearings on penal reform in the City Council Chambers in New Orleans on Friday and Saturday, February 18 and 19.

"I am particularly happy that Mr. Sanger Powers, director of Wisconsin's prisons, has agreed to appear at the two-day conference. That conference will investigate and focus attention upon the savage problems of treatment and living conditions in our Federal, state and local prisons.

"The conference will emphasize the problems of Black prisoners because they make up a disproportionate number of the prison population in this country.

"We see a vivid illustration of this vicious fact in the cases of Miss Angela Davis and Miss Heidi Ann Fletcher. Miss Davis, charged with supplying the guns in the fatal shooting of a California judge, has been languishing in prison for 15 months awaiting her murder trial. She has repeatedly asked for bail and has been repeatedly turned down, even by one judge who said in open court she would be a good bail risk.

"That's the story of a Black girl accused of murder. Now hear this story of a white girl charged with murder. Last summer, Miss Heidi Ann Fletcher was charged with being the driver in a $7,900 robbery of a savings and loan association in Washington, D.C. During that crime, a policeman was murdered.

"Was she confined to prison to await trial? No, Miss Fletcher, the daughter of the city manager of San Jose, California, was freed without having to pay any bail. All the court asked was that she be home by 10 p.m. and get a job.

"How considerate! A few months later, Miss Fletcher, whose family had money to hire a top lawyer, Edward Bennett Williams, pleaded guilty to 10 counts of first degree murder, armed robbery, robbery and illegal possession of dangerous weapons. She got a maximum sentence of nine years and the possibility of release at any time. So if Angela Davis is acquitted, that Black girl may still have served longer for not killing that judge than Miss Heidi Fletcher, the white girl, will have for having killed her cop.

"So that's one example of the reasons Black legislators have decided to discuss penal reform in the New Orleans conference.

"But many white convicts also suffer from the brutality afflicting their Black brothers. When our conference attacks the problem, we will be striking a blow for all oppressed men."

At the weekend conference, former inmates, noted penologists like Mr. Powers and correction institutional officials will testify. "The Black State Legislators will follow up this hearing with recommendations pressing for prison reform at the state and local levels," Barbee said.

DRUGS AND NARCOTICS, PRESS RELEASE, WISCONSIN ASSEMBLY, FEBRUARY 10, 1972

"Our present system of handling drug and narcotics offenses is exactly wrong," according to State Representative Lloyd Barbee (D-Milwaukee-6).

Barbee made the comment while introducing Assembly Bill 1552, which radically alters present statutes covering these offenses. "Rather than lock drug users up, where they are exposed to concentrated prison population and confirmed drug advocates, I recommend in my bill that these offenders be treated psychologically in approved institutions."

Barbee continued, "Detention should be a last resort for those few in imminent danger of harming themselves or others. Even in those cases, rehabilitative care must be provided if we are ever to eliminate this problem from society.

"Criminal penalties are completely ineffective. It is essential that we recognize the failure of our penal system and the inadequacy of rehabilitative facilities if we are ever to eliminate our drug problem," Barbee noted. "My bill prescribes a minimum 90-day treatment period and a maximum 2-year treatment period.

"Certainly we should be able to cure physical drug dependency in this period, and reinforce it with psychological help."

Right to Change Venue and Judge, Press Release, Wisconsin Assembly, February 15, 1972

A defendant would have the right to change the place and judge of his or her trial at least three times under a bill introduced by State Representative Lloyd A. Barbee (D-Milwaukee-6).

"This bill seeks to give defendants a better chance for a fair trial where press coverage or community prejudice has made it impossible to get a decent jury or judge," Barbee explained.

"At the moment, defendants who are charged with a felony or misdemeanor have a right to only one change of place and judge. If they want further changes, they have to show cause. This is not always easy to do, particularly when the defendant is poor and has neither the influence nor highly-paid lawyer to make his case.

"So my bill seeks to improve the defendant's chances for a fair trial. He could change the site of his trial three times and he could change judges three times. Any further changes could come only after he has demonstrated that prejudice does exist.

"The bill would also give a defendant the right to bail when he has appealed a conviction to either the Supreme Court of this state or of this country. The logic of this bill is quite obvious. Actions on appeals to either of these two courts do not happen overnight. To permit a judge to keep a man in prison while his appeal is pending is cruel, primitive, and inhumane treatment. This is what usually happens to poor defendants.

CONSTITUTIONAL RIGHTS TO JURY OF PEERS AND LEGAL REPRESENTATION

Throughout his career as an attorney, Mr. Barbee was cognizant that African Americans were not fairly represented in jury pools. Very few blacks served on juries in the 1950s through the 1970s. In *State v. Burnett*, 30 Wis 2nd 325 (1966), Mr. Barbee challenged the jury panel when no blacks were included. The court denied the challenge. In *McKissick v. Wisconsin*, 182 N.W. 2d 288 (1971), Mr. Barbee again argued against impaneling juries with no black juror (see appendix C, page 270). African American defendants were not receiving juries of their peers when Blacks were excluded from jury panels. In both cases, white judges did not agree that African Americans were unfairly excluded and not represented in juries. The defendants were found guilty by all-white juries. In 1986, the US Supreme Court made it clear in *Batson v. Kentucky*, 476 US 79 (1986), that jurors may not be discriminated against on the basis of race, when a prosecutor systematically excluded blacks from serving on a jury.

In *Sparkman v. State of Wisconsin*, 133 N.W. 2d 776 (1965), Mr. Barbee

"In short, this bill is another attempt to make our so-called justice fair. When the poor in this country see the justice for them is the same as that for the rich, we'll not have only a more just country but a more secure one."

PRISON REFORM, LEGISLATIVE COMMENT, MARCH 2, 1972

Last week the Assembly took action on a measure which has the potential to be a significant first step towards true prison reform. I refer to Assembly Bill 797.

According to the unamended provisions of this bill, any prisoner in a state penal institution would have been allowed to leave prison for up to thirty days to visit a dying relative, to attend the funeral of a relative, or to contact a prospective employer. This provision was amended to read 10 days instead of 30.

appealed the right of a defendant in a criminal case to have a court-appointed counsel at the preliminary stage of a felony charge. The court agreed with Attorney Barbee's argument and ruled: "On grounds of public policy we adopt a rule for prospective application only that an indigent is entitled to appointed counsel at or prior to a preliminary hearing unless intelligently waived."

The case paved the way for all persons charged with felony crimes in Wisconsin to be entitled to a court-appointed attorney without costs at the preliminary stage of the charges.

Following on the heels of *Sparkman v. State of Wisconsin*, Mr. Barbee represented a defendant in *Burnette v. Burke. Warden of Wisconsin State Prison*, 126 N.W. 91 (1964). In this case, the Wisconsin court ruled that an accused has a right to an attorney before a guilty plea is accepted in a criminal case. This case involved an accused who had limited intelligence and who agreed to plead guilty before meeting and discussing his case with an attorney. Before a defendant can plead guilty to a criminal charge, he or she must be provided a court-appointed attorney and be given an opportunity to discuss the charges and possible defenses.

In itself, the 10-day leave provision is not really a reform. It is simply another manifestation of a peculiar syndrome I have noted previously in this space: the collective jail keeper feels guilty. Consequently, to assuage his guilt, he extends minimal considerations of human compassion to his prisoners, as if to make up in this inadequate way for the unmitigated horror of life behind bars.

In point of fact, the approval for prisoners to leave their cells to look for jobs is about as compassionate as throwing them to the wolves. If an "ex-con" is to get a job, he must have contacts in the first place. If he has the contacts, he does not need to leave prison; he can get a job by mail. If he does not have the contacts, he might as well stay in prison and save himself the humiliation of having door after door closed in his face. So once again, the vicious cycle is encouraged to perpetuate itself by the self-appointed protectors of law and order.

There had, however, been in AB 797 a move toward meaningful reform. The bill had read: "The department (of Health and Social Services) may allow an inmate who qualifies to leave his place of confinement for such other specific purposes as are not inconsistent with the public welfare."

In terms of penal institutions the "public welfare" is generally considered to be rehabilitative efforts, attempts to reassimilate the prisoner into life beyond prison walls. By striking the provision quoted above, the legislature threw away a priceless opportunity to initiate a practical, guaranteed-to-work rehabilitation plan at no cost to the state, other than perhaps a little loss of face in admitting they have been wrong about penal institutions for so long. But once again, the omnipotent powers of the status quo have had their way, producing yet another empty victory, the shell and not the substance of reform.

On a brighter note, the Assembly Judiciary Committee last week held hearings on my bill eliminating [prisons] and requiring all state prisons to be sold.

As far as I am aware, this is the first time that such a proposal has reached so advanced a stage in the legislative process anywhere in the country. While I do not kid myself that this bill will immediately become law and that the state will sell all its prisons at public auction, nevertheless I am pleased that at least the public has been given a chance to be heard. At the hearing no one argued against abolishing all prisons and freeing the prisoners. One woman registered against the bill.

ARRESTS OF PROTESTERS, LEGISLATIVE COMMENT, APRIL 21, 1972

The scheduled opening of the special session of the legislature was delayed by an all-white beer lobby occupying the Assembly Chambers. This is reminiscent of another such sit-in years ago.

In September of 1969, a group of welfare rights marchers and Father Groppi occupied the Assembly Chambers. They were jeered and cursed by the elected officials then in office. Several were arrested.

In the demonstration last week, the protesters were allowed to remain, unmolested and unreviled, in the Representatives' seats. There was almost a chivalric politeness when the Assembly leadership suggested to them that they might want to leave the chambers. Later threats of arrest were also made in a subdued and apologetic manner.

It was the purpose of the welfare marchers to obtain nothing more than a decent living wage. Their only request was a more humane treatment from the Legislature, which had ruthlessly cut payments and set up insulting red tape procedures in order to receive meager and inadequate benefits.

The beer bar lobbyists were demanding special treatment from the Legislature because the Age of Majority Bill at 18 passed earlier this year may potentially interfere with their profits. They wanted a liquor license to place them in competition with the present tavern owners, in violation of present quota on the number of liquor licenses in the state.

There is no question that the beer bar owners should pursue their own interests of selling liquor and beer. I am pleased that they appear to be learning something from their youthful customers (18–21) about the politics of protest. They are actively petitioning for something they believe in: their pocketbooks, not the goals of freedom, peace and equality for all.

Another striking feature of the day's events was the materialization of an armed force outside the Capitol later in the day, a symptom of the over-protective paranoia that has gripped security forces around the country as a result of Black, student, anti-poverty, welfare rights and peace demonstrations in the last decade. Yet the touted security forces had failed completely in keeping the demonstrators out of the Capitol. They were white, middle-class appearing, so they slipped right in.

Even the tiger-like Sergeant-at-arms of the Assembly and his staff acted like pussycats and let the demonstrators into the Assembly Chambers proper. After they were in, they became too mousy to kick them out.

This is in distinct contrast to the peace demonstration later on the same day, when blacks and bearded college students tried to enter the building. They were kept out by the aforementioned army, swinging their clubs and shooting their teargas guns. All at considerable expense to the taxpayer.

Some of my Black constituents and long-haired, bearded white acquaintances had difficulty gaining access to the Capitol until I personally vouched for them. People with legitimate business in the building were detained and interrogated before being allowed in. Many were told they needed a pass to walk into the Capitol building. A Black reporter was made to wait 45 minutes before he was allowed to proceed to my office.

The double standard in effect was applied with even-handed discrimination. All Blacks and students were harassed. The white middle-class was allowed in un-harassed. This goes to show that the power of the white middle-class pocketbook is unchallenged, while freedom, peace and racial justice must still be fought for vigorously and relentlessly.

Angela Davis, Legislative Comment, June 6, 1972

I join other freedom and justice lovers celebrating the Free Angela success.*

In view of the years of mental anguish and physical suffering imposed upon one of our most beautiful and brilliant sisters, I don't consider the jury's acquittal a vindication of America's judicial system. A government which punishes before it convicts is unjust. Amid the fog and smog of California's legal oppression of an excellent Black teacher some things are clear. The government never had a case against Angela that could be proved beyond a reasonable doubt before any impartial jury or judge. The real people knew that.

Therefore, the government's political imprisonment and harassment of Angela boomeranged because people power was marshalled and acted for real justice in the courts. The outcome, a not guilty verdict, is a triumph of the people.

Liberation fighters should acknowledge this victory as they prepare to continue struggling for more victories for all political prisoners and oppressed people. We must not forget the public hysteria created by government and the press; the frantic woman hunt; the so-called capture; jail; no bail; excessive bail; the pattern continues without fail.

White justice will continue administering legal and extralegal force to

* Political activist Angela Davis was tried and found not guilty of first-degree murder and aggravated kidnapping in the death of Judge Harold Haley. Davis had purchased the guns used by the three men who carried out the attack in a California courtroom. One of the men, Johnathan Jackson, had worked as a bodyguard for Davis and was killed by police during the crime. See Earl Caldwell, "Angela Davis Acquitted on All Charges," *New York Times*, 5 June 1972, www.nytimes.com/books/98/03/08/home/davis-acquit.html.

maintain a white establishment unless the people remain vigilant and act against tyranny of the majority.

Angela Davis, Huey P. Newton and others will only be temporarily free unless their victories are seen as battle successes in a continuing war against love, freedom and fairness for all of humanity.

Rehabilitation, Legislative Comment, June 28, 1972

The Governor's Task Force on Offender Rehabilitation has made proposals which it claims would reform the prison system in Wisconsin. These proposals include shutting down most of the state's major prisons and replacing them with community treatment centers. On the surface, this may look like reform but it is not.

The only true reform by way of rehabilitation is the complete abolition of the prison system. By calling for the transfer of prisoners to treatment centers, the self-proclaimed reformists are just trying to cover up the basic flaw in the present system. It is a failure.

The Task Force report maintains what is already proven. "Corrections" is just a name. Twenty-nine percent of the prisoners who are released return to prison within 12 months. Even for those "model" prisoners paroled and under supervision, 29 percent still come back. This is hardly the mark of a successful corrections system.

Prisons, rather than stemming the skyrocketing crime rate, do much to perpetuate criminal acts. A cell does not rehabilitate, it does not deter, it only further corrupts. An individual in prison on a minor charge will often pick up the tricks of the trade from the more hardened criminals.

The response to the task force recommendations are interesting and quite revealing. The diehard conservatives took an expected stance: outright opposition with mild claims that murderous criminals would be let out on the streets to kill and rob men, women and children. Their approach is right out of the dark ages: "lock 'em up and throw away the key."

The qualified approach of Governor Lucey and other do-gooders was different, but not unexpected, either. In fact, they are much like the task force members themselves. In a political attempt to pacify both the reformers and hard-liners, they devise a plan of reform which is not reform at all.

Their idea of replacing prisons with treatment centers is like putting a cast on a broken leg without setting the bone. It makes the problem look better, but does nothing to solve it.

Implementing the report's recommendations will only worsen the situation. Why? Because so many people will be fooled into believing that the system has been made good. The basic idea of our penal system is to punish and lock people up, which we've seen does not work. Thus, the only way to reform [the] system is to drop it altogether.

Under no circumstances should we allow human beings to be caged up like animals—with or without bars. Real change will only come about when the concrete walls and iron bars are torn down and unjust laws are removed from the statute books. Poverty, racism, and frustration all breed crime. These ingredients are found largely in ghetto communities. Rehabilitation and an end to crime will be realized only when poisons are removed and when prisoners and offenders are dealt with as humans in or out of their own communities without the hindrance of walls, bars, guards and revengeful people.

TRAFFIC VIOLATION CASES AND JAILING OF MENOMINEE, LEGISLATIVE COMMENT, DECEMBER 13, 1972

Several curious things have transpired in Wisconsin in recent weeks. Their unusual nature demands a few observations.

In Milwaukee, Assistant City Attorney Herbert F. Sonnenberg was accused of dismissing too many traffic cases before the court commissioner. Sonnenberg allegedly had upped the dismissal rate from ten to 50 percent.

I say kudos to Sonnenberg. May his tribe increase. Not even the Police chief or his deputy inspector in charge of traffic publicly supported individual compulsive ticket-writing by the "men in blue." The police officers were the individuals who loudly complained about Sonnenberg's actions. These law enforcement officers, deep into an identity crisis, believe they can and should stop citizens, write tickets, prosecute and judge the case, and then jail or fine the so-called guilty party. They don't want to accept the game rules that the city attorney alone who prosecutes has a higher duty to see that justice is done.

Further traffic codes are for public safety not for punishment. It is an injustice by those entrusted to maintain justice. The second peculiar happening involves the continuing dispute between Menominee Enterprises and DRUMS (Determination of Rights and Unity for Menominee Shareholders). These two groups have been working to end the hoax that the Menominee Reservation was terminated when Menominee County was formed in 1961. In reality, the slave status of the Menominee goes on at this very moment. Menominee County has no district attorney of its own. The white D.A. from the adjoining county performs the function, but the people of Menominee County cannot vote for him.

They are frequently jailed in the adjoining county far out of proportion to their number. It is worthy to note that these individuals—acknowledged to be the original Americans—still refer to themselves as Indians and accept that description by white America. Certainly, the place which Columbus discovered was not India. India was the place that Columbus tried to reach by a short route from Spain with the help of Queen Isabella's jewels. Yet, the natives of this nation continue to live with the name white America has mistakenly and racistly given them.

One international event stands in contrast to this non-white acceptance of white imperialism, racism, and conquest. The people of the Philippines, drafting a new constitution, have recently decided to rename their nation Maharlika, a Tagalog [word] meaning "noble or dignified," closer to their original designation before White Western Civilization was forced upon them. The name Philippines came from Prince Philip, later King of Spain, whose pirates invaded the islands in the early sixteenth century.

It is refreshing to note that people are throwing off their slave names and choosing their own nomenclature. It will be even more refreshing and lead to more fundamental group awareness, development, achievement, innovation, and liberation if more minority ethnic groups follow the example being set by the Philippines, or more appropriately, Marharlika.

POLICE VIOLENCE IN NEW ORLEANS, PRESS RELEASE, WISCONSIN ASSEMBLY, JANUARY 11, 1973

Now that the shooting is over in New Orleans and the count has been made on the dead and injured, perhaps we can now look at the tragic incident in a more reasonable manner.

Mark Essex, a 23-year-old navy veteran, was killed on a motel rooftop in New Orleans during a shooting spree which left six dead and 20 injured. There were charges made by many officials, calling the incident a black conspiracy, "the result of an underground national suicidal group bent on creating terror in America." Yet the cries of conspiracy and selective white murder have come from the very same people whose whole career has been based on "open season against blacks."

Many local authorities have attempted to cloud the issue by stating that there were other people involved in the incident. Statements have been offered that substantiate this claim. Yet the only person found after the shooting stopped was the body of Mark Essex, a young sensitive intelligent Black man. It is possible that others might have escaped. But there were about 600 police and other law authorities at the scene. One reason given for implicating more than one person is the fact that several policemen were wounded after the lone sniper was killed.

Apparently the police not only shot up the motel, but also shot some of their fellow members. The New Orleans police superintendent even admitted the possibility that some of the Police officers were wounded by gunfire from fellow officers stationed in surrounding buildings. In the final assault, newspapers said five policemen were injured by flying concrete chips and ricocheting bullets fired by their own comrades.

Why did Mark Essex feel that it was necessary to kill? If one objectively looks at the treatment of Blacks in the US military it is understandable that they would not respect white American democracy. The racism which young Blacks experience in the military is a shaping influence for their attitudes and emotions.

The causes of violent actions in our country go much further than what is practiced and preached in the military. Violence pervades our entire society. We are fed and bred with it every day. Black Americans are expected to act rationally in an irrational society. Most of us find it relatively easy, but only because we have grown insensitive to many of the problems which we are faced with each day. Many young people have retained their sensitivities toward many intolerable problems.

It is later than a lot of people think. Old solutions to old problems are not proper now if they ever were. New Federal and state institutions must

POLICE BRUTALITY

Eighteen-year-old Clifford McKissick was shot in the neck and killed by police in Milwaukee in 1967, an event that sparked huge protests against police brutality. Such incidents frequently involved white officers shooting and killing black men without answering to any police commission. As in McKissick's case, the officers were usually found to have been "justified" even when the victim had been shot in the back. Like other outraged members of the black community, Mr. Barbee joined the protests and an organized march to city hall. He spoke to McKissick's parents and gave speeches to draw attention to the issue.

By this point, Mr. Barbee had become involved in another case of police brutality. Leroy Payne had been beaten extensively after his arrest for shooting two police officers in Michigan in 1962. The two police officers had previously harassed and beaten Mr. Payne. One evening after Mr. Payne was stopped by the same police officers who had continuously harassed him, shots rang out. Mr. Payne was charged with assault with a deadly weapon. He went to trial and was found guilty by an all-white jury and sentenced to life imprisonment. While in prison in Michigan, Mr. Payne wrote to the NAACP concerning his victimization by the police officers.

Mugshots and other photographs of Mr. Payne taken at the police station clearly showed he had been severely beaten. The NAACP referred the matter to Mr. Barbee, who went out to meet Mr. Payne at the prison. Mr. Barbee was able to obtain a Michigan attorney on behalf of Mr. Payne, who sued the police for the assault. Through Mr. Barbee's help and assistance, Mr. Payne was granted parole after ten years of imprisonment. After being granted parole, Mr. Payne moved to Wisconsin and became a respected citizen. He worked for the Social Development Commission, became a responsible landlord, husband, and father, and volunteered his time with others who had been victims of police brutality and discrimination.

prepare to deal with the needs of its people, starting by redressing past wrongs and assuring the rights of all citizens.

Our system of law and justice isn't based on solving the problems of crime. It is more interested in revenge through selective punishment.

We need to provide treatment for offenders of criminal law through a rehabilitative process. We also need to take the guns away from those who are most inclined to use them for the wrong reasons. One of the groups who have such inclinations are the police authorities themselves. Government should take the first step in eliminating individual and mass murder.

Excessive Use of Force and Police Killings, Legislative Comment, February 8, 1973

On the night of January 31, 1973, Milwaukee once again, became the scene of racial violence and bloodshed. I hadn't realized what the noise and commotion was about, until early the following morning, when I heard the news that two policemen were shot just four blocks from my home.

There's been an immense outcry against this double killing of two white policemen, who were slain while making an arrest of a young Black person. Yet the results of the incident were more than just words and emotions.

The immediate aftermath of the shooting was quick illegal searches and seizures in the immediate surrounding area, and a number of Black arrests, young and middle-aged. In some cases, police broke down doors to gain entrance into homes, and beat up certain individuals. Probable cause was not a motive for their actions.

After receiving a police beating, one man was so badly injured around the head and hands that certain public officials were sickened by his appearance four days later. The beating took place in the street and at the police station.

Murder, at its best, is always bad in my opinion. Yet in this time of high emotion and polarized opinions, I feel compelled to comment on the causes of these latest symptoms of white racism, arrogance, paranoia and malignant aggressiveness.

A brief look at the facts of Wednesday night, January 31, will reveal that the two white police officers, one from Alabama, drawl and all, and the other an arrest-happy officer were major precipitators of the incident.

Assigned to Milwaukee's overwhelmingly Black area, 5th police district, they chose to stop a Cadillac which was occupied by several Black residents. These officers presumed that this car was stolen. However, the ownership was verified as belonging to one of the occupants. Did they check the license plates before proceeding? I doubt it.

However, the police officers pursued the vehicle until they harassed the occupants to the point of panic. Since the young Black occupants' car was stopped in their neighborhood, some started running. The officers caught up with one of the youths. They attempted to make an arrest by handcuffing an individual and giving him a customary Milwaukee police beating. One major difference occurred. Another Black person, or persons, saw the beating and killed the two policemen.

If the justice-loving people in Milwaukee do not learn the real lesson from this incident, and demand the service from law enforcement officers, neither piety, tears, medals, nor speeches honoring the deceased policemen, will erase the resentment and hostilities of ghetto-dwellers against the harassment, brutality, and needless arrests by the Milwaukee police.

The cries for protective legislation, safe streets, money, and gun control do not impress me one bit as solutions until the police, themselves, are disarmed and reoriented along with the remainder of the majority population. We need to insist on better education of policemen. We should also have psychological screening and an emphasis on civilian control of our police.

The recent police murders are a symptom of a much greater problem. The present police organization in Milwaukee has been unreceptive to the needs of all the people for too long a period.

The police chief has consistently ignored the complaints of the Black population in Milwaukee. He has supported the past actions of his personnel, giving them a free reign to "stop the crime in our streets." Instead, he has precipitated violence. Law and order ought to start by enforcers setting the example first with justice for all.

UNEQUAL JUSTICE, PRESS RELEASE, WISCONSIN ASSEMBLY, FEBRUARY 16, 1973

Representative Lloyd Barbee commented angrily on the decision by Dane County Circuit Judge W. L. Jackman to suspend proceedings against

David W. Norgard. Mr. Norgard had been charged with the murder of
David Scott, a Black, 19-year old [University of Wisconsin] sophomore.*

Representative Barbee said this was one more example of a dual system
of justice, one for whites and another for blacks.

"A black man similarly accused would have provoked a violent reaction
by the wheels of white justice. The black would have been immediately
hunted down, his neighbors' houses broken into, and his neighbors detained for questioning. The accused would be portrayed as a vicious killer
and a threat to society.

"The reaction to the murder of a black is hardly more than a yawn. The
only thing that surprises me about the incident," Representative Barbee
said, "is that Scott wasn't blamed for his own death."

IMPRISONMENT OF THE POOR, LEGISLATIVE COMMENT, JUNE 11, 1973

Last week at an Assembly Judiciary Committee hearing, some of my fellow
legislators and lawyers were surprised to learn that Wisconsin still allows
imprisonment of people for the non-payment of debts.

The new awareness came about when we discussed a bill that I authored
repealing the section of the statutes relating to the civil arrest of persons
for failure to pay debts.

A number of Blacks and poor people have been placed in jail, not only
in Milwaukee, but in other counties as well, as a result of dubious debts
where a judgment has been granted in a small claims court against a
debtor—many times without a court appearance.

The person said to owe the money is given insufficient time to pay off
the debt, so the court sentences the debtor to a term in jail.

An even more onerous and oppressive provision of Wisconsin statutes
requires attorney, court and collection costs to be added to the debt. Those

---

* Two weeks prior to this comment, Norgard had been moved from the Dane County Jail
to Central State Hospital for mental evaluation. Four months later, he was found innocent
of first-degree murder by reason of mental defect and pled no contest to a reduced charge of
second-degree murder, for which he was sentenced to a maximum of twenty-five years at
Central State Hospital. ("Murder Suspect is Innocent on Mental Ruling," *La Cross Tribune*,
7 June 1973; and "Madison man will get mental exam in murder of student," *Waukesha
Daily Freeman*, 2 Feb. 1973)

who are unable to pay back the money within the time limit allotted through discretion of the court are charged additional money for food and upkeep while in jail.

The whole reasoning behind such discriminatory laws seems lacking. Once the debtor concludes his jail sentence, he or she still owes the money which was awarded to the plaintiff during the small claims trial. In fact, he must pay back even more than when he was first brought to court. In addition, placing a person in jail for nonpayment of a debt does nothing for speeding up the payment to the claimant. It, therefore, seems that the only rationale for such a law is punishment for the sake of revenge. Revenge is an archaic and insensible attitude that has no legitimate place in our judicial system.

The history of debtor statutes is bleak and grim. During post Civil War times, such laws were used to keep newly emancipated Blacks in jail, on debt farms and under the authority of the people who they owed. In many situations, Blacks were forced back into slavery so they could work off the money debts alleged by whites.

Today, such statutes still act unfairly on the Blacks and other minority groups. The poor and uneducated fall victims to unscrupulous money lenders, high pressure salesmen, and read-between-the-lines type of credit applications.

Since the poor usually pay more for the same services and products enjoyed by everyone else, these debtor imprisonment statutes are discriminatory. Our state and Federal constitution should prohibit such laws, but until we get them declared unconstitutional, the legislature must repeal these unfair laws. The poor should use their money wisely by not hocking their future earnings before the money is in their hands. In short, you people beware of credit. It will keep and even get you into jail.

ACCESS TO LEGAL SERVICES, LEGISLATIVE COMMENT, MAY 3, 1973

The poor have a right to justice equal to that of the rich.

To assure justice to the poor, they must have equal access to competent lawyers and other legal services.

The problem is that justice is all too often directly proportional to the money which one has available to him.

Knowledgeable people in this country realize that justice is expensive.

This fact, if not altered soon, will doom the poor and deprived to injustice forever.

The government under President [Lyndon] Johnson, took a step in the right direction by creating a federal legal services program. This program expanded the traditional legal aid services to include advocacy for the poor by identifying those areas of the law which work against the poor and providing reform through class action suits and legal counsel to poverty groups.

Among the many War on Poverty programs that President [Richard] Nixon is abandoning is the Office of Economic Opportunity which houses the legal aids services. Although the courts ruled that Nixon could not impound funds for the Office of Economic Opportunity, another administrative hatchet man, named [Howard] Phillips, is planning to remove the legal services function from OEO. His plan is to transfer this program to an independent agency, or have it swallowed up by the old-fashioned, conservative, local groups. Notwithstanding the suits against Nixon for attempting to end OEO, the central question of justice to the poor should be faced now, before it is too late.

Are the poor receiving adequate legal aid services? The answer is no, not only at the present, but also in the past. Since the poor have problems in getting their needs met by attorneys, the solution lies in a combination of a better understanding of the role of this country's legal establishment, and retaining good lawyers.

In order for the government to play a more effective role in providing legal services for the have-nots to have what the haves have, it must provide money. With the cash to hire their own lawyers, the poor would be in a position to choose them directly. The amount spent by government to prosecute the poor, and the amount spent by the private sector to conduct an ongoing battle against the deprived, can be redressed better by this approach.

I am preparing a bill implementing this approach on the state level. However, I suggest that some of our federal government representatives begin effective action on a nation-wide basis. Only then can the poor be given an equal chance in our judicial process.

MINORITY REPRESENTATION ON POLICE DEPARTMENTS, LEGISLATIVE COMMENT, JULY 18, 1973

The Marquette University made initial plans for hiring Daniel Hanley, executive secretary for Attorney General Robert Warren, to a program which would promote minority representation on police departments. But their hopes were dashed when opposition was made over the appointment. It didn't matter for bureaucratic party-goers, however, for a celebration was held anyway last Friday at the Loraine Hotel in Madison in honor of Hanley's retracted appointment.

It was no surprise that Madison and Milwaukee Blacks opposed Hanley's appointment. After all, a conservative Republican being appointed to work for minorities is analogous to using a screen door on a submarine.

Daniel Hanley impresses me as a good man personally. However, he does not appear to have either the rapport or the expertise in the area of Wisconsin minority needs. For example, the Council on Criminal Justice had been trying for quite some time to obtain data from the Milwaukee Police Department regarding their hiring practices. Not only were the efforts of the council stifled as a result of Police [Harold] Chief Breier's totalitarian attitudes, but also because the Attorney General's office refused to represent the Council in this matter.

The Council then recommended that they proceed with enforcement of minority hiring by allowing all future grants to the Milwaukee Police Department on the condition that they would have to comply with requests for minority hiring, placement, and promotion. Hanley, however, came out in opposition to this proposal by the Council.

Hanley appears to be a strong law-and-order advocate and a Nixon-supporting Republican. And in this respect, Marquette officials showed gall and disrespect when they chose to confirm his appointment despite opposition from concerned and affected groups.

The Law Enforcement Assistance Administration of the US Department of Justice which provides grants to operate the Marquette Center was all too eager to approve Hanley's appointment. This was done without consideration to the sensitivity of Blacks, Latin-Americans, American Indians and other minorities who were concerned with adequate representation on police departments in Milwaukee and in other parts of the state.

When higher education continues to conspire with white racist bigots and big city police forces, no self-respecting minority member recruited in a law enforcement agency would remain a part of such a dehumanizing situation. Worse yet, Attorney General Warren and his executive secretary, Hanley, indulged in the criticism of those Blacks of a non pro-minority who were still attempting to affirmatively promote minority employment of a police system.

Once again, Blacks had to oppose the leanings of white bigotry. And as a result, whites were forced to back down. The only consolation was that Hanley and his supporters still had their party.

Here's to their being drunk with liquor, rather than with power.

QUESTIONING JUSTIFIABLE HOMICIDE,
LEGISLATIVE COMMENT, AUGUST 24, 1973

This past weekend, another Black man was killed by policemen in Milwaukee, and, as usual, the most articulate witnesses were the police who did the shooting. The victim was 22-year old Andrew Friend.

According to reports, police had seen Friend walking in the vicinity of 60th Street and Silver Spring Road. He was supposedly babysitting during this time at a home in the West Lawn public housing project. Because the two policemen who were patrolling the area had thought his actions to be rather peculiar, they decided to stop Friend for questioning. Friend ran, and finally went back to the home where he was babysitting. When the police arrived at the home, he was reputedly holding three of the children as hostages with a butcher knife. Policemen then shot Friend. The medical examiner reported that Friend died instantaneously from two 38 caliber bullets; one wound, in his head and one in his back.

Despite the stories which appeared in the establishment press and the District Attorney's opinion of "justifiable homicide," I urge all concerned citizens, once again to support a unilateral disarmament of law enforcement agencies. As it is now, it seems apparent that we are placing our own lives, limbs, and health in jeopardy by allowing armed police to patrol our streets with weapons and chemicals as in war. Without weapons of destruction and harm, these officers would not have over-reacted to the situation. Instead, they would have found a sane approach, using imagination and human psychology to solve the problem encountered.

What really comes to my mind in this incident was the use of weapons in such close quarters for the purpose of subduing a person who was presumably risking the lives of small children. Instead of a sure solution for ending the risk, this incident could have easily resulted in the death of the children. It was more luck than anything else that saved these children, especially when the so-called heroics were performed by impulsive, trigger-happy men-in-blue whose motto seems to be shoot first, rationalize second, and leave it up to other law enforcement and injudicious officials to temporize homicide last.

I urge readers to reconsider an earlier incident occurring on Monday night, June 25, when Milwaukee police answered a call about a Black who was allegedly drunk and causing a fracas at a local gas station. After being arrested for disorderly conduct and placed in a paddy wagon, 24-year old Warren Pettis was brought to the district police station. Once the doors of the station garage were closed, police said, he tried to take a pistol away from an officer and started shooting wildly. Immediately, of course, he was shot and killed. When the confusion had ended, four policemen were found slightly wounded, hospitalized and released almost immediately. Brother Pettis was entombed forever. Once again, all the witnesses were policemen. A number of Milwaukee Blacks considered this action "unjustifiable homicide" by the police, the DA's office did not. Nothing came of this charge. How many more killings by the State shall we take?

Time and again, Milwaukee statistics consistently show that police *have* injured and abused more citizens than the citizens, themselves. Murder is a bad, immoral act, no doubt about that. But most non-governmental murders are usually committed out of heat of passion and irrationality. Killings committed by police are worse, since they are supposed to be acting in a wise and rational manner during the performance of their duties, protecting life, liberty, and property.

Barbee discusses politics with close friends and political allies Isaac Coggs, a representative in the Wisconsin legislature, and Marcia Coggs.

Official portraits used in campaign literature in 1964 (left) and 1972 (right).

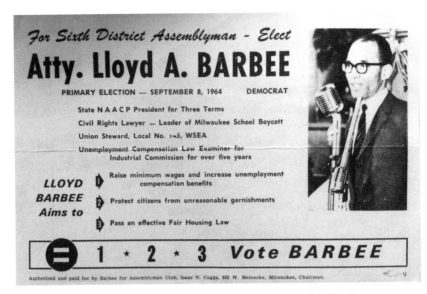

A campaign flier distributed before the September 8, 1964, primary election.

A pamphlet from his campaign to represent the sixth district in the Wisconsin State Assembly highlights Barbee's support for open housing, integrated schools, unemployment benefits, and criminal justice reform.

Barbee with Bobby Seale while promoting the free lunch program run by the Black Panther Party in Oakland, California, in 1972.

Speaking as a state representative in the Wisconsin Assembly Chambers.

With Speaker Mark Lipscomb in the Assembly Chambers.

At his desk in the Wisconsin Assembly Chambers.

Barbee (right) with his brother Quinten and son Rustam on a trip to Jamaica.

Barbee attends the dedication of West Barbee Street, named in his honor, in Milwaukee in 2000. Pictured with Barbee are Leon Young, Quinten Barbee, Marcia Coggs, Priscilla Coggs-Jones, Vernice Nabrit, Rev. Henry C. Nabrit, Chloe Coggs-Jones, Davinia Coggs-Jones, and several others.

Barbee poses, fist raised, with a statue of himself at the Wisconsin Historical Museum in Madison in a display about the fair housing protest.

Barbee attends the 1996 Milwaukee Community Brainstorming seventh annual award ceremony, where he is pictured with Marcia Coggs (seated to his left), Elizabeth Coggs (far right), Vel Phillips (back row, third from left), and others.

The University of Wisconsin–
Milwaukee awarded Barbee an
honorary doctorate in sociology
in 2001. He taught in the school's
Africology department from 1978
to 2000.

Barbee with his grandchildren Leah and Aaron Barbee, children Daphne Barbee-Wooten
and Rustam Barbee, cousin James Gordon, and friend Marcia Coggs (front) after receiving
his honorary doctorate in sociology from the University of Wisconsin–Milwaukee in 2001.

A painting given to Lloyd A. Barbee in 1977 by his client and friend Milton Gee depicts the civil rights leader as an active force.

7

Women's Rights

Women's Rights vs. Minority Rights, Legislative Comment, February 15, 1973

The [University of Wisconsin] System's Board of Regents recently planned a secret executive session on enforcement of the affirmative action program for equal employment opportunities.

The portion of this meeting held without notice to the public was expected to be a victory of the women's faction for equality over the racial minorities. This sneaky victory appears to be engineered by the University administration's fear that white middle class women are more politically powerful as one entity than all the minorities in Wisconsin.

Thus, the Black man, who was hired as a result of a national talent hunt to be the enforcement officer of the affirmative action program, appears to be getting the short end of the deal from the get go. The Board of Regents realized that he is being undercut by a thoroughly political device of having a women's rights enforcement officer who is equal or superior to the Black man's authority and responsibility.

With this sexual and racial split, nobody will be able to enforce the equal employment program effectively. We will be witnessing a hen-and-cock fight over who is first in the pecking order. The University seems to be determined to set the worst example for positive, meaningful change.

We must be careful while we fight for justice and equality that the current ascendency of women's liberation is not permitted to defuse the war against white racism. Blacks know that white middle class Americans from the president down or up are practicing benign neglect.

So, it is essential that we work harder for affirmative action to be made a reality by setting standards, goals, deadlines, and techniques which will bring about concrete results.

BIRTH CONTROL, LEGISLATIVE COMMENT, MARCH 8, 1973

In a recent hearing before the Senate Veterans Affairs Committee, State Senator Gordon Roseleip presented a speech opposing the liberalization of Wisconsin's birth control laws.

This is nothing new. The astounding characteristic of his presentation, however, was the illogic and irony which he employed in the speech. From the premise that "the sons of the poor were the primary source of man power for the Vietnam War," Roseleip said: "Now you want to give contraceptives to poor people. Where are we going to get men for the armed forces if we have another conflict? It's a good way to destroy an army."

During my whole tenure as a legislator, Senator Roseleip has been an amiable opponent of mine who inanely spouts criticism concerning my efforts toward eliminating civil injustices and inequalities.

While some people may be shocked over his comments, it is no surprise to me that the Darlington Republican would make a statement concerning the establishment's use of the poor. If he had his way, Senator Roseleip would more aptly employ the poor as a sex machine to produce recruits for the war machine. Yet, if Mr. Roseleip thinks that the disenfranchised minorities in our society will continue to be fuel for the war machine, then I advise that he take another look.

This should serve as a clear lesson for Blacks and have-nots to become involved in ways to change the system through planned political action. Either that, or accept Roseleip's plan to make the poor people partners in making love for war.

EQUAL RIGHTS AMENDMENT, LEGISLATIVE COMMENT, MARCH 29, 1973

On April 3, 1973, Wisconsin citizens will have the opportunity to vote in city and statewide elections. One of the more important issues on the state ballot is the equal rights referendum.*

Although the amendment is a much needed piece of legislation, many individuals have reflected an opposition to it either out of ignorance or misinformation. Some feel that the equal rights amendment will force women to work. Such is not the case. But women who desire to work and be liberated should be given the opportunity to do so under the protection of the law.

Some fear that a "yes" vote on the referendum would mean that women would be deprived of alimony. This is not true.

Nor will the same restrooms necessarily be provided for both men and women. The right to privacy still holds in most situations. It is obvious that the principle equal justice under the law, which has guided our country for two centuries, has never been realized. Just as separate laws for race and religion are unconstitutional, so are separate legal provisions for men and women.

Equality is not a limited entity. Its extension to one group does not mean loss to another. Equality is the essence of a free democratic society.

EQUAL RIGHTS AMENDMENT VOTING RESULTS, LEGISLATIVE COMMENT, APRIL 12, 1973

Wisconsin polling places received record voting turnouts on April 3, but the results of the voting presented some not too pleasant surprises for freedom lovers. The rude awakening comes as a result of the failure of the equal rights amendment.

---

*The Equal Rights Amendment, first proposed in 1923, stated that rights would not be denied or abridged on the basis of sex. It was passed by Congress in 1972 but needed to be ratified by at least thirty-eight states to be added to the Constitution. See "The Equal Rights Amendment," http://www.equalrightsamendment.org/.

Ironically, the amendment which would have granted equal protection under the law to persons regardless of sex failed to pass in the same election in which a woman was elected as State Superintendent of Schools. In many respects, its failure was due to the misinformation and untruths intentionally spread about the state by rightist organizations such as the John Birch Society and Protect Our Women.

Believing that the unequal status of women in America was ordained by God, and therefore should not be changed, these confused, embittered women have chosen to be slaves to their white, male counterparts. Their negative reaction to women receiving equal treatment under the law can best be represented in their claims that the equal rights amendment would have legalized rape, eliminated alimony, integrated toilets and forced women to work.

Nothing in the equal rights measure would have prevented these bewildered conservatives from continuing their own subservient positions in society. Their efforts, however, may prevent other women from seeking equal protection under the Constitution, blocking concerted legal efforts of others from receiving equal treatment in housing, education, employment and recreation.

The failure of the equal rights amendment can only serve as another example of white affluency forcing their narrow values on the rest of the people. The fight for equality under the law is not over. It takes more than a few months to wipe out the prejudices which people develop concerning themselves and others around them. The long struggle of Blacks for equality should be ample proof of this. The struggle still goes on.

Women who wish to advance the course of humanity, take heed.

Wives, mistresses, and lovers of white fat cats and crass materialists will sell not only their birthright of freedom but yours and mine for a pat on their anatomy from exponents of white male supremacy. They are killers of justice and must be dealt with accordingly.

The time has come to educate the masses, not with propaganda as that spread by hard core opponents of equal rights, but with intelligent arguments, discussion, and facts concerning the impact of equal rights.

Equality of opportunity is feared by tyrants, oppressors, and demagogues, not freedom lovers or believers in a democratic way of life.

EQUAL RIGHTS SETBACK, LEGISLATIVE COMMENT, OCTOBER 17, 1973

Failure of the equal rights referendum last April was a setback and disappointment for advocates of freedom and equality. The fallacious arguments and falsehoods directed toward the equal rights controversy, however, failed to degenerate the influence of the majority of my Assembly colleagues.

This was especially evident with the recent approval of Assembly Bill 23, a comprehensive measure that eliminates distinctions in the Wisconsin statutes based on sex. The vote which sent the bill scurrying to the Senate, was by a 69 to 28 margin.

It is much too early for rejoicing, however. When the bill was first received by the Senate, it was referred to the Senate Committee on Health, Education, and Welfare. A later action by the Republican-controlled Senate, though, resulted in sending the bill to the Senate Governmental and Veterans Affairs Committee. Chairman of this committee is the long-time supporter of white America, motherhood, and apple pie, State Senator Gordon Roseleip.

If you recall, Senator Roseleip came out frothing at the mouth in opposition to the bill that would legalize birth control devices and information to unmarried adults, calling the measure a sure way to eliminate the needed manpower for our Armed Forces. Senator Roseleip is also an outspoken opponent of equal rights for women. Considering this viewpoint of libertarian politics and democratic justice, you can rest assured that Roseleip will not be at all fired up to get this bill reported out of his committee for floor debate unscathed; at least we can safely assume that Mr. Roseleip won't be treating Assembly Bill 23 in the same manner as he treats legislation relating to veterans benefits.

The situation, sarcasm aside, is saddening. The equal rights bill is a very deserving piece of legislation. It is a fundamental measure that, rather than removing or providing special privileges for either men or women, provides for equal treatment of both in most areas of the law.

It has become obvious that opponents of AB 23 will use a false comparison of the bill with the ERA referendum as their main tactic in attempting

SEX DISCRIMINATION LAWSUITS

Lloyd Barbee represented Christine Ward against the Milwaukee Board of Fire and Police Commission in 1974. Ms. Ward filed sex discrimination charges with the Equal Employment Opportunity Commission (EEOC) stemming from the Milwaukee Board of Fire and Police Commissioners use of physical agility tests to discriminate against women. All the women who had applied to be police officers or firefighters failed the physical agility test. Specifically, in July 1974, thirty-eight women took the physical agility test and all of them failed. All of the women passed the written tests.

After Mr. Barbee filed the lawsuit, the EEOC joined the suit. After the US EEOC joined the complaint of discrimination, the defendants entered into a consent decree agreeing not to discriminate against women by use of the physical agility test, and to immediately hire women as police officers and firefighters. This was one of the first successful sex discrimination cases in Wisconsin.

to defeat the measure. The constitutional amendment defeated last April is an entirely different measure procedurally and substantively from the recently approved bill. In fact, I fail to understand how an attorney or a legislator can in good conscience, without violating the ethical responsibility of either profession, stand and make grossly misrepresentative statements in comparing Assembly Bill 23 to the defeated Equal Rights Amendment.

The equal rights bill passed by the Assembly does not force a position on an individual. The measure simply allows either sex to choose the role he or she wants. Certain people prefer slavery to freedom, subservience to equal status. Assembly Bill 23 will continue to allow these individuals to live their own lives in the way they see fit. Without it, however, many other persons will be legally forced to conform to narrow lifestyles. In what has been often assumed to be a democratic society, this is intolerable.

Therefore, government should insist that people who are willingly serving as slaves in society do not infringe on those desiring freedom and equality. Individuals have the right to be their best selves freely and should have opportunities to develop their potentialities fully. Laws must exist which guarantee this right and strongly implement it.

Public Funds for Abortion, Legislative Comment, March 10, 1976

Anti-abortionists achieved a hollow victory when seventy-eight members of the State Assembly passed legislation preventing the expenditure of public funds to pay for abortions.

Even if the State Senate uses the same stingy, shallow judgment in concurrence, the measure is likely to be declared unconstitutional by the courts. Assembly Bill 421 is rank discrimination at its worst.

Ever since the US Supreme Court decision in 1973 to allow abortions during the first trimester of pregnancy, the view that mere existence is more important than the quality of life has grown. At the same time, the rights of women and the poor have been flouted, if not ignored by the pro-life doctrines of moral, dogmatic imperialism.

A prohibition on the expenditure of public funds to pay for abortions is bad public policy from a number of standpoints. It's saddening that so many elected officials lacked the courage of their convictions to face this fact.

From the economic point of view, Wisconsin stands to lose at least $264 million in federal funds because of their noncompliance with federal requirements if the proposed law is enacted, prohibiting public funds to subsidize abortions.

From a legal point of view, Assembly Bill 421 is unconstitutional.

A case recently decided in a federal court in South Dakota held that a state cannot constitutionally deny Medicaid benefits for the performance of nontherapeutic abortions. The case has been appealed to the US Supreme Court. The outcome of the appeal should be obvious.

From a social point of view, the anti-abortion bill which passed the Assembly is a slap in the faces of the poor and disadvantaged. While the measure doesn't altogether prohibit abortions in Wisconsin, it does restrict them to those wealthy enough to afford the medical cost.

Those who must rely on Medicaid and other forms of public assistance to pay their health care costs would again be helplessly placed in the situation of resorting to back alley butchers for terminating unwanted pregnancies, a situation which the Supreme Court successfully eliminated in 1973.

One would think that a lesson was learned about two years ago on the abortion issue when the Legislature enacted law last session giving public and private hospitals and medical clinics the right to refuse to perform abortions. That law was struck down by the courts as being unconstitutional.

The recent Assembly action on the abortion issue is one more example, of the futile attempt by the anti-abortion lobby to impose their self-righteous moral will upon others.

The decision to terminate an unwanted pregnancy should rest solely with the pregnant woman and her physician. The courts have affirmed this. The law of this land must demand it.

Certainly, the decision to abort an unborn child is many times a difficult one. For many, the decision is a moral one. While the final decisions of individuals should be respected, the final choices should not be mandated upon others as the only acceptable alternatives.

While pro-life advocates incessantly stress the immorality of abortion, they fail to recognize the immorality inherent in discrimination of the type approved by my colleagues in the form of Assembly Bill 421.

Anti-abortionists may applaud the Assembly's action on this bill, but the Wisconsin Legislature supported a bill which mocked our political process, challenged the judicial system, and insulted the poor again. The hypocrites, sadists, masochists and sexually repressed persons should recognize that abortions are matters of health care as well as matters of female choice. If only the wealthy persons can have abortions, the Legislature practices and condones economic discrimination.

It is my hope that further consideration of this bill will cease. Let the poor decide for themselves the morality of abortion as a means to terminate unwanted pregnancies.

EQUAL RIGHTS BILL, LLOYD A. BARBEE 1982 MANUSCRIPT

Another example of people fighting among themselves occurred last week during the Assembly Judiciary Committee's public hearing on an equal rights bill for women.

As Chairman of the Committee, I found much of the opposing testimony a total departure from rational and reasonable thinking. The throngs of bickering biddies and Bible-thumping Birchites who appeared in opposition to the bill adequately demonstrated the inability of people to reason and compromise with themselves and one another.

As long as people fight among themselves, governments will continue to make decisions based on their own findings of the particular situation at hand. The equal rights bill introduced in the Legislature this session could become a good indicator of this trend if the emotional rhetoric continues to replace rational analysis as a means of addressing individual or governmental problems and proposals. This is ironic because the bill is modest and inadequate in its coverage.

Women who want to be slaves to dumb and inadequate men who pose as the dominant of the species should not object to and fight women who wish liberty and freedom to develop the fullest of their potentialities regardless of sex.

8

HEALTH CARE, ENVIRONMENTAL, AND ECONOMIC ISSUES

POLLUTION, LEGISLATIVE COMMENT, APRIL 26, 1971

The attitude of a number of people toward the pollution of the atmosphere, the water, and the land is now due for some comment.

For a long time I have been trying to promote some better utilization of anti-pollution devices on automobiles as well as some more assessable waste disposal and recycling actions.

The Government itself is a large polluter. We are going to recognize this more when we see what Milwaukee is doing off Jones Island and what it is permitting some of the suburbs to do in terms of sewage disposal.

I am not in sympathy with a number of the ecology buffs' great concern about the physical condition of the earth to the exclusion of real cancer about the daily plight of human beings, particularly the blacks and the browns.

However, I did show my interest by having sponsored, in another session of the legislature, measures to cut down on pollution by trying to see that something is done against pollutants.

Assembly Bill 194, which was signed by the Governor this week, is one indication of my interest.

I would like to remind my fellow legislators and agitators for an end to physical pollution to help those of us who have to be concerned about that portion of humanity which is being maimed and in a real sense destroyed

195

by the daily actions dehumanizing Black and Brown people both in subtle and blatant ways. Pollution of the environment is bad, but mistreatment of blacks is worse. Genocide is worse!

TREATMENT OF HEART DISEASE, PRESS RELEASE, WISCONSIN ASSEMBLY, JANUARY 18, 1972

Assembly Bill 1456 introduced by State Representative Lloyd A. Barbee (D-Milwaukee-6) that would permit trained, non-physicians to administer heart disease injections has been heard before the Assembly's Health and Social Services Committee.

"This bill would lay the medical and legal framework for a new program that would permit us to treat coronary victims in their homes while there's a chance to save them and before we can get them to a hospital," Barbee said.

Barbee said a Milwaukee industrialist recently considered such a plan but dropped it for legal reasons.

"The president of the Vilter Manufacturing Corporation, Albert Silverman, had a plan to train employees to give heart drug injections so that they would be able to help people in their own neighborhoods, but the plan was dropped because of fears that the firm could be held liable if death or injury was claimed as the result of someone other than a physician giving the drugs."

The Milwaukee lawmaker discussed the dimensions of heart disease.

"Heart attacks are the leading cause of death in this country," Barbee said. "They account for one-third of the deaths every year. Of these, two-thirds die outside the hospital and two thirds of these victims last as long as three hours before dying.

"The main delay in providing early treatment stems not from a delay in getting them to a hospital but from the victim's reluctance to call for help.

"Furthermore, most persons having their first or second heart attack die because the heart suffers a short-circuit, causing unusual and quickened heart beats, not because of a defective heart muscle." If a victim or his or her relative placed a call to a central directory, we could get a trained layperson in the area to his home quickly. This so-called heart-watcher could give either of two drugs which are used to stabilize the heart-beat.

"This program promises a breakthrough in the area stifled by conventional medical practice. In the past, we have been burdened with the idea that we can't give heart victims help until we get them to a hospital and a physician. This heart-watcher program would help us bring the latest developments in medicine to the victim in the neighborhood."

Barbee said the program's success would rest largely on the medical profession's response. "Too often in the past, the self-proclaimed official spokesmen for American medicine have been resistant to change. But times are changing. The young doctors care as much about service and the community's health as they do about their pocketbook. And so I'm confident of the medical profession's support of the program."

Barbee paid tribute to the man who originated the idea. "Dr. Walter D. Shapiro, an internist and a cardiologist and past chairman of the Wisconsin Heart Association's prehospital care committee, suggested the proposal to Vilter's president Silverman as an in-plant program. In turn, Silverman conceived of extending heart watching into the community." Community participation in health care is the best way to assure health delivery to everyone.

G6PD DEFICIENCY, LEGISLATIVE COMMENT, FEBRUARY 9, 1972

Glucose-6-Phosphate-Dehydrogenase deficiency. That is a real tongue-twister. It is known, for short, as G6PD deficiency. The name then becomes easier to handle but the problem does not.

G6PD deficiency is a medical term, meaning a lack of that compound in the blood. This problem is genetically inherited, as are eye and skin color and height. In general, females carry the genes and males exhibit the problem. However, some females can have the disease as well.

The G6PD deficiency is found in people who can trace roots to areas with malaria-bearing mosquitoes, including Africa, China and Mediterranean countries. Frequently, people who carry an immunity to malaria also carry the G6PD deficiency.

Ordinarily, the deficiency in itself is not a serious problem.

It is only when it is aggravated by another illness or the administration of certain drugs that it needs medical attention. It is a metabolic deficiency which slows the absorption of drugs by the bloodstream. In general, as each red blood cell grows older, its ability to metabolize drugs as a result of the G6PD deficiency is diminished. Consequently, when the G6PD syndrome appears, it destroys the older red blood cells. Younger cells are not affected, as long as the drug dosage which caused the initial attack is not increased.

Medical experts maintain that these attacks are self-limiting in Blacks so long as the drug dosage is not increased. In whites and Orientals, the disease is arrested only when the causative medication is discontinued, according to the same medical and genetic experts.

Relatively common drugs can set the G6PD cycle off. Some of them are aspirin and compounds containing aspirin and phenacetin, quinine, and sulfanilamide.

If the attack is severe enough, for instance when it is coupled with sickle cell anemia or a virus such as hepatitis, so many red blood cells are destroyed that the kidneys are unable to remove them from the bloodstream. Possible kidney failure can result if the disease is not reversed.

Studies have shown that roughly 100 million Blacks throughout the world have this genetic imbalance. Approximately 10 percent of all American Blacks are estimated to suffer from G6PD deficiency. This includes a very small percentage of black women.

The G6PD deficiency can be determined through a blood test. Once the presence of the disease itself or of its genes has been established, genetic counseling can be utilized to minimize the possibility that offspring will inherit the syndrome.

Thus—testing and screening is as great for this genetic problem little known to the general public as [it is] for sickle cell anemia.

Extension of Daycare Funding, Press Release, Wisconsin Assembly, September 25, 1972

The recent extension of special needs payments to AFDC [Aid to Families with Dependent Children] recipients comes as good news to all of us concerned about eliminating poverty. But the difficulty we experienced in achieving this extension is a sad commentary on the operation of state government.

Special needs payments are made for the purchase of household goods and clothing, and before 1969, were made to AFDC recipients and those receiving aid to the blind, disabled and old age assistance.

But then, the 1969 State Legislature got into the act. The lawmakers retained the allowances for the adult programs, but restricted their availability to those receiving AFDC. Luckily, the 1971 Legislature corrected this inequity and adopted identical benefit provisions for both programs. But the policy was never implemented by the Department of Health and Social Services. Because of their resistance, the Board on Government Operations (BOGO) was forced to step in. BOGO, of which I am a member, is an interim state agency which operates when the Legislature is not in session.

This discriminatory and unfair distinction had a profound effect on welfare recipients. Those benefiting from AFDC are essentially children, and to be without adequate clothing and beds is a distinct hardship for them. The elderly and the disabled and the blind deserve and need the special need payments; but a child must attend school and cannot go without the shoes and clothing these payments provide.

The actions of the Department of Health and Social Services reaffirms our previous observations concerning the mishandling of programs by bureaucratic misfits. The department's blatant refusal to carry out the legislative intent was accompanied by an absence of consultation with the Department of Health and Social Services Board or BOGO. The department proved they had been intimidated by the anti-welfare, anti-poor corps, led by State Representative John Shabaz of New Berlin. Shabaz fought hard against my proposal to approve the identical provisions policy. Fortunately, his obstructionist tactics failed and we were successful in restoring the benefits.

The opponents of decent and adequate standards of living for all argued that the policy would cost too much money. There is no way that lifting the poor to a realistic subsistence level can be viewed as too costly. Unless we spend whatever it takes to do the job, then the entire welfare program [remains] as wasteful and non-productive as many other government programs. It is not welfare if we only spend 50 cents when a dollar is needed.

Actually, the federal government will be picking up the major portion of the cost—54 percent or $2.4 million. The county and state share will not be that great.

And yet, Shabaz has called upon the Governor to veto this proposal. I hope the Governor will reject Shabaz's suggestion for what it is: a move to deny the poor the right to basic needs taken for granted by middle and upper income families. If others sock it to the poor and welfare recipients seek a veto, I hope Governor Lucey tells them to beat it.

The department's abdication of its responsibility is a slap in the face for not only the poor, but for all citizens who recognize the need of meeting all the needs of each person as a minimum goal of good government.

RIGHT TO HEALTH CARE, LEGISLATIVE COMMENT, NOVEMBER 16, 1972

If there is any one right that has been denied to the people of this nation, it is the right to decent health care. But in typical fashion, only certain persons have been denied this right: the Black, the American Indian, the poor and the elderly. In general, the have-nots. The rich, of course, have decent health care. But they do not need rights—they can purchase needed service while others cannot.

The most gross example of injustice in the delivery of health care is the emergency care available in Milwaukee County. For instance, one private hospital in Milwaukee which claims to offer emergency services closes these services at eight o'clock at night and is not open at all on weekends. What this means, of course, is that if you're going to have an emergency, make certain you have it during office hours.

Hospital officials try to excuse the lack of emergency facilities by sending people to the county hospital or hospitals in Wauwatosa. These officials neglect one basic point: emergencies usually do not wait until the victim can travel from one hospital to another. Secondly, taxis are very reluctant to accept sick persons as fares.

There are two alternatives to this tragic situation. All hospitals should be required to offer 24-hour emergency services. Any additional cost would be overshadowed by the benefit of saving human lives and providing each person with a decent state of health.

The other alternative would be preferable. That is to support—financially and otherwise—the black hospital in Milwaukee, Misericordia Community Hospital at McKinley and 22nd. This facility is controlled and operated by members of the Black community. It is a sad, but true, state of affairs when a race must resort to its own private facilities because the white community cannot and will not provide needed services.

The Governor's health task force has been charged with conducting a thorough review of health care in Wisconsin. The panel has recognized that health care is not accessible to all persons, especially the poor Blacks who live in the inner city. While it has called for state laws regulating ambulance services, I do not feel the task force has sufficiently looked into what can be specifically done to enhance emergency care in general. The accident, disease and death rates for Blacks are much higher than for middle and upper income groups. So is discrimination by hospitals and other health organizations.

It is obvious that a special committee should be named to identify minority health problems and plan efficient solutions. Unless action is taken to improve emergency care for Blacks, minorities will face greater economic and social hardships as well as poorer health.

Preventing Overpopulation, Press Release, Wisconsin Assembly, May 2, 1973

Representative Lloyd A. Barbee (D-Milwaukee) today introduced a far-reaching bill (A.B. 928) designed to assess the impact that expanding population has on the quality of life in Wisconsin. The bill also provides means to confront the problems that overpopulation poses for our environment.

Barbee's proposal would create a population and environment board with broad powers to analyze the whole spectrum of population—and resource-related trends, including such timely issues as air and water pollution, depletion of open spaces and natural resources, and the energy and waste disposal crises.

The board would be charged with charting the probable course of all demographic tendencies from the present to the year 2000, including trends in education, transportation, health, housing and employment.

Another board responsibility would be to develop educational programs on sex education, birth control, and the relationship between population and environment.

A further responsibility of the board would be to study "the immediate or eventual necessity for mandatory population control programs, including limitations on family size and required sterilization."

Barbee stressed the need for a continuing, interdisciplinary board, and noted that the short-term committees and commissions in vogue today have failed to grapple effectively with the interlocking problems of a fast growing population and a rapidly deteriorating earth-wide life-supporting ecosystem.

Other major provisions of Barbee's bill sharply alter the course of public policy. Tax exemptions for children would be abolished, and replaced by positive tax incentives NOT to have children. Adopted children would be exempted from this change. Barbee noted that "it has become obviously irrational to continue to use the tax system to subsidize childbirth."

Another provision of Barbee's bill would deny state aids to any school district which did not incorporate the board's sex education and birth control programs in its courses of study.

Barbee said that he was led to introduce this comprehensive and controversial measure through the realization that the wealthy were consuming energy and resources at a disproportionate and untenable rate, and the disparity in the level of such consumption between rich and poor was growing day by day.

"The crises that assail us daily, and that are growing in frequency and severity—from the price of meat to the incidence of emphysema—are screaming at us that we must act at once to stabilize our population and redistribute our state and global resources to achieve an equitable balance among all people. The quality of life in the years ahead is at stake now. We must plan and act," Barbee concluded. "It would be insane to delay."

JUVENILE DRUG ABUSE TREATMENT, LEGISLATIVE COMMENT, JUNE 14, 1973

The Legislature this week still quibbled over the issue of whether children should be given treatment for drug abuse without parental consent.

Unlike a few weeks ago when the measure was indefinitely postponed, the results on Thursday were more favorable. The drug treatment bill was passed by the Assembly after a motion was made to reconsider the indefinite postponement, thereby taking it from its deathbed.

A few of the more prudish legislators had argued that children should receive medical treatment for drug abuse only if the parents were notified and approved of the treatment first. They claimed that by eliminating parental consent, we would cause a disintegration of the family structure. This is outright bunk. American families need more honest updated respect for human development.

People who know the realities of society in this country realize that young people become involved with drugs in an aura of clandestine-ness. The use of drugs and related activities are done often in secrecy eluding the grip of parents and authorities. Therefore, those who go on drugs without the permission of his or her parents should also be able to get off of drugs without parental consent.

The major purpose of the bill, however, was to allow for emergency treatment of minors resulting from drug overdoses. Youths who take street drugs such as mescaline, LSD, and other assorted chemicals have too often found that what they had taken was strychnine or some other poison. Requiring parental consent for treating such cases would waste those precious few minutes where immediate treatment is most crucial. Overdoses resulting from harder drugs also require speedy treatment.

Three weeks ago, we debated a bill that would allow for treatment of venereal disease in minors without parental consent. Both the drug treatment and the VD treatment bill were at that time discussed, but only the VD treatment of minors was approved. The same outspoken critics who opposed this week's action also denounced the VD treatment measure. It seems evident that some of my shortsighted friends and law makers were more concerned with a breakdown of family relations than with the health of our children.

We have reached a time in history where all persons should be able to receive the highest quality of medical treatment which our medical profession can provide. A part of this high quality medical care involves emergency treatment as well as long term diagnosis, care and/or cure. Our commitment to providing health care must go beyond the pre-fabricated worries of allowing the treatment of minors without parental consent.

Youths have rights to good health regardless of parental interference. Through legislation such as that which was approved in the Assembly, the state should make this right clear and legitimate now and forever.

HEALTH CARE REGULATION, LEGISLATIVE COMMENT, JUNE 21, 1973

A bill establishing a regulatory health care commission was recently put on the Assembly calendar for debate soon. The measure, which I co-sponsor, is a product of the Governor's Health Planning and Policy Task Force.

The more conservative elements of the medical profession have already started an organized drive in opposition to this bill. This is no surprise, since the medical establishment has discriminated against poor whites, Blacks, and other minorities for many years in our country and state.

Assembly Bill 489 gives the three-member health care commission regulatory powers over health care services and institutions, except those provided by private practitioners. Within the commission there would be created nine-member advisory councils in such areas as institutional licensing, quality assurance, and rate review and approval.

The three-member commission would be given four very important functions. One, the commission would be empowered to review rates.

No health care institution could establish or increase a rate without the consent of the commission. However, an annual allowable percentage increase to recognize inflation and other factors would be provided by the commission.

A second function of the commission would be to approve facility expansion or modification when costs exceeded a certain amount. Those institutions receiving certifications of need would be required to comply with other requirements, such as the ability to provide adequate medical staff.

Thirdly, the bill would require that all health care institutions be licensed annually. The license would designate minimum services that must be offered by each institution, determined on the basis of community need.

The remaining function of the commission would be to establish guidelines and standards for health care by 1977 and along these lines make an annual assessment of each health care institution.

Weakening amendments to the bill may pass. A great deal of opposition has been generated by the State Medical Society and the reactionary establishment. They have misinformed too many people in this state through their claims that the health care commission bill will drive physicians out of the state. Their comments seem to imply that doctors are more interested in the money earned than the medical care provided patients. Instead of taking the Hippocratic oath when they become part of the profession, they are taking a hypocritical oath, materialistic to the extreme.

Ironically, the Wisconsin Hospital Association, whose members would be most directly affected by the bill, has endorsed it on the condition that the commission structure be altered. This is, at least, more digestible than what the stronger opponents would like to see done with the bill.

The poor in Milwaukee receive good medical care only when the affluent have received an oversupply.

Poverty groups who are not entitled to Medicaid are being prevented from receiving health care necessary for the enjoyment of other basic rights, and those receiving Medicaid are inadequately treated by private and public practitioners.

The poor are welcomed as guinea pigs for experiments, but when it comes to getting their basic health needs met, they are treated in an inhuman, impersonal and insulting manner.

Regulation of health care services in our state is absolutely necessary if the goal is for everyone, regardless of income, race or color, to receive good health care as a basic right. Yet, the only regulation existing thus far is by Blue Cross-Blue Shield doctors and hospitals, amounting to another example of conspiracy against the poor.

Surely, something must be done in the public's interest. The State should start the job soon.

MILWAUKEE COUNTY DAYCARE FUNDING CUTS, LEGISLATIVE COMMENT, OCTOBER 10, 1973

A proposal by the Milwaukee funding for potential and former AFDC [Aid to Families with Dependent Children] recipients has received some discussion in local newspapers. The reasons for the cuts as stated by the Board and the newspapers, however, is misleading.

The Board claims they are faced with welfare program cutbacks because of decreases in state and federal welfare funding. I view this as sheer bunk.

The state has not cut back on welfare funding for Milwaukee. Rather, they have increased state aid for Milwaukee welfare programs by $14,391,165, resulting in a total of $88,715,637 in state welfare aids for the County.

The restrictions on the County Board come as a result of federal funding guidelines which now require "sum certain" expenditures for welfare programs, rather than "sum sufficient" expenditures. The difference here is that, previously, counties were not limited as to how much they could spend. They would still be guaranteed a federal reimbursement. Now the federal government says it will give counties a specific amount of money for their welfare programs, the limit of which is supposedly based on previous spending.

As a result of these new federal spending procedures, the State Department of Health and Social Services placed limitations on various sum certain expenditures. These limits affected the state funding of the purchase of services within welfare programs. Daycare funding happens to belong in this "purchase of services" category.

The Milwaukee County Board, nevertheless, claims that these different funding procedures have resulted in state and federal cutbacks in welfare funding. Not true. The changes did, however, make it necessary for the Board to employ economic reasoning and fiscal responsibility in drawing up the county welfare budget. This they haven't done.

Why, in the name of economic logic, did the Board propose to cut off daycare funding for potential and former AFDC recipients when this, in turn, would force many working mothers back on welfare?

Although several cuts were made in the proposed county welfare budget, economizing should have been directed toward excessive bureaucratic overhead. The Board claims that daycare for potential and former AFDC recipients is a lower priority program. I disagree. The poor should not have to choose between inadequacy or inferiority. Welfare must be reformed to become adequate and humane. If private individuals will not voluntarily share their wealth, government should redistribute goods and services equitably. Cutting this program employs a contradicting philosophy.

One reason the Board chose the daycare program as the victim for cutbacks is because welfare funding for former and potential AFDC recipients is considered an optional, not a mandatory, program by the federal government. Although the federal government presently gives reimbursement for this optional program, new proposed federal regulations, if adopted, would take away this reimbursement. Their logic is in need of review.

One might also assume that the County Board has taken the new proposed federal regulations into consideration during their deliberations on a county welfare budget. Without federal reimbursement, the County would have to pay even more for the purchase of daycare for potential AFDC recipients. By eliminating the program and forcing these mothers back on welfare, the County would then continue to receive this federal funding at a lower total cost. Economically speaking, this might perhaps be good for the County Board in the short run, but it adversely affects all the people served by government in the long run. It further plays into the hands of stingy and greedy bigots. Which is more important—children and human dignity or political expediency?

During public hearings on the proposed daycare cutbacks, all colors of people came out in opposition. People who are supposed to be represented by these rum-dum politicians. What good did the public hearing serve? The County Welfare Committee heard all the opposition as if they were hearing it for the first time, as if they didn't know already the repercussions of their proposal. Nevertheless, it seems they are going ahead with daycare cutbacks disregarding those who expressed disapproval to the proposal.

Not only is daycare a method of keeping many mothers off the welfare rolls, but it also prepares children for environmental changes resulting from public schooling. Daycare helps children to be more intellectually curious and better attuned to learning. Considering the way in which Milwaukee County generally administers its welfare programs, there are other alternatives to cut down on costs without taking away a part of daycare funding. More will be said on other cuts in service to the poor on the State and County level in a future comment. Meanwhile, I mind my readers of the following: "Intellectually, the descent into hell is easy. One false step, and logic will do the rest."

Tax Reform, Remarks to Senior Action Coalition at Milwaukee Area Technical College, November 15, 1975

The problems experienced by the elderly in Wisconsin are in many ways similar to the problems experienced by blacks and other minorities. Fixed incomes in a world of rising prices, poor nutritional diets, inadequate housing in a deteriorating city environment, a need for better health care, improved energy use, and an anti-victimization program.

Any way we look at the situation, the taste of poverty is the same, whether it's experienced by people who are retired and over 65 years of age or whether it's experienced by people of a different race or nationality, hunger and poverty know no bounds.

Some organizations and public officials in recent weeks have made statements implying that the plight of Wisconsin's elderly is being ignored. The problems faced by senior citizens are not being ignored; it's just that the solutions proposed are nearsighted and superficial. Rather than major reforms of our tax structure and in the delivery of public services, reforms that bring benefits for all poverty and low-income people, only tokens of relief are provided.

Granted, the Wisconsin homestead tax credit program is a significant program. How will the average tax credit of $206 given in one lump sum provide an adequate level of supplemental assistance for those experiencing the day-to-day brunt of our economic troubles?

Such arguments might also be made for many of the proposals which are now pending before the legislature.

One bill increases income tax credits for older adults from the present $25 to $40.

Another provides a $12 to $18 increase in state supplemental benefits.

As stop gap measures to provide small sums of relief, these proposals may serve a good purpose. However, much more will be required of government before significant headway is made on solving the financial crunch faced by the elderly.

Thus far, I have only mentioned programs and proposals relating to tax benefits for the elderly. Obviously, there are other measures which are also being discussed by the legislature and state government as a whole.

One is a program already underway under the direction of the Lt. Governor' s office. The program will establish community care services as alternatives for nursing home care. Another proposal is a foster grandparents program allowing low-income elderly the opportunity to work for wages in our public and semi-private institutions which care for children and the developmentally disabled. Still another proposal is what has been referred to as the Omnibus Aging Services Act.

While these are measures which I hope each of us on the panel will support, I would like to see a push for greater reforms.

During the budget debate this session, one of the amendments that was introduced would update and reform our income tax structure in Wisconsin by changing the existing income tax brackets.

On all taxable income from $14,000 to $17,000; the tax rate would be 12 percent, on taxable income from $17,000 to $20,000, the tax rate would be 13 percent, between $20,000 and $25,000, the tax rate would be 14 percent, and so on, until incomes over $100,000 would be taxed at a rate of 17 percent.

In my own opinion, I don't believe this amendment was that radical of a proposal. Yet the large majority of representatives in the assembly rejected this amendment. For whatever reasons or motives my colleagues had for their choice of votes, it will become more and more apparent as the years go by that a major reform of our tax structure will be necessary.

Wisconsin's corporate and income tax brackets have changed very little since our state's progressive tax structure was first adopted around 1913. It has become out of focus with the realities of present-day incomes. It cries for change and the state's revenue coffers are now beginning to show this.

Each of us here today must also be concerned with the situation now developing on the federal level of government.

In recent weeks, we've heard the [Gerald] Ford administration discuss plans for instituting permanent tax cuts for public taxpayers while cutting back on federal spending. While this might seem to be a plan developed in the public interest, people must first ask the question where the cuts in government spending will be made.

The Ford administration's latest proposal to reduce federal spending would make massive cuts in the nation's food stamp program. By tying eligibility for the program directly to the official poverty mark, the Ford plan does little more than rob from the poor and give to the poorer.

Under the present system, food stamps represent a supplemental program. If a family or an elderly person is having temporary financial problems, the family is able to receive food stamp assistance during these times to assure healthy diet maintenance.

The Ford administration, however, wants to reduce the scope of the program by making it strictly a poverty program. Under his proposal, the most a family of four could earn to be eligible for food stamps is $6,550. An elderly person living alone would have to have incomes that are substantially less to be eligible for food stamp benefits.

Even more disturbing is the fact that his food stamp plan is only one of many more human services cutbacks which he'll propose over the upcoming months. Anywhere from one-third to one-half of the Ford administration's proposed $28 billion reduction in 1977 federal budget spending may be chopped from human services programs. The programs which are almost certain to be victims of this poor perception of priorities include social security, supplemental security income, Medicaid and Medicare.

Obviously, there's been considerable criticism lodged against government spending. Whether justified or unjustified, reducing our commitments to the poor and elderly is not the way to deal with the problem. The pressures of our current economy are felt most by the unemployed, the elderly, and those who are forced to live on fixed incomes, meager or no wages at all. Concern must be focused on these levels.

Time for both state and federal government to end the practice of funding the rich and taxing the poor.

ENERGY, LEGISLATIVE COMMENT, NOVEMBER 16, 1973

The reaction of the Nixon Administration to the so-called energy crisis was predictable. The poor and have-nots of this country are being asked to pull in their belts one more notch so that Nixon and his fat-cat cohorts will be able to continue living in comfort.

Nothing has made this more clear than the call to increase the gasoline tax which is now being promoted by some of Nixon's closest advisers. The focus of this issue is rationing heating oil and gasoline. It appears that everyone in the White House has a different method for rationing.

One is taxing heating oil and gasoline to provide an incentive not to waste valuable fuel that is in short supply now. The other suggestion is rationing these petroleum products through the use of ration coupons. White House energy czar, John Love, suggests that the Nixon Administration impose both tax increases and caps on rationing.

Neither the fat-in-the-belly owner of the chauffeured limousine, nor the bureaucrat who drives a government automobile will be affected by this regressive sur-tax. The reasons they won't feel the pinch are simple. First, a fifty cent tax on each gallon of gasoline will have little effect on his pocketbook. Second, because the government bureaucrat doesn't have to pay the tax. He just writes it off on his allowance sheet and lets the government pay for it.

But the average worker in Milwaukee, who must drive the automobile to work because of a woefully inadequate transit system, will no longer be able to afford the luxury of taking a car to work. The cost of gasoline would make such a practice economically impossible.

It is the poor family that will have to walk to the grocery store, not the rich dude. And as usual, it is the poor who will also pay so that the privileged class can lead their lives "normally."

This same situation applies even to the energy situation as a whole. It is the rich class in this country, the conspicuous consumers, the luxury lovers, who waste the most energy with their frost-free Amanas which use 60 percent more energy than the conventional refrigerator. It is the rich class which uses automatic dishwashers and have a second or third family car. But it is the poor and have-nots who consume far less energy, yet are being required to pay more than their share for necessities.

The problem inherent in the proposals so far to deal with the fuel shortages is that they are being implemented too late and with too little effect on the total energy question. Concerned citizens have been clamoring for many years that if we continued our energy-wasteful ways, we would be faced with severe shortages in our natural resources. But too few listened. Rather than taking preventative measures to deal with the problem before it affects us, government officials wait until the crisis is breathing down our necks. When will we learn? When the public chooses wiser persons to teach, plan and lead.

The Energy Crisis and Its Impact upon the Low-Income and Black Community in America, Speech, November 29, 1982

Nature of the Problem

The present situation presents a confusing array of facts for the average American consumer. Fuel oil prices have for the most part stabilized between 1981 and 1982—and in certain areas of the country have even slightly reduced. The cost of electric utilities continues to rise at a gradual rate of somewhere between 4 percent and 10 percent as it has since 1975. On the other hand, the cost of natural gas has risen approximately 5 percent over 1980 levels and by the end of the heating season of 1983 or at least the end of 1983, will have gone up another 25 percent.

There are many reasons underlying the present pricing situation. Between 1975 and 1981, the price of fuel oil quadrupled; a temporary glut in the fuel oil market has worked to maintain this price at its 1981 level. For electricity, the situation has remained basically stable over the last seven years. Increased fuel and labor costs have led to a gradual acceleration of prices. The rapid growth of natural gas cost is due primarily to the fact that natural gas has been "deregulated" by the federal government and the cost passed on immediately and abruptly to the consumers. If present policies continue, the natural gas cost will probably accelerate at the same rate, i.e. 25 percent, for the next two to three years until it reaches a parity with fuel oil prices.

All of these temporary price adjustments, however, should be put in the context of a basic understanding of the situations with fossil fuels, both in the United States and in the world. Clearly, the amount of available natural gas and oil is decreasing and recent discoveries have not led to appreciable findings in terms of the world supply. In the United States the amount of gas and oil available is clearly at one of its lowest ebbs. On the other hand, a great deal of coal exists. Given the present situation and the inability for the flexible uses provided by coal, there has not been a wholesale shift to this fuel. In addition, problems caused by the polluting aspects of coal have greatly retarded the use of this fuel.

The options for replacement of oil and gas and/or more extensive use of coal have not been seriously developed in recent years. The present [Ronald] Reagan administration has, in effect, ceased to invest in alternative sources of energy such as solar, wind, coal gasification, tidal generation of electricity and/or other forms of fuel. A philosophy of "conversion through price" has been prevalent and all indications are that more extensive exploration of oil and gas will not occur in the near future.

The overall result appears to be a limited supply of gas and oil, the continuation of gas and oil as the prevalent fuels and increased or at least a stable high cost for these fuel sources.

The high cost of fuel has had a deleterious effect on the nation's economy; the increased cost of energy has led to overall increases in cost production. In addition, high energy cost has had a severe impact on the consumer since more and more of his/her income is used for that source; this impact has been more strongly felt in the northeast and midwest sections of the country where not only is more fuel used but the money expended for fuel quickly leaves this section of the country and returns to the "producing states" of the west and southwest.

Clearly, the most severely and immediately impacted group has been the low income consumer. With heating and utility costs accounting for somewhere between 30 percent and 40 percent of the average household's income at least during the winter months, the energy crisis has put upon low income communities a burden which they are unable to bear. Given this situation, there has been a national response to deal with the energy problems of low income persons. The extent of the impact upon the low-income and minority community can be shown from some examples from Milwaukee, Wisconsin:

A. Low income households are spending 40 percent to 50 percent of their income . . . during the winter months for fuel cost and utilities. Obviously, the lower income, the greater portion of the family budget that heating and utility costs accounts for. Since 30 percent of the Black population and approximately 20 percent of the Hispanic and Native American population in Milwaukee are in poverty, the overall impact of the high utility cost on these households is indeed greater.

B. Due to the lack of readily available income, many low-
   income households are required to pay cash on delivery
   for oil and cannot receive oil until they have such cash available. The result is interruption in heating service for low
   income persons. During 1982, some 2,500 households were
   forced to seek emergency assistance payments to either return heating to their homes or to avoid a crisis of running
   out of fuel oil.

   The cash on delivery approach also has some negative impacts such as buying oil in small quantities so that the price
   per gallon is up to $.20 higher than were a person to buy 150
   gallons or more; the payment of an additional $25 for turn-on
   charges once heat has gone off.

C. Dangers to health and safety due to low temperatures, the
   negative impacts of which are especially strenuous upon older
   adults and very young children.

D. An increase in utility disconnections among low income persons prior to this winter, i.e. the winter of 1982–83; some
   4,500 gas users were disconnected for lack of paying arrear-
   ages. They therefore entered the heating season without any
   heating source for their home.

   In Milwaukee as in other communities, the high cost of energy is creating innumerable problems. Those immediately
   and most harshly impacted are low income persons. They are
   unable to obtain adequate energy and/or if they do, they obtain it with a price, both in terms of the actual cost for the fuel
   and for the overall impact it has on their households.

Current Programs to Assist with Energy Problems

Prior to 1980, the programs designed to assist the low-income households
were for the most part concentrated in the Community Services Administration, a federal agency which is now defunct. In 1980, the final transfer
of weatherization activities to the Department of Energy occurred and the
Low Income Energy Assistance Program, a program designed to assist with
emergency needs and to provide financial aid payments to low income

households, was transferred to the Department of Health and Social Services. The programs for energy education and for energy advocacy were for all intent and purpose eliminated. While the weatherization program was transferred to the Department of Energy, its budget was also reduced from $200 million to approximately $125 million nation-wide. Such a reduction occurred despite considerable Congressional and Senatorial debate and controversy.

On the other hand, the Low Income Energy Assistance Program became a full-fledged national program. For the 1980–81 year, $1.4 billion was appropriated nationally. For 1981–82, approximately $1.875 billion was appropriated and for 1982–83 approximately $1.85 billion has been appropriated. This program, which is strongly in place and run primarily through the state governments, seeks to assist low-income persons with their home heating bills and also to provide crisis assistance.

In this regard, however, it should be noted that the program also allows for 25 percent of the funds provided for energy assistance to be transferred to other programs; 10 percent for energy conservation, primarily weatherization, and 15 percent to other social services programs, i.e. those formerly funded under Title XX.

Some Policy Perspectives and Suggested Recommendations

Present energy policy in the United States with perhaps the exception of the Low Income Energy Assistance Program does not seem to be designed to meet the needs of the low income community either in terms of energy use or in terms of employment opportunities for low income persons. Perhaps the major change in energy policy under the Reagan administration has been a clear switching from conservation and a reliance upon price to cause savings. Funding has not been provided in this area in any extensive way and efforts are now under way to eliminate weatherization as a federal program. In addition, alternative energy, research and demonstration, has for the most part been eliminated, except for those areas which relate to nuclear and in most cases defense applications. Also energy education and immediate application of alternative technologies has been eliminated from federal policy.

In attempting to develop a policy related to the low-income community, the following considerations should be made.

A. A policy of conservation would not only assist the low income community in terms of saving energy in the household but could have very positive effects in terms of creating employment opportunities.

B. Much of the energy conservation work requires labor intensive and moderate to low skilled persons to carry out the activity. Such opportunities are especially crucial to many of the persons in the low income and particularly the minority community. The conservation of energy would not only assist the national government in maintaining its energy use down but would also have very positive effects in terms of providing employment and necessary revenue to the government to continue its other efforts. The Low Income Energy Assistance Program which has now taken a place as part of federal statutes, should clearly be continued. It offers the only major source of revenue to assist low income persons.

However, in this regard, there appears to be a wide range of the use of the funds provided by the federal government. The Low Income Energy Assistance Program is now one of seven "block grants" provided by the federal government. Many states have utilized the money to assist low income persons in some proportion to the cost of energy while others have tried to hold down their costs and transfer energy funds from it . . . to offset federal cuts in other areas; for example, in social services. Such usages, while to a limited extent being reasonable, also have decreased the amount of energy assistance made available to low income persons.

C. More extensive energy education should be available to low income persons. While a great deal of controversy surrounds the issue as to whether low income persons should be forced to conserve, it is clear that at least those persons should be given the option to conserve energy where appropriate and where such energy conservation could assist them without endangering their health and safety. The elimination of energy conservation from the list of federally funded programs

along with the other reduction in funding and educational
and social service areas has resulted in a great deal of elimination on this item. Also, the temporary "glut" of availability of
energy has in some ways lulled the consuming public into not
taking conservation steps.

D. Protection of low income persons against unwarranted price
increased. When a federal policy of protection of conservation
through cost is put into place, those who have no available resources are clearly the most in jeopardy. Such is the case with
the low income population. While their use may be low, the
increased price may force them into situations where they
cannot afford an adequate amount of fuel or utilities. If conservation through pricing has occurred, some fail-safe mechanism must be in place so that the rights of low income
persons are protected.

E. The low income and minority community should take an active interest in energy policy. Since a disproportionate number of low income persons are minority, particularly Black,
Hispanic and Native American, it is critical that elected officials look at energy policy from at least two vantage points:
the necessity of solid energy policy to protect the health and
safety and the economic development and employment opportunities which energy policy can offer.

If the low and minorities community can unite around a
conservation policy which protects the low-income person
and assures that their basic needs are met, it can have an important impact upon the direction of policy in our country.

9

PRESS AND PRIVACY RIGHTS

RIGHT TO PRIVACY, PRESS RELEASE, WISCONSIN ASSEMBLY, JANUARY 27, 1972

A strong right to privacy law which in most instances would require government agencies to notify a person about all records it has on him has been proposed by State Representative Lloyd A. Barbee (D-Milwaukee-6).

"We live in a time when government is increasing its files with information about the private lives of people," Barbee said. "Whether it is the US Army, the FBI, the CIA, or local police forces, government surveillance is becoming as common as it is in communist and fascist countries.

"Now all Americans are potential victims of these snoopers, eavesdroppers, picture takers, and file keepers," Barbee stated.

"The complacent, non-revolutionary suburbanite can someday be the object of government spying. He too can have this information used against him for whitemail or blackmail purposes. He can also find himself blocked from employment and advancement based on a file or dossier containing inaccurate and/or irrelevant information about his person.

"But the new American spy apparatus, directed against its own citizens, concentrates mainly on the loud critics of American society, the people who want to change the system including the spy apparatus.

"And these critics usually happen to be social activists, many of them civil rights and Black freedom fighters. At the moment, these people, these critics of society, are trailed, photographed and spied on secretly by police forces. It's not deserved, it's not right, it's not American.

"And so I have introduced a bill that would order government agencies to advise persons of the records it has on him in its investigatory files.

"Further, the surveillance agency could not disclose that information without that person's permission. A record would have to be kept of all persons who inspect the records. And finally, any individual may examine his own records and make supplement comments of a corrective or protesting nature.

"In short, this measure seeks to make people aware that the Federal Bill of Rights is still in force."

Divorce Proceedings, Press Release, Wisconsin Assembly, January 27, 1972

A bill that would speed up divorce proceedings and the remarriage process for divorced people has been introduced by State Representative Lloyd A. Barbee (D-Milwaukee-6).

"This bill reflects my view that we have too much state interference in private lives, too many laws restricting an individual's freedom," Barbee said.

"At the present time, the attorney for the person suing for divorce must wait sixty days between the time he serves a summons on the defendant notifying him or her of the suit and the time he serves the complaint outlining the alleged grounds for separation or divorce.

"In addition, once a divorce is granted, the divorced persons must wait one year before they can remarry.

"Now all this makes a silly, oppressive law. The sixty-day wait between summons and complaint is unnecessary. And the one year wait before remarriage is an outrageous restriction on a person's freedom.

"It not only discriminates against divorced people but against people who have never been married. In either case, one person may be pregnant, an even stronger reason to wipe out the one-year wait and let people marry when they want to."

CONFLICTS WITH THE PRESS, LLOYD A. BARBEE
1982 MANUSCRIPT

My difficulties with the press as an elected official were relatively minor when one considers that many of my civil rights activities were covered regularly. After having to fight to get a letter published which criticized the establishment of a community action agency by the Mayor of Milwaukee which did not permit the poor to select their own representatives, I ceased writing letters to the editor, or Op-Ed articles.

The Black press in Wisconsin was consistently sympathetic and supportive of my legislative and community efforts. On several occasions when reporters from both the Black and white press covered speeches which I made, the printed stories looked as though I had made two speeches. The stories in the white press would lead readers to conclude that I was an iconoclast zealot, baiting whites. The stories in the black press would lead readers to conclude that I was telling a predominantly white audience something and they were refusing to listen.

The last flap that I had with the Milwaukee establishment press centered around their refusal to carry a story in which I criticized McDonald's Restaurant for charging 5 cents more for its hamburgers sold in my district than in the rest of Milwaukee.

My district was predominantly Black and poor. I retaliated by refusing to act on a press shield bill which was in the Judiciary Committee which I chaired. The press responded throughout the state pointing out the need for a shield law and either criticized me for tying a First Amendment freedom of speech privilege and news reporters shield proposals together with the price of hamburgers or requested that I be a good friend and release the bill, arguing that the news reporters and the public of the state of Wisconsin and the entire United States are being hurt every day . . . carry the story of the nickel discriminatory increase, while the state-wide press had given ample publicity to my concerns about this discrimination to my constituents.* I finally released the shield bill and we all lived unhappily thereafter.

---

* A line of text is missing in the document here.

Two of my weekly articles that drew the largest number of letters from people outside the state were the ones dealing with Hoover's death, which began, "The runt shall grunt no more," and the shooting of [Alabama Governor George] Wallace by Arthur Bremer, a Milwaukee native.

Writers who identified themselves as black were complimentary; writers who identified themselves as white were condemnatory. I'm as firm in my opinion now on these two incidents as I was then.

Another of my articles which capped enimity on a continuing basis is the one relating to Handley's [Daniel Hanley] appointment at Marquette University. He was on leave at the time from the *Milwaukee Journal*, our largest monopoly newspaper entity in Wisconsin, serving as public relations writer for our state Attorney General [Robert W. Warren], who was appointed a U.S. District Judge. Mr. Handley was being considered for a position at Marquette for blacks and other minorities. Handley didn't get the position, for which he was patently unqualified, but he did return to the *Milwaukee Journal* as an investigative reporter.

In 1976, he masterminded a story implying that I falsified some hours which were reportedly spent on the public interest school desegregation law suit. The truth is that I underreported the time and expenses spent on that lawsuit, covering a period of about 16 years at that time. This so-called investigative reporter is still engaged in moonshine.

NEWS SHIELD, LEGISLATIVE COMMENT, JANUARY 19, 1973

We've finally begun consideration on some important proposals this legislative session that will help to insure the rights of many Wisconsin citizens.

The Committee on Judiciary will be reviewing four such proposals in its committee hearings on Tuesday, January 23. The proposed bills would establish the state's first shield law for newsmen.

Three bills which are competing for the shield law would grant newsmen full privileges for protecting their information and sources from disclosure to any government body or person. The law would make no exceptions to the rule, which has been the problem with most shield laws in other states.

As chairman of the Committee on Judiciary, I am in total support of the proposal without any reservations. My support for the bill is not only for civil libertarian reasons, but also because most newspapers are lacking in good investigatory reporting. One of the reasons for the lack has been the pressures on news staffs as a result of the recent jailings of newsmen for refusing to disclose their sources.

Not only has the White House been managing the news through spoon-feeding, manipulating and intimidation of the news media, but courts and other branches of government have also pressured the press. One of the methods that have been used and abused is the grand jury proceedings and the threat of contempt charges for those who refuse to reveal their information and news sources.

I am ever mindful of the bad publicity which certain Black groups have received, especially the Black Panther Party, not to mention the unjust accusations which the Milwaukee establishment press has directed toward this excellent organization and leaders in its past issues.

Hopefully, the shield law proposals will change the situation, giving newsmen the freedom to report in an investigatory manner without the fear of reprisal. In this respect, perhaps, we'll have newspapers which would use means at hand for countering unjust criticisms by the private and governmental power structure against persons and groups who work for just changes.

The other bill to be discussed in Tuesday's hearing would eliminate and prohibit distinctions in the Wisconsin statutes between persons based on sex. The proposals would also make statute changes which would extend more rights and privileges to women.

As a beginning for providing the rights to all individuals, this bill is a needed piece of legislation. Nevertheless, we must strive for much more. No concerted effort has been made yet to erase racism from the wording and implications of Wisconsin statutes. The changes to eliminate distinctions of race, sex and sexual preferences are long overdue.

Let us work to effect such changes vigorously and expeditiously.

10

NATIONAL FIGURES

MALCOLM X, LLOYD A. BARBEE 1982 MANUSCRIPT

I first saw Malcolm X at the University of Wisconsin Memorial Union Grand Ballroom early in 1962. He spoke of white blue-eyed devils. The white man was destructive of all that was good and an enemy of humanity. The audience was predominantly white. During the question and answer period, he insulted young students of the Right and Left indiscriminately.

I considered myself a human being seeking more justice for those who were denied it. A one world, one race person. It was astounding for me to see an overflowing crowd in a crystal chandeliered ballroom applauding the man Mike Wallace and CBS TV featured in a 1959 program called "The Hate That Hate Produced," and *Life Magazine* depicted as a new leader of Elijah Muhammad's Nation of Islam, better known to me as the Black Muslims. I could not decide whether Malcolm X was a serious separatist or shocker performing before and/or on masochists in public. His religious expressions reminded me of negative, hate-filled sermons preached by Protestants. His doctrine was black supremacy. His charisma was direct and his appearance without extraneous gestures or grandiloquence. After his speech I remember telling a good friend how ignorant and narrow his myths were and how divisive his religion was. The only logical solution to the issues posed by him were to establish a Black Nation within the USA or mass immigration to Africa. Both solutions were antithetical to my views of resolving racism here.

I was in Flint, Michigan, doing some work for NAACP and was invited to meet with Malcolm X and some other Black people of influence and affluence at some Bourgeoisie home. Malcolm X arrived at the appointed time, spoke of the "need of unity," an all-out strategy against racism, and the like. My inviter, a young attorney, attacked Malcolm X as a Black separatist sponsor of violence, etc. Malcolm X quietly, systematically explained his position without becoming defensive, rude, or negative. I was won over by Malcolm X that night.

The next time I saw Malcolm X was in Washington at the NAACP National Convention. CORE [Congress of Racial Equality], NAACP, SNIC [SNCC; Student Nonviolent Coordinating Committee], SCLC [Southern Christian Leadership Conference] and others were planning the March on Washington in the Stadler Hotel. He was ostracized from the meeting and stood alone in the foyer. I told my cousin Sloan Williams that I was going over to greet Malcolm X. He agreed to join me. We met Malcolm X and visited with him briefly. He said he just stopped by to see what was going on and wished the convention and meeting well.

He shook our hands and called us brothers. As we left I was struck by his modesty and dignity which was real. I noticed his eagle eyes. While he appeared to be alone in the hall, he moved his head from side to side and then front center and left to right. When he spoke, a bull in the china closet appeared.

Of course Malcolm X was not invited to speak at the March on Washington nor did he invite himself. As a State Planner and Marcher on Washington, I was delighted to hear that Malcolm X said that while Martin Luther King Jr. was having his dreams, Blacks in Harlem were having nightmares.

When Malcolm X spoke at the Group on Advanced Leadership [GOAL] early November 1963 in Detroit, I began to pay even more attention when he said, "America's problem is us. We're her problem, the only reason she has a problem, she doesn't want us here. . . . What you and I need to do is begin to forget our differences." I recommend listening to the recording of this speech. It is powerful even today.

Shortly after the GOAL speech, President John Kennedy was assassinated, and Malcolm X made his comment about chickens coming home to roost to the press. As a result, Elijah Muhammad silenced him.

MUHAMMAD ALI, LEGISLATIVE COMMENT, JULY 15, 1971

On July 14, I introduced a motion under Joint Rule 26 that reads as follows:

"Whereas, Muhammad Ali refused military induction April 28, 1957, because of his belief in the Nation of Islam faith; Whereas, Muhammad Ali was prosecuted by the U.S. Justice Department as not having sincere religious beliefs; Whereas, Muhammad Ali was convicted by an all-white jury in Houston, Texas; Whereas, the World Boxing Association stripped the undefeated champion of his title; Whereas, for 3½ years Muhammad Ali was barred from fighting; Whereas, the U.S. Supreme Court unanimously overturned Muhammad Ali's conviction June 28, 1971; Now, therefore, under Joint Rule 26, commend Muhammad Ali for continuing to fight for his religious beliefs, for behaving like a champion of life and his race, as well as his sport and wishing him well."

After this resolution was read State Representative Gerald Greider (R–LaCrosse–1) moved to reject the motion and after he was informed that such a motion was improper because you can't reject a motion, State Representative Earl McEssy (R–Fond du Lac–1) moved to table the motion. This motion succeeded on a vote of 67 to 32.

In my remarks to the Assembly prior to tabling the motion, I urged the Assembly not to deviate from its tradition of commending individuals and events recommended by their fellow legislators. No more outstanding person has ever been congratulated by a legislative body. Muhammad Ali's principles and courage to say "no" was vindicated by the U.S. Supreme Court. I specifically indicated that Muhammed Ali deserved commendation for his principle techniques which he used to maintain his religious beliefs, the consistency of his fighting in the ring and his clean living.

Nevertheless, the Assembly did table the motion for commendation and then went on to commend cowboy riders and a rodeo that was held last weekend. They must have known that cowboys use spurs on the horses and inflict other physical and psychological harm on rodeo animals in their continuing attempts to prove man's dominance over the "animal world."

Not only are priorities out of wack, but so is political morality and expediency. May the Great White Hope forever fail!

J. Edgar Hoover, Legislative Comment, May 16, 1972

The runt will grunt no more!

J. Edgar Hoover died in his sleep last week. While the FBI bulletin issued Tuesday morning stated that Hoover died of natural causes, it is interesting to note that the specific cause of death was not determined, or at least none was given. So in the death of Chief Hoover, the FBI continued to live with the same contradictions he had established during his reign. He increased the size of his agency and expanded its activities from investigation to surveillance and killing. From all this "we the people" must insist that if the FBI remains its Chief must be accountable to us, the US people.

Many former critics of Hoover and his personal views on crime prevention detection, surveillance methods and policies as well as his fight against political activists both foreign and domestic have proceeded to eulogize and praise this narrow minded, pig-headed, senile septuagenarian.

I do not believe in fighting dead men. But neither do I adhere to the superstitious notion of not speaking the truth as I see it. While there is death there is hope.

With the timely death of the old FBI chief, who died with his badge in his hand amid reports of illegal dossiers on celebrities' sex lives for the bedtime entertainment of Presidents, I have reason to feel that there is faint hope for improvement in this agency's philosophy of justice. While Mr. Gray, a political crony of President Nixon, offers no long-range improvement, at least he is not an immutable and unchallengeable institution. He is actually uttering good rhetoric for the time being.

With Hoover's passing I am also led to wonder whether anyone has delved into his voluminous personal files and removed the white male, extortionist material which kept him securely in office long beyond his usefulness to a free and open democratic country's principles of law, order and justice. I hope that the files were burned or put into ITT's [International Telephone and Telegraph] paper shredder before Nixon's political operatives were able to get their hands on them. With his personal hatchet man in charge now, the short run future looks rather grim for blacks, for the peace movement, for political progressives and activists, in short, for decent people in general.

While his gross cadaver putrefied under the Capitol dome, profaning President Lincoln's bier, no doubt many Washington VIPs were heaving sighs of relief. Perhaps they will take steps now to insure that we never see the concentration of so much secret police power in the hands of one man again.

A good first step would be the abolition of both the CIA and the FBI. Short of that, which I concede is unlikely, Congress should make the Civil Rights Act apply to the FBI as well as to the rest of the country. The employees of the FBI should be a representative cross sample of the entire country, not just white, Protestant America. Finally, a white woman has been assigned as an FBI Special Agent. For too long, these sado-masochistic chauvinists, racists and jingos have gone unchallenged.

These are goals that the black movement and other activists should push for. The FBI, under a director who has read and believes in the US Constitution, must become a humane organization with a concept of fair play and freedom for all.

In Hoover's 47-year reign, he did not increase his stature, but he did increase his girth. He often denounced Black liberation but seldom showed leadership in solving the astronomical number of anti-civil rights bombings and murders. FBI agents are too friendly and sympathetic to white bigoted oppressors to effectively fight them.

George Wallace, Legislative Comment, May 23, 1972

One could say it was inevitable, only a matter of time before a bigot and reactionary was shot down. After the rash of political assassinations in the 1960's, not to mention the numerous anonymous blacks and whites killed trying to change an oppressive political system, it was almost anticlimactic that a bullet should find its target in the gut of such a lightning rod for hate and divisiveness.

The ironic thing about previous assassinations, of prominent and anonymous alike, is that nearly all had preached and practiced nonviolence in seeking change. While Wallace had never openly preached violent methods, nevertheless his attitude and manner condoned and invited violence.

Recently he had taken to styling himself a new "populist," as a spokesman for the common man. This was a clear attempt to hide his bigotry and racism under a blanket of respectable rhetoric. But his rhetoric is all that changed: From openly opposing black quality education to simply opposing Bussing, the result is the same—segregation and racism. It is only his fellow racists and the establishment press who are beguiled by such nonsense.

Whether it is committed by guys with white hats or guys with black hats, it is unfortunate that violence is chosen as the solution.

But the incompetence of such attacks as the attempt on Governor Wallace's life last week, if indeed that is what it was, serve only to make living martyrs out of vile demagogues. Wallace lives with paralysis in the nether portion of his anatomy. Diarrhea of the mouth testify to Wallace's mental ossification and flamboyant compensation of an inferiority complex. Remember his reaction to the Sunday Birmingham bombing of a Black church which left children killed, Selma marches, etc.

If it is true that Governor Wallace's assailant was a Milwaukeean, then he behaved in keeping with the Milwaukee character—always missing but often coming close. Perhaps the would-be killers (there must have been more than one based on ballistic reports alone) succeeded ironically. Relative immobility and long suffering rather than a quick death may humble Wallace and teach him some lessons in humanity which Blacks learn at birth and live through daily.

PRESIDENT RICHARD NIXON, LEGISLATIVE COMMENT, MAY 9, 1973

President Nixon's public explanation of the Watergate affair last Monday night is undoubtedly true to his hallmark. (How else do you think he is called Tricky Dick?)

After having knowledge of the facts surrounding the break-in and conspiracy at Watergate for about a year, he finally decided to take the responsibility for the unethical, criminal espionage and cover-up which occurred, but without taking the blame. This is undoubtedly a contradiction and a vain hope not to bear the shame.

Worse yet is that, during his speech, Nixon made a number of innuendoes implying that such criminal behavior goes on within both parties. Essentially, he is attempting to destroy the credibility of his opponents for an ounce of redeeming grace of his own corrupt administration.

Some of the middle class public reaction to the whole Watergate affair, however, has been that of indifference. Some say it doesn't affect them. Watergate was just another political strategy. Wake up, America.

When people in power use every means at their disposal, including the supposedly "nonpartisan" organizations such as the CIA, the FBI, personal staff, and the U.S. Attorney General's office, to crush their opponents, then the entire democratic process is undermined.

The Nixon administration believes that it can do anything it wants and then deny its intentions, replacing true reasons and motivations with some type of artificial justification, hoping that the majority of people will fall for it. This has gone on for five years. The Watergate revelation proves to be the destruction of this strategy.

It is my hope that people in this country require the President to bear the blame, not only for the nefarious activities of his personally selected campaign committee during the actual burglary, but also of the large scale cover-up perpetrated by his administration. Nixon's opposition is growing, and his attempts to crush this has gone deeper than partisan gamesmanship. It has even reached into personal lives.

The administration's prosecution of Daniel Ellsberg is an example of this. Ellsberg's psychiatrist had his office burglarized by Nixonites for the purpose of getting more information for the Pentagon Papers prosecution. Even worse, the Federal administration offered the federal judge presiding in the case the position of FBI Director. This offer was made not long before Nixon presented his speech before a nationwide audience. It seems likely, too, that this deal was made with the President's knowledge.

The Nixon war against political opposition has reached into every part of our country. Black militants in ghettos as well as members of the Black bourgeoisie have been intimidated, jailed, crucified, and killed by the administration's tactics. Rural dwellers, white radical student elements, and most of the less represented groups in our society have felt the brunt of the Nixon administration's antics. Crass white racist middle class Americans will ruin us all unless decent people act wisely and rapidly to clean house and disinfect the vermin.

The federal government is going backward in its attempts to meet the needs of all its people. It is ignorance, arrogance, stinginess, selfishness, and an unwillingness on the part of people to become involved with life and death issues which has aided this trend.

When the majority of this country is not cutting its own throat under "law and order," it is giving weapons to the White House for the murder of democracy. I hope this is perfectly clear. Think Impeachment. Act now!

VICE PRESIDENT SPIRO AGNEW, LEGISLATIVE COMMENT, SEPTEMBER 1, 1972

Vice President Agnew, that verbose peddler of disapproval, has indicated his campaign tactics and rhetoric will be somewhat different this campaign year. The Vice President says his mood will be more conciliatory and that he will no longer be the President's meat-axe man.

However, through his appearance on nationwide television last week, the nation's number two executive became a meathead when he lambasted Black leaders in the U.S.

For the second time in his four-year rise to national fame, Agnew has advised Blacks that they can learn a lesson from their "brothers" in Africa. It is no surprise to me that Agnew and other whites feel they are in the best position to advise Blacks on the appropriate methods for liberation from the evils of racism and poverty which the whites themselves perpetuate.

The Vice President criticized U.S. Black leaders for their "querulous complaints and constant recriminations against the rest of society." Claiming they do not reflect the real opinion of the Black community, Agnew charged the leaders with constantly harping on the inadequacies and just as constantly overlooking the constructive changes.

He further states that Blacks in this country could learn much from secondary Black leaders in Africa. What the Vice President is actually saying is despite the plight of Blacks, despite their oppression, and despite all the broken promises, they should keep their chin up and look on the bright side. In the past, Agnew has not hesitated in citing specific individuals to support his criticism of the press, student activists or the poor. However, in a departure from previous haranguing, he refused to be specific in this case and would not name the Blacks to whom he was referring.

The former governor of Maryland surely makes a fitting running mate for Nixon, who has nixed more programs and progress for Blacks than anyone. It will be interesting to see how recently purchased Black mouths and bodies will explain the new Agnew-Nixon team to garner Black votes.

Perhaps a moral can be drawn here. If you are a white in general, you don't have to be for any Black in particular—lump 'em all!

11

INTERNATIONAL CIVIL RIGHTS

COMMUNIST CHINA, LEGISLATIVE COMMENT, OCTOBER 29, 1971

I have felt since I was a student that Communist China should be recognized by the "United" States government. I therefore think it appropriate to comment at this time on the current reaction and overreaction to the recent U.N. decision to admit Communist China to the U.N. while removing Chiang Kai-shek's exiled military government from that body.

It is important that people recognize realities of government. One of these realities is that Chiang Kai-shek, who is supported by the United States, and his military government, which supposedly represents the Chinese people, in fact have been installed and forced upon the people of Taiwan.

One clear explanation for the U.N. vote was the heavy handed boss tactics used by the United States in an attempt to force the adoption of a two China policy. America will have to rely on right not might in the future.

More importantly I think that the world, represented in the U.N., has finally recognized that the Chinese people threw out the corrupt Chiang Kai-shek government years ago and the true government of the Chinese people are on the mainland where it belongs.

A legitimate motion to the U.N. that should be made and sponsored by the United States government is for Taiwan to be admitted to the U.N. and represent itself. The Taiwanese are aborigines and constitute 80 percent (12,000,000) of the Formosan population.

British Occupation of Ireland, Legislative Comment, February 17, 1972

Two weeks ago I co-authored Assembly Joint Resolution 150. This measure calls for the immediate withdrawal of all British occupation forces from Northern Ireland.

By a curious political circumstance, I found myself actively allied with several Assembly members who had previously opposed my straight-forward position on Black liberation and individual rights. This alliance came about because my co-authors are white, American-Irish and proud.

They are now experiencing, if indirectly through their Irish brothers and sisters the kind of oppression and persecution that American blacks and Indians have lived with for centuries. Perhaps they will be able to summon more empathy through this experience and eventually become radicalized.

The British army was called in to Ulster in 1969 to protect the rights of the Catholic local minority. As is the case with too many similar situations, the liberator became the oppressor in a very short time. To my mind, the efforts of the Irish Catholic local minority in Ulster to retaliate, following the failure of other attempts to solve their problem, are entirely justified.

In this struggle we can see many parallels to the Black liberation movement in America during the sixties:

- The police and the army have joined forces to intimidate peaceful and legitimate demonstrations—thus perpetuating violence and counter violence.

- The authorities have resorted to summary arrests on quick flimsy or non-existent legal grounds.

- Illegal searches are commonplace.

- Illegal seizures frequently follow.

- Unlawful detention of hundreds of dissidents is standard. Silent and hostile press calls civil rights activists "terrorists."

- Singing of "We Shall Overcome" has become a symbol for Irish Free movement as it was for ours.

In one respect the old country—Britain—is ahead of the new—America. Their army has resorted to the wholesale suspension of civil rights in Ulster as they detain and intern hundreds of civil rights activists and protesters in concentration camps without trial or any vestige of due process. Since England is the birthplace of our system of civil rights and due process (which are frequently more theoretical than actual for Blacks and poor people), I am sorry to see this happen, although not surprised.

The name of the game is preservation of the status quo, and when that status quo is threatened all steps are taken by the establishment to maintain itself. Liberation and freedom fighters, while not necessarily imitating the oppressors, must wage their battles until the war ends in victory. The British may have taken a cue from their cousins in Canada, who slapped their country under martial law for six months as a result of the Quebec separatist movement's activities. Former United States Attorney General [John Newton] Mitchell and the D.C. police have tried the same thing on a small scale, herding thousands into a stadium during an end-the-war protest, simply because of the threat of changing the status quo slightly.

In light of these acts by the British, I understand why the Irish destroyed the British embassy in Dublin. I am pleased that they continue to take appropriate and unrelenting action against the enemies of freedom.

Some authors of the Resolution have agreed to wait until St. Patrick's Day to consider the measure. They did this without my consent. I object to waiting for a religious holiday to petition for the redress of grievance against human liberty and dignity as a publicity stunt.

VIOLENCE AND REPRESSION IN NORTHERN IRELAND, PRESS RELEASE, WISCONSIN ASSEMBLY, MARCH 9, 1972

In a recent Comment, I discussed the conditions of repression and violence in Northern Ireland. Contemporary colonialism continues to manifest itself throughout the world, often despite expressed opposition to world public opinion and the passage of laws supposedly freeing former colonies.

To some extent, colonialism and imperialism is evident on every continent. The U.S. in Asia. The USSR in Eastern Europe. Britain, Portugal, and Belgium in Africa.

All these instances of present-day colonialism stem from that unfortunate age of discovery concept known as hegemony. Hegemony is the sphere of influence within which one government is predominant over another or other countries. For example, throughout most of Eastern Europe, the Soviet Union is predominant; thus one refers to this area as the Soviet Union's Sphere.

Hegemony, however, does not simply mean political influence. Hegemony can be achieved—and frequently is—by the use of economic power. It is through this means that, despite nominally divesting themselves of their African colonies, such nations as Portugal, England, Belgium and the U.S. continue to control the destinies of millions of Black people.

The United Nations recently renewed their sanctions against the illegal regime of Rhodesian Dictator Ian Smith. Smith and a small white clique run the government of Rhodesia by force and terror, subjugating the Black majority to the force of their will.

However, by an act of Congress, despite the sanctions of the U.N. against trade with Rhodesia, we continue to import chrome from Smith's fiefdom, justifying it by calling it a "strategic material." I have difficulty considering the cosmetic trimming on automobiles and refrigerators, both toy and real, as anything short of superfluous and irrelevant. But our government, itself not immune to economic influence, brands it "strategic" and subsidizes a corrupt, racist regime.

Despite the continuing racial problems in America, we defy our own people and world public opinion in trading with Smith. This is tempting fate twice. First, by giving reasonable cause for Black protest on racial grounds. Second, by needlessly compounding our already overwhelming solid waste disposal problem.

Our coming Black National Convention in Gary [Indiana] will try to come to grips with the realities of the international situation.

The incessant pattern of white exploitation of Black people and their resources must be challenged by this country at home and abroad. We must begin to move towards solidarity with other western-white-oppressed peoples as well, especially American Indians, Spanish-speaking minorities, and Asians.

The roots of this problem are insidiously deep. They subtly and sometimes ingratiatingly pervade every stratum of American life. The extent to which this is true was demonstrated after the recent state black convention.

I accompanied several other delegates to a restaurant in the black community. There happened to be a Portuguese wine listed on the menu. A black elected official from Madison requested that the tavern owner remove this wine from his stocks.

It was our feeling that to buy this wine or sell it in the Black community is to give tacit support to the repression and exploitation practiced by Portuguese whites in Angola and Mozambique. So in the way it was necessary to boycott grapes and lettuce to help Cesar Chavez. It is necessary to apply economic sanctions against Bigoted Imperialist Nations and boycott products which represent the subsidizing of humiliation and suffering for our brothers in other countries.

FAMINE IN WEST AFRICA, LEGISLATIVE COMMENT, JULY 26, 1973

The famine disaster currently affecting large portions of West Africa impels us to act quickly. Unless assistance is brought to these African nations, an estimated six to ten million human lives will be lost by October.

I introduced Assembly Joint Resolution 104 urging that the federal government take immediate steps to assist the people of these African nations in alleviating mass starvation. Support is necessary from all parts of our country to get our federal government and the private sector to assist in solving the food and water shortages in Western Africa.

African nations most affected by the famine are part of the ever-creeping Sahara Desert, the southern fringe of the Sahara Desert. These Sahelian countries include Mauritania, Mali, Senegal, Upper Volta, Niger and Chad. Worse yet, the disaster is seriously affecting other parts of the continent. By going further south into Africa, the disaster is spreading into Nigeria, Ethiopia, Ivory Coast, and Ghana, to name just a few.

What is being done by the federal government so far?

Worrying more about low fund appropriations than human lives, Nixon has committed only $24 million in relief to these impoverished

African nations. An additional 450,000 tons of grain have also been provided as relief. This is not enough.

The amount of U.S. aid to Africa represents only 10 percent of the total
foreign aid budget. This money, however, goes only to 10 of the 41 African
nations. At the same time, the federal government provides approximately
$436 million to Portugal which uses these funds to butcher innocent Blacks
in Mozambique.

An additional $30–50 million is needed in West Africa to relieve the
general famine which the native people are experiencing there. Only the
U.S. government has the apparatus to provide immediate relief in the area.
If relief is not forthcoming, African people will drop like flies.

The African nations in the western portion of the continent have suffered through three consecutive years of drought. The rainy seasons have
not occurred as frequently or to the extent which has occurred in the past.

The people in this area thrive on cattle as the sole possession and chief
source of income. Yet millions of cattle have died. As cattle die, people will
die also. Mauritania and Mali have already lost 80% of their livestock and
cattle; Niger and Senegal have lost 50% of their herds. The crop production, which is off by thousands of tons, further adds to the problem of
starvation. Worse yet, much of the production is seed crops. Because of the
food shortages, this is being used as food instead of for planting purposes.
This means that next year, food shortages will multiply, and there will be
very few crops to harvest.

The physical climate has not been the only factor leading to famine in
West Africa. To see what has given rise to this human tragedy, we must
examine West Africa in its true political and economic picture. The murder
and forcible removal of many of its people, the establishment of racist,
bureaucratic governments which fail to meet the realities of the majority
peasant populations, the subdividing of its lands . . . all have contributed
to Africa's present state of economic poverty and downfall.

We need a program of massive action to demand that the U.S. government respond to this crisis. Direct assistance in the form of food, water,
and medical supplies is the first necessary item to halt the spread of death
and starvation. This, however, will only be a stop gap measure for solving
the overall problems existing in West Africa. Priorities in our country are
in desperate need of re-arrangement. It is time that we also begin an aid

program for the development of this impoverished land. The government and private enterprise have the materials. But the people must provide the impetus and support.

Write to your federal representatives calling for the passage of an amendment to the foreign aid bill which would make special provisions for relief and reconstruction of the Sahel region of Africa. Also urge your congressman to support the passage of a proposed amendment to the House Foreign Assistance bill now awaiting action which would permit U.S. funds to be used in the African nations most in need of assistance.

Private profiteers who raped, pillaged, and exploited human and natural resources of the African continent should make amends now, there.

VIETNAM WAR, PRESS RELEASE, WISCONSIN ASSEMBLY, APRIL 25, 1972

Below is the text of a resolution prepared by anti-Vietnam War demonstrators, drafted and processed through the Legislature in obtaining signatures of the Governor as well as 27 Representatives and 4 Senators:

> WHEREAS, President Nixon was elected in 1968 largely on the strength of his campaign promise to end the United States' involvement in the Vietnam war; and,
>
> WHEREAS, after more than 3 years of office, the President has not only failed to end our country's tragic military involvement in Southeast Asia, but has recently renewed the bombing of North Vietnam to an intensity which amounts to a major escalation of the United States military involvement; and,
>
> WHEREAS, without the continued presence of U.S. naval and air power in Southeast Asia, the Nixon administration's policy of Vietnamization would be a total failure; and,
>
> WHEREAS, public opinion at home and abroad is mounting in opposition to the President's dangerous re-escalation of the U.S. military effort in Vietnam; therefore,
>
> BE IT KNOWN, that the Governor and undersigned members of the Wisconsin State Legislature hereby memorialize the Congress

of the United States to prevent further American military involvement in Vietnam by refusing to appropriate funds for military operations in Vietnam, and,

BE IT KNOWN, that the Governor and undersigned state legislators urge the Congress to take immediate action to bring about a swift halt to all aerial and naval bombardment and demand an immediate withdrawal of all American troops and materiel from Indochina.

OLYMPICS, LEGISLATIVE COMMENT, SEPTEMBER 19, 1972

It should not be surprising to observers of the international scene that the games of the Twentieth Olympiad in Munich mirrored the problems and ills of the world.

It is ludicrous for serious-minded people to expect politics to be missing from the actions of nations represented at any international competition.

Munich was a fitting scene for prohibiting white Rhodesia from participating in the international sports events. Shades of Hitler would not have faced otherwise. After all that happened, Blacks from Africa and the United States came off well by high-lighting the evils or racism and the folly of nationalism throughout the world.

The former head of the International Olympic Committee, Avery Brundage, appears to have played the crucial role in banning from further Olympic competition two Blacks: Vince Mat[t]hews and Wayne Collett, both of the U.S.A. His reasoning behind the dismissal was that the pair did not stand at ramrod attention in deadly silence during the playing of *The Star-Spangled Banner*.

Flag worship and super-reverence for the U.S. National Anthem—which is based on an old English club song—is no test of patriotism. Collett and Mathews have no reason to apologize for their actions.

Fortunately, there are four years before the next round of Olympic contests. This should give promoters and organizers of the Olympics enough time to update the basic concept of the games starting with the tossing out of unreasonable and peculiar rules dealing with amateurism

versus professionalism: They and others should also be able to deal with
international issues such as racism and nationalism on a more forthright
and honest basis.

Because of the victories won by Blacks, the results of the September
12th primary are also deserving of some comment. The election of a black
Senator and another black representative is assured in this fall's general
Wisconsin election. The Black membership of the State Legislature will
thus increase from one to three.

Credit for this long overdue progress must go to those of us who worked
hard to remap the state's legislative districts to give blacks political power
at least proportional to their population in the state.

I have already given myself credit, but I would like to advise the readers
of this column of the special contribution made by two men: Frederick P.
Kessler, former State Assemblyman and now Milwaukee County Judge,
and retiring Senator Mark Lipscomb. Both played key roles in seeing that
"equal representation" and not solely party politics were the basis of the
new district boundaries.

It is one of the ironies of politics that one of the first political casualties
of the new districts was Senator Lipscomb himself. The price of progress
for some is often at the sacrifice of others.

DUAL CITIZENSHIP, LEGISLATIVE COMMENT, DECEMBER 28, 1972

A few points need to be stressed regarding the often made proposal to
grant dual citizenship to Blacks, a suggestion most recently voiced by
Roy Innis of the Congress on Racial Equality (CORE). The idea is to allow
Blacks in this country to be citizens of the United States and of Africa at
the same time.

The curious thing about Innis' proposal is not the idea itself but his
reaction to Jesse Jackson of PUSH [People United to Save Humanity, later
called People United to Serve Humanity]. Innis has complained that Jackson stole his suggestion. Jackson is apparently saying he made the proposal
more than two years ago.

At the same time, Innis has made several statements regarding the
fact that Black leaders are often named by white liberals. Additionally, he

is calling for a national convention of Black leaders to map strategy against some of the programs of the Nixon Administration.

It is highly regrettable that Innis and CORE are not sufficiently secure to realize that when another group accepts a so-called original proposal, this is the best form of flattery. Indeed, it is strange that all persons do not realize the truth regarding this proposal. From my viewpoint, dual citizenship for Blacks stems back to my own childhood, which is more than two years ago.

By the same token, it is not a new phenomenon that white liberals have been able to designate the leaders of the Black movement. Such Black leaders as Booker T. Washington, Innis and Jackson have been so designated by some whites, and not all Blacks. Being called a leader, however, does not make an individual a leader.

If an acknowledged leader chooses to fight with other Black leaders, any victory is relatively meaningless unless the Black community as a whole permits the so-called victor to represent them. The power for Blacks does not come from stand-ins or prima donnas but from the people themselves who need individual spokesmen or representatives who reflect their needs and aspirations.

My observations have convinced me that Blacks will tolerate strong leadership when it is human, efficient and benign. Cut-throat, bellicose, and mafia type leadership rarely progresses beyond a temporary handful of people.

I am mindful of the problems faced at this time by revolutionary, national cultist and evolutionary groups regarding Black needs. Their screaming, ranting and raving regarding whose idea has been pirated by whom is ironic. In one breath, they are calling for a strategy of togetherness and unity, in a national convention while on the other hand, they seem to be engaging in an exchange of hot air halitosis and ego trips. We need substance, not theatrics, to solve the problems faced by blacks.

The Bahamas' Independence, Legislative Comment, July 12, 1973

The Bahamas, an archipelago consisting of approximately 700 islands between Florida and the island of Haiti, became an independent nation on Tuesday. By becoming the world's 143rd sovereign country, the Bahamas ended more than 300 years of British rule and eventually white domination.

Change for independence became manifest when Lynden Pindling became prime minister of the Bahamas and leader of the majority Progressive Liberal Party in 1967. This was the first time that a Black was chosen to lead this country. Considering the fact that 85 percent of the island group's population is Black, it was about time.

Now that the July 10, Independence Day celebration is over, I cross my fingers in hopes that the country will now be able to deal with its economic development besides the promotion of white tourism. Pindling, it appears, is already on the road to solving the economic situation in the Bahamas. The new leader is planning on negotiating with Cuba about the new country's sea boundaries and fishing rights, as well as settling with foreign investments.

The prime minister of the Bahamas is also considering raising the rent on the U.S. government for the military bases which are situated on the islands. Because of past British-American relations, the U.S. government was getting off easy as far as reimbursing the Bahamas government for use of their land for military installations. Now, hopefully, the Bahamas will be able to settle for a more adequate reimbursement.

Racism, however, still exists in the Bahamas. A secessionist movement was started just prior to the island group's independence on the island of Abaco. Approximately 3,000 whites, comprising about half the population on the island, want to become a separate unit attached to the British Commonwealth. Some observers say that certain U.S. interests have come out in support of this move because of the fear that the islands will become a "second Cuba."

Critics of the Bahamas' government have charged that Pindling has been carrying out a "Blacks only" policy, especially in regard to employment. Government policy there bans the importation of foreign workers to perform jobs that Bahamians can do just as well. Previously, however, when the Bahamas were under white rule, the majority of Blacks were in a state of economic deprivation solely because very few native Bahamians were given decent employment opportunities. Most good jobs were taken over by foreign workers.

It is appropriate to congratulate Pindling for the liberal advances which he made within his political party and for the bloodless revolution resulting in the island group's independence. His accomplishments have done a great deal for making the country's future much more optimistic.

The [Associated Press] and Milwaukee papers say the Bahamas were discovered by Christopher Columbus. This I must note with wry curiosity. Considering that the islands were already inhabited around 1492, it would be more appropriate to say that Columbus discovered that he and the white western world were ignorant about geography and people. Some of his descendants still are.

Appendix A
Racial Discrimination in Housing
Film Transcript

Selected Scenes from Film Produced by Lloyd Barbee, Filmmaker Stuart Hanisch, and Photographer George Allez, 1962, Madison, Wisconsin

Miss G and Miss H stand in front of house by door. Door opens, woman is hidden by door.

MISS H: Hello. We are interested in renting the apartment upstairs, and we were wondering if the rental agent had been around.

MISS G: We had telephoned before and he was supposed to be here at 2:30.

MISS K: Oh, that was Mr. L—

MISS G: Is that—Oh—(laughs)

MISS K: I am sorry he isn't here

Girls turn and greet agent as he walks up.

MISS G: Hello.

MISS H: Hello there.

MR. L: Hello.

MISS G: My brother called before about our renting the apartment.

MR. L: Oh ya, ya. I'll see if I have the key

MISS K: Here.

MR. L: The key? Thank you, [first name].

MISS G: Thank you.

MR. L: Do you want to grab that key, [name]?

MR. M: Ya, I do. I'll see if—if it's—

MISS G: Could you tell me—

The girls go into the apartment with the agent.

NARRATOR #2: Although the girls were shown the apartment, they were later told that it could not be rented to them. The reason given by the landlord was that he had decided not to rent to single girls before he made the appointment to show them the apartment. Another couple then went out to see the same apartment.

Mr. and Mrs. C in studio with interviewer.

Exterior view of house in Scene 79.

INTERVIEWER: Two girls were turned down by a landlord who told them he did not want to rent to them. When you went to see this same apartment, what happened?

MR. C: We told him we were the couple who had called him earlier about the apartment and which he said it was still vacant and to come out and he would be glad to show it to us, but when we got there he called us over to his car and then he said that he was sorry, and he didn't think that he could accommodate us.

INTERVIEWER: He didn't say why?

Window of house with "For Rent" sign.

Detail of fence in front of above house.

Front door of house.

MR. C: Well he did, he said that he felt that the people in the community, uh, would complain and he didn't want any trouble about the people in the community. I asked him if he had, uh, if there had been any previous incidents of trouble in the area or had any negroes lived in the area for him to be able to make such a statement and uh—

MRS. C: He said there were no negroes living in the neighborhood.

INTERVIEWER: And so the apartment was not available to you?

Miss G and Miss H approach and enter office of apartment building.

MISS G: Hi! We are looking for—

NARRATOR #2: On Friday the girls were told that the office was closed. They could not see an apartment until the following Monday. However, a white couple called over the weekend and they were told to come right out. The manager who showed them through a vacant apartment told them that it was no trouble showing it on a weekend; they always did this.

White couple enter apartment.

Miss G enters office of apartment building. The camera holds on a shot of the door.

MISS G: Hello.

MISS N: Hello.

MISS G: I came by on Friday about an apartment which you had listed and thought . . . is it possible that I might see it?

MISS N: Well, I can show you one.

Miss G: We wanted to see it together, but we were told that . . . you wouldn't be open Saturdays or Sundays—so—

Miss G and Miss N, a clerk, leave the office.

Door of office. Pan to view of apartment building.

Narrator #2: On Monday, one of the girls returned. This time she was shown an apartment. She was told that utilities would average about $25 a month. The white couple had been told that it would run around $15. When the girl called back in the evening she was told that the apartment was the last available and that it had been rented to someone else that afternoon. However, when the white couple called that evening they were told that the apartment they had looked at over the weekend was still available if they wanted it.

Mr. and Mrs. O (negroes) and Mrs. P approach a single family residence in a neighborhood of new homes. They enter.

Mr. O: This is the one advertised for fourteen nine?

Mr. P: Fourteen nine—ya—ya—Hello.

Mr. Q: Hello. Come on in.

Camera holds on exterior view of home.

Narrator #2: While the true reasons of a turn down of a rental are sometimes difficult to pin down, because of the dodges and evasions used, the sale of a home is an even more difficult thing to check. This is true because of the greater number of people involved in the sale of a home. The first hurdle is access to the broker's listings—being able to find out what is available. Then there is the making of arrangements to be shown the home by the broker. And if the home is seen and liked there is the bid to submit to the agent who then passes it on to the owner. The financing still remains as another step to be completed. If the deal is blocked at any one of these stages it is probably blocked for good. The local realty industry has stated that they have no policy written or unwritten regarding the sale of housing to negroes. And they further state that they act only as agents for the owner, that any decisions to sell or not to sell are made only by the owner.

Mr. and Mrs. O leave the house.

Exterior view of home.

"For Sale" sign is on the lawn.

Mr. R: Hello there.

MR. O: Mr. R? How do you do.

MR. R: She isn't home so I don't know what we can do.

MR. O: She isn't home yet?

MR. R: No. The kids are getting out of school over there. She is always home by this time. Ought to be home by this time. May not be home til 4 or 4:30. I don't know.

MR. O: I would like to see it, I don't know—uh. Well, there somebody is inside there.

MR. R: A little kid might be home.

NARRATOR #2: At another home the salesman quickly and superficially showed the potential buyer through the house. While doing so he frankly stated that he wouldn't have come out to show the place if he had known the buyer was a negro. He said he has a license to worry about. He doesn't want to jeopardize it.

MR. S: Called again before I left the house.

MR. T: Hello.

MR. S: Hi! I just called—did you just get home?

MR. T: Just now—ya—just got home now.

Mr. O and Mr. V talk in front of a single family residence.

MR. V: . . . one way or another. But—uh—I am sure she should be home tonight. In fact, I would even come over with the guy—and—I will give her the pitch and the background and everything. But, uh, when you people come up . . . then the property values—you know how it is.

MR. O: The problem is they don't stop to ask their neighbors. The neighbors might not even care. They don't even know for certain.

MR. V: Oh! Ya? [Pause for 3 sec.] I think you will learn if you haven't looked around this town much—you haven't, obviously, have you?

Front window of real estate office. Pan across pictures of homes for sale.

MR. O: Uh—no—

MR. V: Ya—you'll—

MR. O: and—uh—I work for [name of company]. [Pause for 4 sec.]

MR. V: Well, I guess we don't have anything. I am sorry, honest to God, we are very low.

MR. O: Well, OK, thanks a lot.

Door of real estate office.

Display of pictures and data on homes for sale in real estate office window.

NARRATOR #2: When the gentleman visited a realty office to see what listings they could show him they had nothing to offer, but when a white person went to the same office asking for the same type of housing at the same price, he was promptly supplied with seven listings to look at, and told that if none of these looked like what he wanted, come back and they would show him some more. In addition, he was told that the present time was an excellent time to be looking. It was really a buyer's market.

A close up of interior in living room of house. Pan to Mrs. W (white).

INTERVIEWER: Last summer you had a rather interesting experience with one of your neighbors, I understand.

MRS. W: Yes, this young neighbor came by as I was working in the yard and happened to mention that he had gone into the real estate business. I happened to ask him whether if a negro family wanted to buy one of the houses in the area, whether it would be possible for the family to do so.

INTERVIEWER: What did he say to that?

MRS. W: Well, he said it would not be possible and I was surprised at this and was interested in exploring why this would be and he said that he himself would have no objection, but he would not be able to carry a transaction like that out because of the rules.

INTERVIEWER: He wouldn't actually be allowed to show property?

MRS. W: No! He wouldn't be allowed to stay in the business and show property to negroes—against the rule whether it was a written or unwritten one of the real estate organization.

Interviewer with Mrs. X (negro) in living room.

INTERVIEWER: You've only been in this city a relatively short time. Where did you come from?

MRS. X: We are from New Orleans originally.

INTERVIEWER: How long have you been here?

MRS. X: Since September.

INTERVIEWER: Do you find that there is much of a contrast between the two areas?

MRS. X: Considerably—uh—our trip sort of pointed it up for us because we have never been out of the south before. We didn't feel we were out of the south until we had gotten out of Tennessee and into Illinois. There's a considerable change in the atmosphere. Maybe we felt it more because we were southerners, but I think the people seemed to be a little more friendly—and the weather change, of course—and, uh, our trip just sort of improved after we had left Tennessee.

INTERVIEWER: How did you happen to end up here instead of somewhere else?

MRS. X: I am studying here on a fellowship in French. This was given by the Woodrow Wilson Fellowship Foundation. I could have chosen any other school in the United States, or I could choose to come here.

INTERVIEWER: You could have gone to a southern school?

MRS. X: Well, yes, I studied in a southern school this summer but I decided I wanted to come here. Well, I mainly wanted to get my family up here. I have two children at home now. I hope by the end of the year to have them here. My husband and I feel they will have better opportunities up here. So I chose to come here.

INTERVIEWER: How do you like this city now that you have been here a couple months?

MRS. X: Well, I think generally we have been very much pleased with it. We are glad that this has been our choice. We have—well—uh, had a few difficulties.

INTERVIEWER: You say you have had a few difficulties?

MRS. X: We have run into a segregation problem, or discrimination problem, whatever you want to call it. We found that some people were very nasty about renting to negroes, and have various reasons for it, tenants' disapproval, this sort of thing, but the basic thing was that we were negroes and couldn't live there, and this was the problem that we had.

INTERVIEWER: In trying to locate housing here, about how many places did you try unsuccessfully?

MRS. X: I would say about 15 or 20 altogether. We didn't do all of them in person. We did 5 or 6 in person, then after being refused for the reasons that were given, some of them good, some not so good, we decided that we would try it by telephone then. We tried one or two times calling by telephone, and not saying that we were negroes but simply saying that we wanted a place, and we were asked to come out and see it and then when we got there we were refused again, so from that time on we decided to say we are here looking for a place to stay and we understand that you have a place. Do you mind renting to negroes? Almost invariably the answer was yes we do. Then we would get the reasons.

INTERVIEWER: Well you did finally locate a place?

MRS. X: Yes we did. A very nice place and we are quite comfortable there. It is rather large and quite suited to what we need and, in fact, a little more than what we need, but . . . it is a very nice neighborhood. We have made many friends with the neighbors and we are settled for the time being. However, as I was telling you, we are going to bring the children up, and that means that in a little while we are going to have a house hunting problem again. We can't bring the children to this place where we are now situated. This is a pretty good place to live until you start looking for a house—which we are going to be doing again next year. I hate to think of having to face the same problem again, but it is there, and we are going to have to face it.

Appendix B

Dick Gregory Trial Transcript

State of Wisconsin—County Court—Milwaukee County Misdemeanor Division, #2-64484

State of Wisconsin, plaintiff, vs. Dick Gregory, defendant.

Disorderly Conduct.

Trial in the above-entitled matter, before the County Court, Branch 4, Milwaukee County, Wisconsin, the Honorable Christ T. Seraphim, County Judge, presiding, on the 22nd day of November, 1967.

Appearances

John H. Lauerman, Assistant District Attorney, appearing for the State of Wisconsin.

Lloyd A. Barbee, Attorney-at-Law, appearing on behalf of the defendant. Defendant in court.

William L. Shimeta—Official Reporter.

Proceedings

(The defendant entered a plea of not guilty to the charge.)

Patrolman Thomas K. Jackelen called as a witness on behalf of the State of Wisconsin, being first duly sworn, on oath testified as follows:

Direct Examination by Mr. Lauerman of Officer Jackelen

Q: Would you state your name, please.

A: Thomas Jackelen.

Q: You are a police officer for the City of Milwaukee Police Department? Is that correct?

A: Yes, sir.

Q: Were you acting on October 8, 1967?

A: Yes, sir.

Q: On that date, Officer, did you see the defendant in this case, Dick Gregory?

A: Yes, sir, I did.

Q: Where did you see him?

A: In the 1400 block of North 12th Street.

Q: That is in the City and County of Milwaukee, State of Wisconsin?

A: Yes, it is.

Q: What time did you see him at that place on that date?

A: Approximately 10:10 P.M.

Q: What did you observe him do, Officer?

A: He was with a group of demonstrators that were blocking the roadway in the 1400 block of North 12th Street. There was a group of about ten squad cars with their red lights on and a wagon attempting to get through, south on 12th Street in the 1400 block. The defendant was standing in the lane of traffic that we were attempting to get through on. I got out of my squad car, asked him to move, and he stood his ground and didn't say anything. I placed my hands on his chest and pushed him back, and then proceeded to move several other parties with Commando sweatshirts out of the lane of traffic. I returned and the defendant was again standing in front of the squad. I told him that he had better move or he would be arrested. He stood his ground again and I forcibly moved him back. I went to my squad and observed the defendant right back in the area, told him again to leave or he was going to be arrested, and he said, "Don't talk to me, white boy." I moved him back a third time and he had his hands in his pocket, but threw his weight into my chest. I then placed him under arrest.

Q: For the most part did this happen in the roadway?

A: It was in the roadway all the time, yes.

Q: Where there are lanes of traffic?

A: Yes, sir.

Q: And when you pushed, you said you would push him out of the way—would you push him towards a sidewalk or some area where there was no traffic?

A: Yes, sir.

Q: And he would then do what?

A: He would come right back again. As I proceeded to move others back, he would return to the position in front of the squad car.

Q: And you said that the defendant was with a group. Approximately how many were in that group, if you know?

A: I would say approximately 250 at that time.

Q: And where was the defendant in relation to this group? I mean, front, back?

A: He was up front of the group.

Q: I see. That's all.

MR. LAUERMAN: You can cross-examine, Counsel.

Cross-Examination by Mr. Barbee of Officer Jackelen

Q: Sir, would you spell your last name please?

A: J-a-c-k-e-l-e-n.

THE COURT: Excuse me a minute—one moment.

(After a recess, the trial proceeded.)

MR. LAUERMAN: Your Honor, I would ask leave of the Court to ask this witness just two or three more questions before cross-examination.

THE COURT (addressing Mr. Barbee): Is that all right?

MR. BARBEE: Yes.

THE COURT: All right.

Direct Examination by Mr. Lauerman of Officer Jackelen

MR. LAUERMAN: Officer, you said there were emergency vehicles on the roadway?

A: Yes, sir, there were.

Q: Where were they in relation to the defendant?

A: The defendant was standing directly in front of the first squad car with the red light on, obstructing—

Q: (interposing): The squad had his red light on?

A: Yes, sir.

Q: Flashing red light?

A: Yes, sir.

Q: On the top of the vehicle?

A: No, sir, on the side of the vehicle.

Q: Were there other emergency vehicles there also?

A: Yes, sir, there was approximately nine other vehicles to the rear of that—automobiles—and there was also one wagon that was at the end of the line.

Q: State whether or not these vehicles were moving.

A: No, sir, we could not. We would have hit the demonstrators if would have.

Q: Now, prior to these vehicles arriving at the point where they could no longer move. Did you observe them prior to this? In other words, were they moving up the street prior to this?

A: The demonstrators?

Q: No, the emergency vehicles.

A: Oh, we were moving south on North 12th Street, attempting to get to West Vliet Street. I was in the second car from the front, and we had to stop for the demonstrators.

Q: Were the demonstrators then moving north?

A: They were stopped midblock in the 1400 block of 12th Street.

MR. LAUERMAN: All right, that's all.

Cross-Examination (Continued) by Mr. Barbee of Officer Jackelen

Q: Officer, about what point on North 12th did the marchers stop moving? And were they on the sidewalk or were they in the street?

A: No, sir, they were in the roadway—the street.

Q: Were they the full width of the roadway or the midpoint?

A: They had all but one lane. It is a four-lane road. They had all but one lane blocked as we approached. When we got to them, they had blocked the whole roadway.

Q: At the time you first observed Mr. Gregory, was the line still in a stopping position? In other words, were they marching? Or were they still?

A: When I—

Q (interposing): Was the line making any progress?

A: When I first approached him, the line was stopped. It was still.

Q: And which side of the street was open? The lane that you said was not occupied by the demonstrators?

A: It was occupied when the squads approached. We approached in the—it would be the east side of the street, the far lane, on the east side of the street, but this was blocked by the demonstrators by the time we got there.

Q: And in what direction was the squad car which you said was at the head of the line and the other vehicles that were behind it going? Were they going in a southerly or northerly direction?

A: Southerly.

Q: In other words, they were going in the same direction as the demonstrators?

A: The demonstrators were stopped.

Q: Which way were they headed before they were stopped?

A: Before they were stopped, they were headed south.

Q: And is 12th Street a one-way street?

A: Northbound.

Q: Was there an officer with you at the time you had your contact with Mr. Gregory?

A: Several other officers were present, yes.

Q: To your knowledge, did they speak to Mr. Gregory?

A: I don't know.

Q: And did you have any conversation with Mr. Gregory other than what you have testified to today?

A: Not on the street, no.

Q: That is, prior to the arrest?

A: No, sir.

Q: And now you are the officer that actually arrested Mr. Gregory?

A: Yes, sir, I am.

Q: And about what distance was this squad car that had the light on to you and Mr. Gregory at the time that you placed him under arrest?

A: I don't understand.

Q: Would you tell the Judge what relationship the squad car, which was at the head of the line of emergency vehicles, was to you.

A: At the time of the arrest, it was in front of the squad car.

Q: So you were ahead of the squad car then?

A: Yes.

Q: And it is your testimony then that other vehicles were behind the squad car; is that correct?

A: Yes, sir.

Q: And is it your testimony that the squad car and all other vehicles were going in a southerly direction on North 12th?

A: Yes, sir, with the red lights on.

Q: And did you have any conversation with Mr. Gregory regarding why he was not getting into the line?

A: The only conversation I had with him was I ordered him back into the line of march and out of the path of the squad cars, three times. A third time I told him this, he told me, "Don't talk to me, white boy," and then he threw his weight into me and I placed him under arrest. This was the only conversation that we had at all on the street. I did ask him why he wanted to be arrested, but he didn't—he didn't give me an answer to that question.

Q: Officer, did you arrest any other people at the time you arrested Mr. Gregory?

A: After I arrested Mr. Gregory, there were several other arrests made by myself, but not at the same time, no.

Q: Now, how far out of the line was Mr. Gregory in terms of distance?

A: I would say he was approximately four feet out of the main body of the march, standing in front of our squad.

Q: And was he going over toward the sidewalk?

A: No, sir, he was standing in the middle of the lane that we were in.

Q: Are you saying there is only one lane that was open, right adjacent to the demonstrators, and that there was a squad car occupying that remaining lane and the rest of the vehicles?

A: Yes, sir. The squad car was forced to stop by the demonstrators.

Q: And you say Mr. Gregory was about four feet to the side of the line. In other words, then be would have been very near the sidewalk, would he not?

A: No, sir, definitely not.

Q: How wide was the lane that was open?

A: I would say about six feet.

Q: So there would have been two feet between him and the sidewalk, then?

A: No, sir.

Q: Well, you indicated he was about four feet out into this lane?

A: There was only one complete lane left for vehicular traffic. There was possibly half of the other lane that was left. He was standing immediately in front of the squad car. It would be towards the right fender but the squad could not proceed south.

Q: And had the squad been moving prior to the time that you first observed Mr. Gregory?

A: The Squad was forced to stop by him, yes.

Q: Did you hear them blow any horn?

A: I don't know if they blew a horn, but I heard sirens. If it came from the front or the rear, I don't know.

Q: But at the time that you talked to Mr. Gregory, you are not aware of aware of whether the driver of the squad or anyone else had spoken to him; is that correct?

A: I do not know.

MR. BARBEE: No more questions.

MR. LAUERMAN: No re-direct. State rests, Your Honor, subject to rebuttal. (Witness excused.)

MR. BARBEE: We will call the defendant.

Dick Gregory, the defendant herein, being first duly sworn, on oath, testified as follows:

Direct Examination by Mr. Barbee of Mr. Gregory

Q: Will you state your name?

A: Dick Gregory.

Q: And where do you live, Mr. Gregory?

A: [address omitted]

Q: In what city?

A: [address omitted], Chicago, Illinois.

Q: What is your occupation, Mr. Gregory?

A: Entertainer, lecturer, author.

Q: How old are you?

A: Thirty-five.

Q: Were you in Milwaukee October 8, 1967?

A: Yes.

Q: And were you in the vicinity of North 12th Street and Vliet? Do you know that area?

A: Yes.

Q: You heard the officer testify today, have you not?

A: Yes, I did.

Q: Were you in that general area that he testified to?

A: Yes, I was.

Q: And about what time was that?

A: Oh, from about 9:00 till about—oh, 10:15.

THE COURT: You mean 9:00 P.M.?

A: 9:00 P.M., yes.

MR. BARBEE: Will you tell the judge what you were doing and what happened, if anything.

A: I was marching down the street.

Q: What direction were you going?

A: I don't know what direction.

Q: Do you know if that's a one-way street or two-way street?

A: It's a one-way street.

Q: And were you going in the direction that the traffic is supposed to move?

A: No, we were going in tile direction—one-way street, where the traffic would have been coming against us.

Q: So you were going opposite the way the arrow would be pointing?

Q: And would you tell the Judge whether you were on the sidewalk or on the street?

A: We were in the street.

Q: About how much of the street were you occupying—what percentage of the pavement?

A: About half of the street when we were marching.

Q: And during the time that you were marching, nearing a street that is called Vliet Street, would you tell the Judge what happened?

A: Yes, there was about two hundred of us, as the officer said, and when I looked to see what time it was, I was getting out of line. So I—

Q (interposing): Why were you getting out of the line at that time?

A: Because I was going to leave town. I had a ride waiting for me. And this is when I got out the line, going to the sidewalk.

Q: And would you tell the Judge what happened as you looked at your watch and got out to go to the sidewalk?

A: This is when the officer—not the one that made the arrest—

Q (interposing): I beg your pardon—did you say not the one?

A: Not the one that made the arrest.

THE COURT: Not Mr. Jackelen, you mean?

A: No, not Mr. Jackelen.

MR. BARBEE: Tell the Judge what happened with that officer.

A: When I crossed over to go to the sidewalk, the officer told me to get back in line.

Q: And did you say anything to him?

A: No, I just said I'm going over to the sidewalk.

Q: And what did he say?

A: He said, "Get back in line."

Q: And what was your response?

A: I was still going over to the sidewalk.

Q: And did you reach the sidewalk?

A: No, I didn't. The officer was pushing me back in the line. When I say push, I don't mean shoved violently—he was just with his hand, pushing me back in line.

Q: And did you make another attempt to go to the sidewalk?

A: I kept on. I never moved. I kept going for the sidewalk.

Q: When did you first see the officer Jackelen who just testified today?

A: He was there at the same time, or got there a little bit behind, after the first officer and myself, and he is the one that told me that I was under arrest.

Q: Did you explain to the officer that you were trying to leave the line?

A: Not to the one that made the arrest, no.

Q: Did you explain to the other officer that you were attempting to leave?

A: I felt it was obvious, I was leaving. As the officer testified, there was two hundred people there and I was over by myself. I was trying to get to the sidewalk.

Q: And did you, at the time you were told you were under arrest, did you have your hands in your pocket?

A: Yes.

Q: Did you explain to the officer that you were trying to leave—the one that arrested you?

A: No.

Q: And was it your intention to leave the line and leave town?

A: Yes, my intention was to. I had already left the line. It was a matter of getting out the street.

Q: Did you notice any of the vehicles referred to by the officer Jackelen?

A: No, I didn't.

Q: Did you hear any siren?

A: Yes, there were sirens down at the corner, of the head of the block where we were marching.

Q: Did you see any light flashing from a vehicle that was to your rear?

A: No.

Q: Did you see the line-up of vehicles that the officer referred to after you were arrested?

A: Yes, after I was arrested, yes, I did.

Q: And how far away were those vehicles from you?

A: By that time they had approached me.

Q: Were you asked to move out of the way so the vehicles could pass?

A: By the time the vehicles had reached me and I noticed them, I was already under arrest.

Q: Were you told that you were blocking the vehicles?

A: No.

MR. BARBEE: Your witness.

Cross-Examination by Mr. Lauerman of Mr. Gregory

Q: Mr. Gregory, from what direction were you walking and in what direction were you walking when you left the line of the march to walk, as you said, to walk across to the sidewalk? Were you walking west?

A: I wouldn't know the relationship. I was walking this way and then we— the sidewalk was to my left.

Q: All right. Do you know what direction the march was proceeding?

A: We were marching—

Q (interposing): South?

A: Towards downtown.

Q: So you were marching south?

A: Right.

Q: Now, when you left, was there a free lane of traffic to your right as you were marching south?

A: There would have been a free lane.

Q: So you were marching on the left side of the street, in the roadway?

A: We were marching in the roadway, right.

Q: And is it your testimony that you left the line of march and walked to your right?

A: I was walking to my left.

Q: You were walking to your left.

THE COURT: You were walking south, were you not?

A: If south is towards downtown, yes.

Q: Yes.

A: Yes, I was walking south, and I was leaving to my left.

MR. LAUERMAN: To get back on the sidewalk?

A: To get on the sidewalk.

Q: Did you notice any construction there?

A: Did I notice any construction there? There had been construction, yes, but you could still get to the sidewalk from the part where we were.

Q: Were you able to notice that there wasn't a sidewalk in that particular area?

A: Was I able to notice it? No, I was not.

Q: Did you notice that?

A: No, I did not.

Q: You didn't notice that?

A: No.

Q: Now, do you remember when you first saw Officer Jackelen, the officer who testified here this afternoon?

A: Yes.

Q: You were standing in the middle of the roadway alone at that time; is that correct?

A: No, there was police officers around me.

Q: How close to you were the police officers when Officer Jackelen first talked to you?

A: Oh, they were all around me.

Q: Well, were they within six feet or something?

A: They were close to me, right up on me.

Q: Had any other officers spoken to you prior to this?

A: Yes.

Q: And do you remember Officer Jackelen asking you to get back in the line?

A: Asking me to get—yes, I do.

Q: And you didn't—did you go voluntarily back into the line? Did you just stand there?

A: Did I? I had to stand there, I couldn't move. It was too many police around.

Q: Were they holding you?

A: No, they weren't holding me.

Q: Was anybody holding you?

A: No.

Q: Did anyone tell you to stand still?

A: Did anyone tell me to stand still?

Q: To stand still.

A: Nobody had to tell me to stand still. I'm surrounded by police and I can't get to where I want to go, so I had nothing else to do but to stop.

Q: Did they form a ring around you? Is that what you are saying?

A: They were all around me. I don't know about a ring around me.

Q: Would it have been possible for you to have walked back to the line of march?

A: If I wanted to get back in the line of march, it would have been. I was through.

Q: All right. And would it have been possible for you to walk on the opposite side from the line of march, if you had wanted to?

A: If I wanted to, yes.

Q: But you just stood there?

A: No, I just tried to get over to the other side where I was headed.

Q: And do you remember saying anything to Officer Jackelen?

A: I don't know who I said it to. I do remember saying something to one of the officers.

Q: Do you remember moving in with your shoulder or your body into Officer Jackelen?

A: No, I don't.

Q: Putting your weight into Officer Jackelen?

A: I remember putting my hands in my pocket when I was being pushed and I was still trying to get across the street so no one would be able to say I was, you know, trying to fight the police. All I was trying to do was get across the street and I put my hands in my pocket and made my way towards where I wanted to go.

MR. LAUERMAN: That's all.

Redirect Examination by Mr. Barbee of Mr. Gregory

Q: Mr. Gregory, do you recall having any physical contact with any officers there on the line?

A: No.

Q: How long had it been from the time that the first officer spoke to you and the officer that arrested you spoke to you? Do you recall?

A: Just a matter of minutes, if that long.

Q: All right.

MR. LAUERMAN: That's all of this witness.

(Witness excused.)

MR. LAUERMAN: The State would like to recall—wait a minute, I am sorry—do you have any other witnesses?

MR. BARBEE: No one.

MR. LAUERMAN: Defense rests?

MR. BARBEE: Yes.

MR. LAUERMAN: State would like to recall Officer Jackelen in rebuttal, Your Honor.

Patrolman Thomas K. Jackelen, sworn previously, was thereupon recalled as a witness by the State of Wisconsin and on oath testified as follows:

Redirect Examination by Mr. Lauerman of Officer Jackelin

Q: Officer Jackelen, you realize you are still under oath?

A: Yes, sir.

Q: Officer Jackelen, when you first saw the defendant, from what you observed, could he have walked freely in any direction he desired?

A: Yes, sir, definitely.

Q: And what was he doing?

A: Standing in the lane of traffic that we were in.

Q: And was there anyone that you observed immediately next to him or right within his immediate presence?

A: Not when I got out of the car. It was just him and the demonstrators to his—it would be to the west of where he was standing.

Q: Was he facing in the direction of the emergency vehicle?

A: Yes, he was.

Q: For what period of time did you observe him standing there?

A: Approximately, at the most, say a minute before I got out of the car and my partner got out, and I went to him and my partner went to the other end of the line, where the Commandos had stopped other squad cars and asked them to leave the lane of traffic, which they did. I asked Mr. Gregory, at which time he refused, and I had to move him back.

Q: And when you first observed the defendant, did you see any other police officers talking to him?

A: Not when I first observed him. There were several other officers there. If they talked to him, I don't know.

MR. LAUERMAN: That's all.

Re-Cross-Examination by Mr. Barbee of Officer Jackelin

Q: Officer, about how many officers were there at the time you placed Mr. Gregory under arrest?

A: I couldn't tell you.

Q: These emergency vehicles, did they all have officers manning them?

A: Yes, sir, they did.

Q: And you have testified that this was a pretty long line of vehicles, did you not?

A: Yes, it was.

Q: About how many officers were on duty watching the line the night of October 8, 1967?

MR. LAUERMAN: I would object to that, Your Honor, as being beyond the scope of rebuttal.

MR. BARBEE: It has to do with the number—

THE COURT (interposing): One moment. Will you read the question first, please?

(The reporter thereupon read aloud the question.)

THE COURT: He may answer.

A: I have no idea.

MR. BARBEE: Was it a small number or large number?

A: I don't know how many were there to begin with.

Q: No, I only want to know the number that were there at the time that you first spoke to Mr. Gregory, the first time when you spoke to him, and when you spoke to him the third time and placed him under arrest.

A: I would say there were several officers outside their automobiles. I don't know how many. I didn't stop to count. We were having enough difficulty with the marchers. I didn't take time to see how many officers had surrounded him.

Q: Do you know how many vehicles the officers had stepped out of?

A: I don't know how many they had stepped out of. There was approximately ten squad cars there and a wagon. Now, how many of these officers got out of their vehicles, I don't know.

Q: You said the vehicles were lined up and they went to the end, where the marchers were, which was about two hundred, right?

A: Yes, sir.

Q: Did officers usually ride inside the patrol wagon when it was moving prior to arresting people?

A: I believe they were inside, yes.

Q: And about how many would be inside the wagon?

MR. LAUERMAN: Your Honor, again I will have to object. That is beyond the scope of rebuttal.

THE COURT: He may answer.

MR. BARBEE: It is not, Your Honor, because he asked about the number of officers that were on the scene.

THE COURT: If he knows, he may answer.

A: Possibly ten. I don't think any more than ten would fit in a wagon. I am not sure of it.

MR. BARBEE: That's all.

(Witness excused)

MR. LAUERMAN: That's all. State rests, Your Honor.

THE COURT: Closing arguments, gentlemen?

Closing Arguments

MR. LAUERMAN: Well, Your Honor, the State would just state that based upon the testimony that was adduced from Officer Jackelen in this case this afternoon, to-wit, that the defendant was standing in the line of traffic, was told by the officer on three separate occasions to move out, that there were emergency vehicles, or just to move out—he refused to do so, he said "Move away, white man," or something to that effect, and then he threw his weight against the officer who was trying to get him out to clear the roadway. I think it is an act of disorderly conduct.

MR. BARBEE: Well, Your Honor, I think it is quite obvious that the vehicles were behind Mr. Gregory and at the time of the warrant, it was alleged that Mr. Gregory was obstructing the vehicular traffic. This time it turns out that it has to do with his refusing to get into line. He was trying to get out of line in order to go on and leave the city, and I don't think that that, in and of itself, is disorderly conduct, considering the things that happened on that particular night thereafter, that if it had been the intention to create a disorder, that it would have been done in a much clearer way by the defendant with his experience, and it is pretty well known that he, at that time, did leave town, and once the marching really was at a standstill, he was trying to leave, that he had a right to leave, and hindsight certainly would have at least dictated an inquiry as to what he was attempting to do since quite clearly he was trying to separate himself from the marchers who were no longer marching but standing at a standstill. There is a conflict as to the direction of the traffic going, but there is no conflict that it was always behind Mr. Gregory.

THE COURT: By traffic, you mean police traffic?

MR. BARBEE: The squad car, paddy wagons and the other things.

THE COURT: Because traffic normally goes from south to north on that street, isn't that right?

MR. BARBEE: That's right, and whether they were going in the downtown area south or going to the northtown area north, the traffic is still on one side of the highway and always behind Mr. Gregory. So it is not a case of any flagrant disorder on his part that is breaching the peace, as far as the conduct of Mr. Gregory as related to the officer who testified, but there were a number of officers there and the fact that the arresting officer arrested Mr. Gregory for not getting into line, I think, shows that there was no disorder or conduct tending to cause a disorder which is under our statute, what the standard for disorderly conduct amounts to, and I don't think we have that degree of disorder to meet the burden that the state has in order to establish that the defendant was committing a crime by not stepping in the line when he was obviously away from the line and trying to move even further from the line. So I move to dismiss.

MR. LAUERMAN: Your Honor, I would just like to, in rebuttal, indicate that I think the State, too, feels it is obvious what the defendant was attempting to do here, but the State feels that it was not as Counsel suggested. He was trying to get across the street and away from the line of the march. The officer testified that he stood still in the middle of the street when he was free to move in either direction or any direction that he chose; he stood there in the line of traffic. I think the officer's testimony on cross-examination was that he was standing directly in front of the squad car—or the emergency vehicle. I think it is obvious that he was trying to impede the flow of traffic and certainly that's an act that tends to create a disturbance, especially when there is a situation where there are a few hundred people there who could react in any manner, certainly in a disorderly manner.

MR. BARBEE: Well, Your Honor, the State's witness did not testify that any horn was blowing. He thought perhaps a siren was blowing. He did say that there was a flashing light, and certainly one who is operating a traffic vehicle, who wants someone to get out of the way, would tell him so, and also then if that's the case, they should have considered issuing a traffic violation warrant. Actually as the case originated, this is what it was, and it has now altered itself from the time of going before the magistrate to the time that it was tried under oath, that it is a matter of not getting back into line as opposed to impeding traffic. And I submit that it should be— the case should be dismissed, and if there is going to be an amendment as the impeding the flow of traffic—

THE COURT (interposing): No, there is no charge here of obstructing the flow of traffic.

MR. BARBEE: This is how it started, but it resulted in a disorderly conduct and I had to leave. My partner took over for me on that particular day. I wasn't here for the initial case, but I do know that it started out as being a traffic thing and it grew into a disorderly conduct, and it looks like to me now that it is going back into an impeding traffic, which I submit, though, the burden for disorderly conduct, beyond a reasonable doubt, has not been met.

THE COURT: Mr. Barbee, I would state this, that the way you state the proposition, there is no question that I would have to make a finding, as you stated it. However, I don't think that you have stated the proposition the way the testimony came out, as far as Mr. Jackelen is concerned, and even Mr. Gregory concedes that—and this was near the end of his testimony— that he just put his weight in the direction he wanted to go, and the officer would tend to corroborate he put his weight into the officer and said, "I'm going that way." I think under the circumstances also it is not a part of this, it didn't come out, but the Court would take judicial notice here that the marchers who have consistently demanded police protection were going against the flow of traffic and made it very difficult for the police to give them the protection that they demand and deserve, in that they were going the wrong way on a one-way street, necessitating emergency vehicles, squad cars, to also go along the south instead of—when the whole flow of traffic is towards the north. I am finding him guilty of disorderly conduct, fine him a hundred dollars.

MR. BARBEE: Your Honor, this is the first time. That is the maximum monetary fine. Do you have any stay? You are actually fining him the maximum. This is the first time.

THE COURT: I am fining him a hundred dollars, and that's what it is going to be in this case, which have been the fines, whites and colored, in this—

MR. BARBEE (interposing): You haven't always on the first offense done that, though.

THE COURT: No—for Mr. Gregory, he can afford more than the average poor defendant.

MR. BARBEE: Is that and costs or including?

THE COURT: I will make it a hundred including costs.

Appendix C

Alvin J. McKissick Appeal Brief

State of Wisconsin in Supreme Court
August Term, 1970; State No. 14
Alvin J. McKissick, Plaintiff in Error, vs. State of Wisconsin, Defendant in Error
Brief of Plaintiff in Error

Nature of Appeal

This is via writ of error by plaintiff in error from a conviction, sentence and judgment for violation of Section 943.10 (a), Wisconsin Statutes. On August 3, 1968, plaintiff in error was found guilty of burglary by a jury. On August 23, 1968, he was sentenced by the Honorable Maurice Spracker, Circuit Court Judge, Milwaukee County, to an indeterminate term of not more than two (2) years.

Questions Involved

I. Is the method of selecting jurors from poll lists discriminatory against blacks?

The Court felt not.

II. Is the state required to give written notice to the defendant that it will rely on admissions or confessions made to the police?

The Court answered no.

III. Should the Court grant change of venue when the accused's brother and family have received wide notoriety through the news media?

The Court answered no.

IV. Is intent, an essential element of burglary, established merely by showing that some articles in a residential dwelling were moved but were not removed from the premises?

The Court answered yes.

V. Do instructions given to the jury concerning a defendant's prior conviction of a crime prejudice the jury when the crime is a misdemeanor unrelated to the accused's crime at bar?

The Court said no.

Statement of Facts

On April 14, 1967, plaintiff in error was accused of entering a residence at 2725A North 15th Street, Milwaukee, Wisconsin, without the consent of the lawful possessor with intent to steal and that plaintiff in error planned this burglary with the plaintiff in error acting as a lookout violating Section 943.10 (a) and Section 39.05, Wisconsin Statutes. After a trial before a jury, the plaintiff in error was found guilty August 3, 1968, and on August 23, 1968, he was sentenced to the Wisconsin State Reformatory in Green Bay, Wisconsin, for an indeterminate term of not more than two (2) years.

Argument

I. Plaintiff in Error Was Tried By A Jury That Was Not Representative of the Community

The jury which tried the instant case was underrepresented by blacks. This is due to the method that the Milwaukee County Jury Commission used in selecting jurors from poll lists. It is axiomatic that blacks are underregistered and their names are disproportionately purged from the poll lists prior to and after recent elections.

Chapter 255, Wisconsin Statutes, has a two-fold purpose. First, it protects the defendant's right to an array "as representative of community character as is practicable." Second, it "assures each person in a county of an equal opportunity to serve upon a jury." *State vs. Nutley* (1964), 24 Wis. 2d 547, 129 N.W. 2d 155, 159. This purpose is based upon the recognition that the defendant's right cannot be protected unless the citizen's right is adequately guaranteed.

Article I, Section 7, of the Wisconsin Constitution requires an impartial jury trial in every criminal case. Chapter 255 of the Wisconsin Statutes requires that this jury be "a truly representative group from the community in which legal controversies are to be tried." This "representative" requirement acknowledges "the fact that those eligible for jury service are to be found in every stratum of society," *Thiel vs. Southern Pacific Co.* (1946), 328 U.S. 217, 66 S. Ct. 984, 90 L. Ed. 1181, and that if any such stratum is ignored the jury is not truly representative.

It follows that any method of jury selection which ignores particular strata of society violates Article I, Section 7, Wisconsin Constitution, and

Chapter 255, Wisconsin Statutes. The selection process beginning with a poll list is such a method.

The jury which heard the above-entitled matter was biased. Milwaukee County maintains a separate criminal and civil jury panel. This is the only county in the state which uses such a system. This case was tried before a criminal jury selected from the criminal jury panel. The criminal panel serves two months at a time and four months over the summer. Civil panels are called for three weeks. Therefore, the criminal jurors have more experience in hearing criminal matters but this amounts to a bias in favor of the state and against the defendants.

II. Plaintiff in Error Was Not Given Notice of the Use of Alleged Admissions and Confessions

Under *State ex rel. Goodchild vs. Burke* (1965), 27 Wis. 2d 244, 133 N.W. 2d 753, plaintiff in error should have been given notice that the prosecution was relying on admissions made to the Milwaukee Police Department. Defendant in error claimed to have given oral notice during the trial over objections of plaintiff in error's counsel that the doctrine of Goodchild was not observed by the Court (R. 132). In the instant case, the hearing became a nullity since plaintiff in error had no opportunity to prepare an attack on the alleged admission or confession.

III. Plaintiff in Error Should Have Been Granted a Change of Venue Because of Community Prejudice

Plaintiff in error's motion for change of venue on the ground of community prejudice should have been granted (R. 62). Plaintiff in error's brother was killed by the Milwaukee Police. The notoriety and extensive press coverage via the total news media made it impossible for the plaintiff in error to receive a fair trial in Milwaukee County. Eight (8) members of the panel, one of whom remained on the jury to try plaintiff in error, recognized the plaintiff in error's name based on such publicity. It was an abuse of discretion on the part of the trial judge not to grant plaintiff in error's motion.

The white presses' coverage of Clifford McKissick's death was so different from the black presses' coverage that a vi[r]tually all white jury would be influenced by articles emanating from the one race press. A hearing should have been conducted on the fact of whether the news coverage was fair or unfair. No factual determination of this issue was made. *Schro-*

eder vs. State (1936), 222 Wis. 251, 267 N.W. 899, suggests that the question that the existence of community prejudice is connected with whether or not the coverage is fair.

IV. The State Did Not Sustain its Burden of Proof in Establishing Burglary

The state did not sustain its burden of proof in establishing burglary, Section 943.10, Wisconsin Statutes. The state never established the essential element of intent. Evidence showed that nothing was taken from the dwelling. It was only established at the trial that articles had been moved.

V. The Instructions Given the Jury by the Trial Court Further Influenced and Prejudiced the Jury

The instructions given by the trial court (R. 240) concerning plaintiff in error's prior conviction further influenced and prejudiced the jury. This is particularly true in view of the fact that the crime was disorderly conduct, a misdemeanor, Section 927.01, Wisconsin Statutes.

Conclusion

In conclusion, plaintiff in error reasserts that the method of selecting jurors is violative of the United States Constitution, Fourteenth Amendment, Due Process Clause, the Wisconsin Constitution Article I, Section 7, and the Wisconsin Statutes, Chapter 255; that the submission of his alleged admission or confession to the jury was in error; and that venue should have been changed on grounds of community prejudice.

In the interest of justice based upon facts, the record, and valid inferences drawn therefrom, the judgment below should be vacated.

Respectfully submitted,

Lloyd A. Barbee

Plaintiff in error's attorney*

---

* Barbee's appeal was denied. On January 5, 1971, the Supreme Court of Wisconsin issued its decision upholding McKissick's conviction on burglary charges. The decision, in part, argued that Barbee had not shown evidence that African Americans had been "intentionally and systematically" excluded from juries and that "the mere lack of proportional representation of races on a jury panel does not constitute discrimination." See "McKissick v. State," *Justia Legal Resources*, 5 January 1971, law.justia.com/cases/wisconsin /supreme-court/1971/state-14-4-1.html.

Appendix D
Wisconsin Senate Resolution
Recognizing Lloyd A. Barbee

February 27, 2008—Introduced by Senators TAYLOR and COGGS. Referred to Committee on Senate Organization.

Whereas, Lloyd A. Barbee was born on August 17, 1925, in Memphis, Tennessee, and died on December 29, 2002, in Milwaukee, Wisconsin; and

Whereas, Lloyd A. Barbee was a tireless freedom fighter, civil rights leader and attorney, Wisconsin state representative, professor, and true leader in the cause for social justice as he lived by the philosophy that the only race is the human race; and

Whereas, according to the Wisconsin Lawyer Publication of the State Bar, "Lloyd Barbee is probably the most important figure of the 20th century in Wisconsin civil rights"; and

Whereas, he graduated from Booker T. Washington High School in Memphis, served his country as a member of the U.S. Navy during World War II , and returned to earn a degree in economics in 1949 from LeMoyne College in Memphis and a law degree in 1956 from the University of Wisconsin–Madison; and

Whereas, he additionally taught at the University of Wisconsin Law School and the Bronx Community College of the City University of New York; and

Whereas, Mr. Barbee founded the Milwaukee United School Integration Committee (MUSIC) and, in 1965, filed a lawsuit in federal court on behalf of both African-American children and white children from Milwaukee Public Schools who were attending segregated schools which were subject to overcrowding and inferior resources; and

Whereas, that lawsuit led to a 2-decade-long court battle and ultimately resulted in the ruling that the Milwaukee Public Schools were unconstitutionally segregated, prompting the Wisconsin legislature to enact a program of school integration; and

Whereas, during the same period, Mr. Barbee was one of the first African Americans to win state office when he was elected to the Wisconsin state assembly, where he ultimately served for 6 consecutive terms from 1964 through 1976 before retiring to focus his time completely on the schools case; and

Whereas, during his tenure in the legislature, Mr. Barbee quickly gained a reputation for being an innovative and unconventional lawmaker willing to push for social change even if there was little chance for political success, as he continually attacked laws that he felt inhibited individuals, especially the poor and minority group members, from achieving their full human potential; and

Whereas, while serving in the assembly and as the chair of the Judiciary Committee he fought to expand personal freedoms by repealing restrictive laws on what he called "victimless crimes" and was an advocate for open housing, ending job discrimination, and providing better medical access for minorities and low-income families, all issues that we are contending with yet in the present day; and

Whereas, from 1969 to 1973, he served as president of Freedom Through Equality, a Milwaukee-based group established to reform laws detrimental to the poor; and

Whereas, Mr. Barbee received numerous awards and honors, including the American Civil Liberties Union of Wisconsin Eunice Z. Edgar Award for Lifetime Civil Liberties Achievement and the Wisconsin Association of Minority Attorneys Award for Inspirational Leadership and Outstanding Dedication; and

Whereas, in 1999, a Milwaukee street was renamed "Barbee Street" by former Mayor John Norquist in Mr. Barbee's honor; and

Whereas, Mr. Barbee received an honorary doctoral degree in sociology from the University of Wisconsin–Milwaukee in 2001; and

Whereas, the adoption of this senate resolution is supported not only by the senate, but also by members of the assembly, including specifically Representatives Sheridan, Schneider, Young, Grigsby, Sinicki, Mason, Fields, Benedict, Turner, Kessler, and Hintz; now, therefore, be it

Resolved by the senate, That the Wisconsin senate honors the remarkable life and achievements of Lloyd Barbee, both in the political sphere and in the various communities in which he dedicated himself to improving the quality of life for all.

Acknowledgments

My father had many friends and supporters who helped make his work possible. I would especially like to acknowledge Isaac Coggs, who preceded my father as a state representative, Marcia P. Coggs, who succeeded my father as a representative, and their daughter Elizabeth Coggs; Arlene Johnson and Ann Tevik, who were my father's loyal secretaries for many years; and Kimberly Davis, LeRoy Payne, University of Wisconsin Africology professor Dr. Winston Van Horne, and photographer George Allez, who were my father's friends.

Ramisha Knight and Sharon Yarbrough provided invaluable help with preserving and printing my father's notes, and the Wisconsin Historical Society helped to make his writings available to the masses. I would also like to thank my brothers, Finn and Rustam Barbee, for their support of this project.

Most importantly, I would like to thank my father, Lloyd A. Barbee, who left his writings to share with all, and the freedom and justice fighters who have followed in his footsteps.

—Daphne E. Barbee-Wooten

INDEX

Page numbers in **bold italic** indicate illustrations.

housing discrimination, NAACP and, 11–12, 13. *See also* fair housing law
housing for poor, and exclusionary zoning, 69–74
Huley, Dorothy, 146
Humphrey, Hubert, 42

Indian, as racist term, 167
Indianapolis, school desegregation in, 107
inner-city blacks, decreasing opportunities for, 70
Innis, Roy, 240–241
Integrated Education, Barbee timeline for Milwaukee school desegregation in, 89–101
Ireland, British occupation of, 233–234

Jackman, W. L., 171–172
Jackson, Jesse, 240–241
Jacobson, Tom, xi
Janssen, John, 28
Johnson, Arlene, 146
Johnson, Ben, 74
Johnson, Lyndon B., 174
judges: attacks on civil rights activists by, 88; bill to allow defendant-requested changes to, 159–160; racist, in Wisconsin, 118–119, 147
juries, inadequate black representation on, 160
justice, Barbee's first contact with concept, 5
justice for minority groups: groups in need of, 17, 26; importance of immediate action on, 18

Kennedy, John F., 57
Kennedy, Robert F., 57
Kessler, Fred, 30–31, 240
Knowles, Warren, 123

labor, declining demand for, and black upward mobility, 37
law and order governments, 66–67, 149, 230

laws, targeting of poor by, 146–147
leaders, black: necessary characteristics of, 241; white appointment of, 240–241
legal representation, right to, 160–161, 173–175
legislation: methods of killing, 18; strategies for, 27–28
legislators: advice for, 18–19, 21–22, 27–28; coalitions and deal-making by, 17, 18–19, 21, 27; evaluating effectiveness of, 18; and matters of conscience, 21; subjective success, measuring of, 19–21
legislators, black and minority: benefits derived from, 16; central issues for, 20; strategies for, 29–30
legislature of Wisconsin: 1969 legislative session, major legislation considered in, 31–35; black representation in, 25, 240; campaign reform proposals, 56; failure to help poor and needy, 35–36; and Milwaukee riot of 1967, 145–146; as reactionary, 123–124; redistricting of, 38–39, 240; Senate resolution recognizing Barbee, 274–276; and Welfare Mothers March, 122–124, 151–153, 162, 163
legislature of Wisconsin, Barbee in, *180*, *181*; bill on divorce, 219; bill on environmentalism, 201–202; bill on government surveillance, 218–219; bill on population control, 201–202; bill on sex education, 201–202; bill to allow defendant-requested venue and judge changes, 159–160; bill to repeal mandatory school attendance, 124–125; bill to suppress arrest records, 155; bills on prison system, 148, 153, 160–161; and bills to require minority history education, 119–122; campaign literature of, *179*; coalition-building by, vii–viii, 19, 25–26, 27, 59; and education reform efforts, 85; and election

Milwaukee Teacher's Education Association, 92

Milwaukee United School Integration Committee (MUSIC): dispute with NAACP, 115–116; protests against intact busing, 85–86; and school desegregation, 94–99, 114

Milwaukee Urban League Board, and fair housing law, 58–59

minstrel shows, protests against, 8–11, 12, 13–14

Misericordia Community Hospital, 200–201

Mitchell, Parren, 104

morality: in democracies, 135; impossibility of legislating, 27, 134–135

NAACP: Barbee as Wisconsin branch president, 6, 11–15, 22–24; and fair housing activism, 113–114; leaders of in 1960s Milwaukee, 113; and Milwaukee United School Integration Committee, dispute with, 115–116; Nick Hall controversy, 115; opposition to Nixon busing bill, 103–104; protests against minstrel show, 8–9; and school desegregation in Milwaukee, 89, 90–96, 100, 103; sit-in in support of fair housing law, 23–24; and Story committee hearing, 115

Nabrit, Henry C., *182*

Nabrit, Vernice, *182*

National Association for Equal Opportunity in Higher Education, 141

National Black Political Convention (Gary, 1972), 36–38, 103, 235

National Black Political Convention (Little Rock, 1974), x

National Council for Black Studies conference (1980), Barbee address to, 138–143

Native Americans: rights of, 20; white oppression of, 167

Near Northside NonPartisan Conference, 93

Nelson, Gaylord, 6

New Orleans, police violence in, 167–170

Nixon, Richard M.: animosity toward black interests, 49–50, 55, 231; attacks on enemies by, 229–230; black supporters of, 53; and busing bills, 103–104; Democratic presidential candidates and, 42; and energy shortages, 210–211; jobs programs by, 37; and legal aid services, 174; manipulation of press by, 222; reelection of, 53–54, 55; support for capitalism, 50; Supreme Court appointees of, 40; and Watergate, 228–229

Norgard, David W., 171–172

North Carolina v. Swann (1971), 103

Northside Community Inventory Conference, 115

nuclear power, efforts to reduce regulation of, 105–106

Olympics (Munich, 1972), 239–240

Oswald, Russell, 148–149

Parish, Clarence, 113

Payne, Leroy, 169

Pentagon Papers, 229

Perrin, Richard, 62–63

Philippines, rejection of white colonialist name, 167

Phillips, Howard, 174

Phillips, Vel, *183*

Phillips, W. Dale, 113

Pindling, Lynden, 242

Pitts, Orville, 49–50

police: and Attica prison riot, 149; and enforcement of laws on sexual behavior, 134; failure to enforce Accommodation Law of Wisconsin, 6–8; in New Orleans, violence of, 167–170; plans to boost minority representation in, 175–176; routine violations of blacks' civil rights, 57

police in Milwaukee: abusiveness and brutality of, ix, 41, 169, 170–171,

police in Milwaukee (*continued*)
176–177; Barbee's calls to disarm,
171, 176–177; black fear of, as road-
block to voter registration, 52, 54–
55; call for civilian control of, 171;
hostilities toward, 171; insulation
from criticism, 28–29; and Milwaukee riot of 1967, 144–145; opposition to defendant discovery
procedures, 35–36; in schools, 125;
sex discrimination by, 191; and
traffic tickets, overuse of, 166–167;
unjustified shootings of blacks by,
169, 176–177
political participation by blacks: and
accomplishment of goals, 46; and
campaign donations, 50–51; and
election of 1972, 48–49; NAACP
efforts to boost, 14–15; need for
increase in, 44, 45–49; and voter
registration roadblocks, 52–53;
and voting, importance of, 48–49
political parties, interests of blacks as
independent of, 49–50, 54
polygamy, arguments for legalization
of, 134
population control, Barbee bill on,
201–202
Powers, Sanger, 157, 158
press. *See* media
prison system: and Attica Prison riot,
148–150; Barbee bill on prisoner
leave, 160–161; Barbee bill to allow
conjugal visits, 148; Barbee bill to
credit prisoners for time on parole, 153; Barbee's calls to close,
150–151, 156–157, 162, 165, 166;
failure of, 149–150, 150–151, 156–
157, 165; high levels of incarceration in US, 148; more severe
punishment of blacks in, 150; proposal for community treatment
centers, 165–166; psychiatric
treatment as alternative to, 151,
156, 158–159
privacy rights, 218–219

property rights, vs. human rights,
58
property taxes for school funding,
110–112
prostitution, arguments for legalization of, 133
protest rights of students, lawsuits on,
120
protesters, black, discriminatory
treatment of, 162–164
public accommodation law of Wisconsin, protests of violations of, 6–8

Racial Discrimination in Housing
(film), xii; selected scenes from,
245–251; University of Wisconsin
suppression of, xii, 11–12
racism: Barbee's early solutions to,
1–2; as ongoing problem, x;
schools in Wisconsin as contributors to, 124–125; white media
opposition to black activists, 220–
221, 222. *See also* criminal justice
system, US; fair housing law;
school desegregation; zoning, exclusionary; *other specific topics*
racism, Barbee's early activism
against: discriminatory restaurant
service, ix, 6–8; minstrel shows,
8–11, 12, 13–14; offensive terms
and imagery, 5–6, 12
Reagan, Ronald, 213, 215
redistricting, to increase minority
power, 38–39, 240
Reischauer, Edwin O., 135–136
religion, Barbee on, 4–5
reparations, Barbee on, 1, 20
Republican Party: hostility to black
interests, 49–50, 54; and roadblocks to black voter registration,
52–53
Reuss, Henry, 97
Reynolds, John, 87
Rhodesia: and Munich Olympics, 239;
Smith regime in, 235
Roseleip, Gordon, 187, 190

About the Editor

Daphne E. Barbee-Wooten, pictured with Marion Loss's portrait of her father on display at Lloyd Barbee Montessori School in Milwaukee.

One of three children of noted civil rights activist, attorney, and lawmaker Lloyd A. Barbee, Daphne E. Barbee-Wooten is an attorney specializing in civil rights practicing in Honolulu, Hawaii. Previously she worked as a public defender and trial attorney in Honolulu and was the first Equal Employment Opportunity Commission senior trial attorney in Hawaii. In 2014, she received a lifetime achievement award from the Hawaii NAACP. In 2016 she received Civil Rights Attorney of the Year award from Sisters Empowering Hawaii.

Having grown up in Milwaukee, Barbee-Wooten earned her bachelor of arts in philosophy at the University of Wisconsin–Madison and her juris doctor degree from the University of Washington–Seattle. She is a member of the Hawaii State Bar Association, African American Lawyers Association of Hawaii, National Bar Association, NAACP, and African American Film Festival in Hawaii.

Her previous publications include *African American Attorneys in Hawaii* (Pacific Raven Press, 2010), a contribution to *They Followed the Tradewinds* (University of Hawaii Press, 2005), and numerous other articles and documents. She and her husband, Andre S. Wooten, also have produced a video series on African American history that has been shown on Hawaii Public Access Television.